Inquiry

⊐L Bradford Books

Daniel C. Dennett. BRAINSTORMS. 1979.
John Haugeland, Editor. MIND DESIGN. 1981.
Fred I. Dretske. KNOWLEDGE AND THE FLOW OF INFORMATION. 1981.
Jerry A. Fodor. REPRESENTATIONS. 1981.
Hubert L. Dreyfus, Editor, in collaboration with Harrison Hall. HUSSERL, INTEN-
    TIONALITY AND COGNITIVE SCIENCE. 1982.
Jerry A. Fodor. MODULARITY OF MIND. 1983.
George D. Romanos. QUINE AND ANALYTIC PHILOSOPHY. 1983.
Robert Cummins. THE NATURE OF PSYCHOLOGICAL EXPLANATION. 1983.
Stephen P. Stich. FROM FOLK PSYCHOLOGY TO COGNITIVE SCIENCE. 1983.
Jon Barwise and John Perry. SITUATIONS AND ATTITUDES. 1983.
Izchak Miller. HUSSERL, PERCEPTION, AND TEMPORAL AWARENESS. 1984
Norbert Hornstein. LOGIC AS GRAMMAR. 1984.
Paul M. Churchland. MATTER AND CONSCIOUSNESS. 1984.
Owen D. Flanagan. THE SCIENCE OF MIND. 1984.
Myles Brand. INTENDING AND ACTING. 1984.
Zenon W. Pylyshyn. COMPUTATION AND COGNITION. 1984.
Daniel C. Dennett. ELBOW ROOM: THE VARIETIES OF FREE WILL WORTH
    WANTING. 1984.
Robert C. Stalnaker. INQUIRY. 1984.
William G. Lycan. LOGICAL FORM IN NATURAL LANGUAGE. 1984.

Inquiry

Robert C. Stalnaker

A Bradford Book
The MIT Press
Cambridge, Massachusetts
London, England

First MIT Press paperback edition, 1987
The Massachusetts Institute of Technology

This book was set in Palatino by The MIT Press Computergraphics Department
and printed and bound by Halliday Lithograph in the United States of America.

Library of Congress Cataloging Publication Data

Stalnaker, Robert.
  Inquiry.

  "A Bradford book."

  Bibliography: p.
  Includes index.
  1. Knowledge, Theory of—Addresses, essays, lectures. 2. Belief and doubt—
Addresses, essays, lectures. I. Title.
BD161.S675   1984   121'.6   84-15453
ISBN 0-262-19233-0 (hard)
      0-262-69113-2 (paper)

MIT Press

0262691132

STALNAKER
INQUIRY

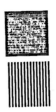

To Nan

You do inspire me with your dedication.
Happy birthday!

Lots of love,
Adima

Contents

Preface   ix

Chapter 1
The Problem of Intentionality   1

Chapter 2
The Linguistic Picture   27

Chapter 3
Possible Worlds   43

Chapter 4
Belief and Belief Attribution   59

Chapter 5
The Problem of Deduction   79

Chapter 6
Conditional Belief   101

Chapter 7
Conditional Propositions   119

Chapter 8
Realism about Counterfactuals   147

Notes   171

References   179

Index   183

Preface

I started this project a long time ago with the naive idea that if only I was free of the deadlines and space limitations imposed by the conferences I was writing papers for, and if only I had some time away from teaching and administrative distractions, I could get to the bottom of the problems I was thinking and writing about. In the succeeding years, including two and a half years on leave, I learned that the bottom was farther down than I thought. I am not there yet, but it is time to stop and make a progress report.

My topic is the abstract structure of inquiry—the enterprise of forming, testing, and revising beliefs. My goal was to provide a philosophical foundation and motivation for an apparatus for describing that structure—an apparatus that might help to clarify the relationships among some problematic concepts in the theory of knowledge and the philosophy of mind, concepts such as belief and conditional belief, presupposition and presumption, probability, counterfactual dependence, causation and explanation.

The apparatus I discuss begins with possible worlds and with an analysis of propositional content in terms of possible worlds. The possible worlds framework is recognized as a technically fruitful theory for doing semantics, and philosophers have found the imagery of possible worlds useful for stating philosophical problems and solutions, but there remains widespread suspicion of philosophical explanations which presuppose an ontology of possibilities. And even setting aside general worries about the ontology of possible worlds, there are serious problems with the possible worlds analysis of propositional content, problems that many philosophers have taken as sufficient reason to dismiss the analysis. But it seems to me that the possible worlds framework has a compelling philosophical motivation. The problems it faces are problems not just for a piece of semantic machinery but for an intuitively plausible conception of informational content and for a persuasive philosophical account of mental representation. I don't think that recognizing this will solve the problems that the possible worlds framework faces, but it does provide a reason for trying to solve them within that framework, and it does help to point the way toward some possible solutions. I tried, in a paper published in 1976 (Stalnaker, 1976a), to sketch the connection that I saw between a pragmatic account of belief and the possible worlds analysis of the objects of belief, and to suggest a strategy for solving some of the problems that the analysis faces. The first half of this book develops this theme in more detail.

The second half of the book focuses on the dynamics of belief and on the relationship between what we believe and our policies for changing our beliefs in response to new information. More specifically, it focuses on the relationship between conditional beliefs, which represent policies for changing beliefs, and belief in conditional propositions, which purport to represent the world. I try to motivate what I call the projection strategy, a strategy of explaining concepts of causal and counterfactual dependence as projections of epistemic policy onto the world. The strategy does not suggest that our concepts of causal and counterfactual dependence are in any way illegitimate, nor does it point the way to a reduction of these notions to something more fundamental. I argue that the projection strategy motivates a semantic analysis of conditional propositions that I first discussed and defended in 1968 (Stalnaker, 1968), and in the concluding chapter I defend a modest form of realism about counterfactuals.

Three very general philosophical prejudices help to motivate the project and to explain why I make the moves I make at various points. The first is a pragmatist prejudice. I assume, for example, that mental representation should be explained in terms of its role in the determination of rational action and that concepts such as causation and explanation should be explained and legitimized, ultimately, in terms of their role in helping agents find their way about in the world. The second is a realist prejudice. I assume that the world is the way it is independently of our conceptions of it and that the goal of inquiry is to find out how it is. I don't regard this as an exciting or controversial philosophical thesis, but it seems to me true. I am not sure that I am what Hilary Putnam calls a metaphysical realist—I certainly do not believe that "there is exactly one true and complete description of 'the way the world is' " (Putnam, 1981: 49), but I don't see why a realist should believe that. The third is a naturalist prejudice. Human beings, I assume, are part of the natural order. They are physical objects whose mental capacities and dispositions—specifically their representational capacities—need to be explained in terms of natural relations between natural objects and systems of natural objects. There are some tensions between these three prejudices, some of which I discuss in the last chapter, but I think they can fit together into a coherent philosophical view.

In the years that I have been working on this project, I have received support, encouragement, and advice from a large number of individuals and institutions. I cannot hope to name them all, but I want to acknowledge and thank some that stand out.

Cornell University granted me leaves in 1974–75, 1978–79, and the fall term, 1982. The first of these leaves, supported by the John Simon Guggenheim Memorial Foundation, was spent in London where I enjoyed the hospitality of the Philosophy Department at University College. The second, supported by a National Endowment for the Humanities fellowship, was spent at the Center for Advanced Study in the Behavioral Sciences in Stanford. Both years were pleasant and productive. They inspired in my son the ambition to be, when he grows up, a philosopher on leave.

Earlier versions of two parts of this book have been previously published. First, a paper based on a draft of chapter 3 was published as "Possible Worlds" in *Nous*, 10, 1976. Second, the last part of chapter 7 was the basis of "A Defense of Conditional Excluded Middle," which appeared in William Harper, Robert Stalnaker, and Glenn Pearce, eds., *Ifs: Conditionals, Belief, Decision, Chance, and Time*, published by D. Reidel in 1981. I thank the editors of *Nous* and D. Reidel for permission to use this material.

Many people have influenced my ideas and arguments. The work of a number of them (for example, Robert Adams, Donald Davidson, Dan Dennett, Michael Dummett, Hartry Field, Allan Gibbard, Gil Harman, David Lewis, Steve Stich, Bas van Fraassen) is discussed in the text. In these discussions, disagreement and criticism are often in the foreground, but this should not be allowed to obscure the common ground I share with the philosophers I am criticizing or the extent to which their ideas have contributed in a positive way to my own.

A number of colleagues read parts of what I have written and provided me with comments and suggestions. Richard Boyd's comments on a draft of chapter 1 helped me to clarify a number of points. Philip Bricker's criticisms, in his dissertation (Bricker, 1983), of some of the claims in Stalnaker (1976b) helped me to correct some mistakes and to get clearer about some issues in chapter 3. Hartry Field sent me detailed and constructive comments on a draft of the first four chapters, which I hope have helped me to improve my discussion of his work as well as to clarify some other points. Gil Harman read the whole manuscript, and his concise and illuminating comments helped me to avoid a number of confusions and obscurities.

My greatest debts are to Rich Thomason and David Lewis. The theory of conditionals discussed in chapter 7 was developed in collaboration with Rich when we were colleagues at Yale from 1965 to 1968. David and I began corresponding in about 1967 when we discovered that we had developed, independently, similar theories of counterfactuals. Correspondence and conversation with both over the years have been important to the development and clarification of my ideas about all the issues discussed in this book. Both have read the whole manuscript and provided extensive comments and advice, for which I am very grateful.

Thanks also to Harry Stanton of Bradford Books for encouragement and advice, to Nan, Tom, and Joanna for putting up with it all, particularly in the last hectic stages, and to Tom for help with the typing.

Ithaca, New York
February, 1984

Chapter 1

The Problem of Intentionality

When a person suspects or supposes, realizes, regrets, infers or imagines, doubts or discovers that something is true, he is taking an attitude or changing his attitude toward a proposition. To understand such propositional acts and attitudes, in terms of which the cluster of activities that constitute inquiry must be explained, we need to be clear about what kind of thing propositions are. Are they essentially linguistic things, or abstract objects, or mental constructs? Do they have constituents and, if so, what kinds of constituents? What are the identity conditions for propositions? That is, under what conditions do two sentences express, or two persons believe, the same proposition? What kinds of relations hold between propositions, between propositions and the sentences that express them, between propositions and the subjects of propositional attitudes? I will begin my exploration of the structure of inquiry with an exposition and defense of an account of propositions which is intended to answer some of these questions. The definition I will defend is short and simple, but it has struck some philosophers as an obscure and unhelpful metaphor rather than a real definition, and it may seem to involve problematic commitments and to have some unpalatable consequences. My defense will try to make clearer the content of the definition, as I understand it, to free it from some of the commitments and consequences that have been attributed to it, and to argue that others of its supposed commitments and consequences are more acceptable than it might seem.

The definition I will defend has its origin in formal semantics, and many have assumed that what interest it has lies in its application to technical problems in semantics. But I think a more important virtue of the definition, and of the framework that it presupposes, is the contribution they make to the philosophical understanding of the foundations of semantics, to our understanding of the notions of mental and linguistic representation. My main task in this chapter will be to tie the definition of proposition that I will defend to an independently plausible general conception of the nature of intentional mental states.

I will begin with a brief statement of the definition and of some of the problems that must be overcome if it is to be acceptable. Then I will sketch, in impressionistic terms, two contrasting pictures of mental and linguistic activity, one of which motivates the definition of propositional content that I want to defend. I will argue that only this picture of mental and linguistic activity provides us with a plausible way of solving the problem of intentionality—the problem of explaining the nature of intentional or representational mental states. I will outline a strategy for solving this problem, and then, in chapter 2, discuss critically some strategies for solving the problem in the spirit of the alternative picture of mental representation.

The analysis I will defend defines propositions in terms of possible worlds, and so one of the burdens of my defense will be to explain and justify this familiar but controversial notion. In chapter 3 I will try to explain what I think possible worlds are and why I think the kind of commitment to their existence which the definition makes is a reasonable one.

A proposition is a function from possible worlds into truth-values.[1] That is all there is to the definition, but to make it clear we need to say something about the terms with which propositions are defined. Discussion of the most problematic of these—the notion of a possible world—will be deferred to chapter 3, but I will make a brief remark about truth-values and functions.

There are just two truth-values—true and false. What are they: mysterious Fregean objects, properties, relations of correspondence and noncorrespondence? The answer is that it does not matter what they are; there is nothing essential to them except that there are exactly two of them. We could formulate the definition of proposition in a way that did not mention truth-values at all without changing its essential character: a proposition may be thought of as a rule for selecting a subset from a set of possible worlds. The role of the values *true* and *false* is simply to distinguish the possible worlds that are members of the selected subset from those that are not. But is there not more to truth than this? Should not an adequate theory of truth include some explanation of why curious people seek it, honest speakers aim at it, and good arguments preserve it? Shouldn't it help us to understand and solve metaphysical problems, such as disputes between realists and idealists? Somewhere in a theory of propositions and propositional attitudes such explanations must be given, but according to the account to be developed here, these questions are concerned less with truth itself than with belief, assertion, and argument, and with the relation between the actual world and other possible worlds.

A function may be thought of intuitively as a rule for determining a value relative to any member of a specified domain of arguments. But the identity conditions for functions are purely extensional: if functions f and g are defined for the same arguments, and have the same values for each argument, then they are the same function. So a proposition is fully determined relative to a domain of possible worlds by the subset of that domain for which the proposition takes the value *true*.

Let me mention two distinctive features of this definition—features that are the source of the strengths of the account, as well as of its weaknesses. First, according to this conception, propositions lack structure of the kind that reflects the semantic structure of the sentences that express them. The account thus contrasts with accounts of content given, for example, by Frege, Russell, and Wittgenstein, according to which propositions are compounded out of individuals, concepts, properties, or senses. Second, according to this conception, propositions are defined independently of language and linguistic behavior. The definition thus contrasts with any account which tries to explain content in terms of the uses of linguistic expressions. The two most serious objections to the proposed definition derive from these two features.

It is a consequence of the first feature that propositions are individuated much less finely by this account than by contrasting accounts. The analysis implies that propositions are identical if they are necessarily equivalent—true together and false together in all possible circumstances. But, it may be objected, these are not plausible identity conditions for the objects of mental states such as belief since it is obvious that one may believe a proposition while disbelieving one that is necessarily equivalent to it. It may, for example, be a nontrivial mathematical problem to see that two expressions are necessarily equivalent, and where a person has not yet solved such a problem, his attitude toward the content of one may be different from his attitude toward the content of the other. The implausibility of the identity conditions imposed on propositions by the definition is particularly striking in the case of necessarily true propositions. Since all necessary truths are necessarily equivalent to each other, it follows that there is only one necessary truth. Since all mathematical truths are necessary, this means that there is only one true thing that can be said in mathematics, although it can be said in many different ways.

The second distinctive feature of the definition—its language independence—opens it to a second objection: the charge of ontological extravagance. It may be argued that if the account is committed to the existence of possible worlds, then it is false, since there obviously are no such things. But if the theory treats possible worlds as only a convenient fiction, then whatever its heuristic value in helping to see the consequences of certain assumptions, it has no real explanatory power. At the very least one can reasonably insist that the elusive concept of a possible world be given more specific intuitive content before it is asked to bear the burden put on it by the proposed definition of proposition.

Both of these problems are serious ones, and I have no final and decisive solutions to them. But I will try to make a case that they are not insurmountable obstacles to the success of the account of propositional content that I will be defending.

Here is one impressionistic picture of the nature of human activities which involve mental representation—call it the pragmatic picture. Rational creatures are essentially agents. Representational mental states should be understood primarily in terms of the role that they play in the characterization and explanation of action. What is essential to rational action is that the agent be confronted, or conceive of himself as confronted, with a range of alternative possible outcomes of some alternative possible actions. The agent has attitudes, pro and con, toward the different possible outcomes, and beliefs about the contribution which the alternative actions would make to determining the outcome. One explains why an agent tends to act in the way he does in terms of such beliefs and attitudes. And, according to this picture, our conceptions of belief and of attitudes pro and con are conceptions of states which explain why a rational agent does what he does. Some representational mental states—for example, idle wishes, passive hopes, and theoretical beliefs—may be connected only very indirectly with action, but all must be explained, according to the pragmatic picture, in terms of their connections with the explanation of rational action.

Linguistic action, according to this picture, has no special status. Speech is just one kind of action which is to be explained and evaluated according to the same pattern. Linguistic action may be a particularly rich source of evidence about the speaker's attitudes, but it has no special conceptual connection with them.

This picture suggests that the primary objects of attitude are not propositions but the alternative possible outcomes of agents' actions, or more generally, alternative possible states of the world. When a person wants a proposition to be true, it is because he has a positive attitude toward certain concrete realizations of that proposition. Propositions, the picture suggests, are simply ways of distinguishing between the elements of the relevant range of alternative possibilities—ways that are useful for characterizing and expressing an agent's attitudes toward those possibilities. To *understand* a proposition—to know the content of a statement or a thought—is to have the capacity to divide the relevant alternatives in the right way. To *entertain* a proposition is to focus one's attention on certain possibilities, contrasting them with others. To *distinguish* two propositions is to conceive of a possible situation in which one is true and the other false.

Here is a contrasting impressionistic conception of mental representation—call it the linguistic picture. Rational creatures are essentially speakers. Unspoken thought is something like inner speech—"saying in one's heart."[2] Representational mental states represent the world because of their resemblance to, or relation with, the most basic kind of representations: linguistic expressions.

Those attracted to this picture are inclined to say things like this: Assertion is "not the expression of an interior act of judgment; judging, rather, is the interiorization of the external act of assertion."[3] "The thought that p is an episode which might also be referred to as the mental assertion that p."[4] "A creature cannot have thoughts unless it is the interpreter of the speech of another."[5] "Representational characteristics of mental states derive from representational characteristics of sentences of the language of thought."[6]

It is not essential to the linguistic picture that every thinking creature be capable of outward speech or that every one of our thoughts be expressible in our public language. All that is essential is that thought be explained by analogy with speech. Every thinking creature, according to this picture, does something like talk to itself in the language of thought, even if it lacks the capacity to translate its utterances into any public language. Our inexpressible thoughts are inner utterances for which no adequate translation into a public language is available to us.

Proponents of the linguistic picture are inclined to be skeptical of any notion of an abstract object of thought and speech which can be identified across languages. Particular episodes of speech and thought have sentences or sentence-analogues as their objects, and there may be various more or less indeterminate translation relations that hold between them. But translation, according to this picture, is not an attempt to preserve some independently understood property like meaning or content. Rather, translation is the notion in terms of which the vague preanalytic notions of meaning and content should be explained—or better, with which those vague notions should be replaced.

I want to emphasize that in characterizing the linguistic picture I am describing a cluster of metaphors and analogies which guide the construction of theses and theories and not attempting to describe even the broad outlines of a unified approach to the explanation of mental representation. As will become clearer in the next chapter, the development of the linguistic picture leads in two quite different directions which emphasize different analogies between speech and thought. One hypothesizes a language of thought, which may be different from any language used for communication; the other argues for the dependence of thought on the social activities of speech. There are sharp conflicts between these different developments of the analogy.

My main task in this chapter is to bring the two pictures into sharper focus by formulating and discussing one issue that divides them. The issue concerns conflicting strategies for solving the problem of intentionality. Let me first say what the problem is and then describe the alternative strategies for solving it.

The problem of intentionality is a problem about the nature of representation. Some things in the world—for example, pictures, names, maps, utterances, certain mental states—*represent*, or *stand for*, or are *about* other things—for example, people, towns, states of affairs. Some philosophers have suggested that the capacity to represent, and to confer representational properties, is a distinctive and essential capacity of thinking things. Persons can represent because they have minds; inanimate objects can represent only because of the way people use and regard them.

For various familiar reasons, intentional or representational relations seem unlike the relations holding between things and events in the natural world: causal interactions, spatiotemporal relations, various notions of similarity and difference. One can, it seems, picture, describe, or think about such things as gods and golden mountains even if they do not exist. And one can picture, describe, or think about a triangle or a sunset without there being any particular triangle or sunset that is pictured, described, or thought about. Some philosophers have used these distinctive features of intentional relations to argue that they are irreducible to natural relations. From this conclusion it is argued that mental phenomena cannot be a species of natural phenomena. Any account of thinking things as natural objects in the material world, these philosophers argue, is bound to leave something out. The challenge presented to the philosopher who wants to regard human beings and mental phenomena as part of the natural order is to explain intentional relations in naturalistic terms.

The linguistic and pragmatic pictures each suggest strategies for giving a naturalistic explanation of representation—both mental and linguistic representation—but the two strategies differ in what kind of representation they take to be more fundamental. The pragmatic picture suggests that we explain the intentionality of language in terms of the intentionality of mental states, while the linguistic strategy suggests that we explain the intentionality of mental states in terms of, or by analogy with, the intentionality of linguistic expressions.[7] If we opt for the former course, then to avoid circularity we need an explanation in terms that make no reference to language of the representational character of mental states. If we opt for the latter course, then we need an explanation in terms that make no reference to mental states of the representational character of linguistic expressions. I will argue that the problem can be solved in the first of these ways and that it can be solved only in this way—that attempts to solve the problem of intentionality in the alternative way are doomed to failure. In trying to make this case, I will discuss a number of arguments from a very illuminating paper by Hartry Field, "Mental Representation."[8] I find this paper useful for my purposes because I agree so thoroughly with the terms in which it poses the problem of explaining mental representation and because I disagree so thoroughly with the solution it offers. Field and I agree in taking the problem of intentionality to be the central philosophical problem that an account of mental representation must solve. We also agree, I believe, that the problem can be solved and that only one of the two options listed above describes a way of solving it. We disagree only about which of the two ways it is.

This informal characterization of Field's project may be misleading, so I will add a qualification. There is a sense in which Field might agree that the intentionality of thought is prior to the intentionality of language: it might be, according to Field as I understand him, that the representational properties of expressions of a *public* language are derived from, and explained in terms of, the representational properties of beliefs and intentions. But Field would insist that the representational properties of beliefs and intentions must be explained in terms of the semantic properties of *a* language or language-like system: mentalese, or the language of thought. Field's essential thesis is that only by assuming that mental states have something like a linguistic structure can we explain how they can represent the world. His strategy, like Jerry Fodor's, is to explain propositional attitudes as nonintentional relations to sentences of the mental language and then to explain the intentional properties of propositional attitudes in terms of the semantic properties of the sentences of that language.

Sometimes the problem of intentionality is posed in terms of the notion of *content*. Some objects, or states of objects, have content, where to have content is to be related to a proposition. Hartry Field, in the paper cited, suggested that the problem of intentionality (at least for those who take mental states such as belief at face value as relations between persons and the contents of the states) is the problem of giving "a materialistically adequate account of a relation between a person and a proposition."[9] This is a problem, I think, and it is closely tied to the problem of intentionality, but I want to suggest that it is not quite the same problem. There may be relations between persons and propositions which are not intentional relations—which do not themselves involve representation—and which are unproblematic from the point of view of the problem of explaining representation. Such nonintentional relations between persons and propositions are important, since one strategy for solving the problem is to reduce intentional relations (such as belief and attitudes pro and con) to nonintentional relations between persons and propositions.

How can a person be related to an abstract object such as a proposition? Let me ask, first, a parallel but easier question: how can a person be related to an abstract object such as a number?[10] Note that while some relations between persons and numbers, such as those that are instantiated when I think about or name the number 42, are intentional, others are not. I take it that height in inches, weight in pounds, age in years, are all nonintentional relations between persons, or other physical objects, and numbers, and that while the existence of such relations may call for some explanation, the problem they pose is not a problem about representation. Nevertheless, I want to look briefly at the question, how can physical objects be related to numbers, in the hope that it will throw a little light, by analogy, on the question, how can persons be related to propositions, and ultimately on the question, how can persons stand in intentional relations to propositions.

The analogy between numbers and propositions, and the examples of physical quantities such as height and weight, are useful, I think, for suggesting different ways that one might understand how people could be related to propositions. Some philosophers seem to assume that we must respond in one of the following three ways to the apparent fact that propositional attitudes relate people to propositions: (1) One might deny that propositional attitudes correspond to such relations, taking the fusion or orthographic accident line. "The fusion story is the proposal that sentences like 'John believes it's raining' ought really to be spelled 'John believes-it's-raining'; that the logical form of such sentences acknowledges a referring expression ('John') and a one-place predicate with no internal structure ('believes-it's-raining'). 'John believes it's raining' is thus an atomic sentence, similar *au fond* to 'John is purple.' "[11] (2) One might hypothesize some kind of mysterious nonnatural connection between persons and abstract objects, for example, that people have "a special intellectual capacity (*theoria*) wherewith one peers at abstract objects."[12] (3) One might suppose that people are related to propositions in virtue of being related to a sentence token, or mental analogue of a sentence token, which expresses the proposition. The first response is obviously unsatisfactory, and the second is incompatible with a naturalistic account of human beings. So we are left with the third response, in which the psychological relation between a person and an abstract object is factored into two relations: first, a psychological relation between a person and a less problematic entity (a sentence token) which will have a physical form; second, a semantic relation between the sentence token and an abstract proposition.

The analogy between propositions and numbers suggests that there may be further alternative strategies for explaining how a person can be related to a proposition. No one would be tempted to tell the fusion story about occurrences of the numerical expression 'two hundred' in the statement 'George weighs two hundred pounds,' nor would anyone be attracted by the hypothesis that George's weight is a mysterious nonnatural relation between George and the number. Are we forced, then, to say that George must weigh two hundred pounds in virtue of containing within him something that counts as a token of a numeral denoting the number?

What is it about such physical properties as having a certain height or weight that makes it correct to represent them as relations between the thing to which the property is ascribed and a number? The reason we can understand such properties—physical quantities—in this way is that they belong to families of properties which have a structure in common with the real numbers. Because the family of properties which are *weights* of physical objects has this structure, we can (given a unit, fixed by a standard object) use a number to pick a particular one of the properties out of the family. That, I think, is all there is to the fact that weights and other physical quantities are, or can be understood as, relations between physical objects and numbers. There is, of course, much more to be said about physical quantities, for example, about what it is for properties to belong to a family and for such a family to have a certain structure. The theory of measurement provides rigorous and detailed answers to such questions. But if one were inclined to think that there is some mystery, in general, about how physical objects can stand in relation to abstract objects, the informal explanation I have given ought to be enough to dispel the mystery.

Some might be inclined to argue that the kind of explanation measurement theory gives of physical quantities shows that they are not really relational properties at all—at least not properties that relate physical objects to numbers. They are instead either intrinsic properties of the physical objects or properties defined in terms of the relations holding between the object and other physical objects. There is a grain of truth, according to this line of argument, in the fusion story since, ontologically if not semantically, physical quantities may be nonrelational properties. On some explications of the rough intuitive distinction between intrinsic and relational properties, this may be right, but the fact remains, as even a nominalist would agree, that the numerical expression that goes in for x in a statement of the form 'George weighs x pounds' is a semantically significant constituent. It is important to keep the extremely counterintuitive *semantic* fusion thesis distinct from a much vaguer, but perhaps much more plausible, *ontological* thesis about what kinds of properties are expressed by certain semantically complex expressions. The thesis that propositional attitudes should be analyzed as relations is compelling only if it is understood as a denial of the semantic fusion thesis.

Fodor, in his defense of the thesis that propositional attitudes should be analyzed as relations, does not clearly separate the ontological from the semantic issue. Discussing an example of Dennett's, Fodor says that the surface grammar of such apparently relational expressions as 'Mary's voice' is ontologically misleading—that it does not really express a relation between Mary and an object, her voice.[13] But I am sure that Fodor would agree that the semantic structure of 'Mary had a little voice' exactly parallels that of (one reading of) 'Mary had a little lamb,' even if voices have a more tenuous place in our ontology than lambs and even if the references to voices are more easily paraphrased away than references to lambs. Whatever a proper metaphysics might say about voices, the semantic fusion thesis is as implausible about voices as it is about weights, beliefs, or lambs.

In a postscript to a reprinting of "Mental Representation," Field discusses the analogy between propositional relations and the relations between physical objects and numbers expressed by physical magnitude terms.[14] He suggests that a solution to the problem of intentionality which parallels the explanation of physical magnitudes provided by measurement theory would support his thesis that mental representation requires a system of internal linguistic representation. A parallel solution, he argues, would "have to postulate a system of entities inside the believer which was related via a structure preserving mapping to the system of propositions. The 'structure' that such a mapping would have to preserve would be the kind of structure important to propositions: viz. logical structure. So the system of entities inside the believer would have to have logical structure, and this I think means that the system of entities inside the believer can be viewed as a system of sentences— an internal system of representations."[15]

I agree that the relations essential to a system of propositions are logical relations, if this is understood to mean relations of entailment, compatibility, logical independence, and so forth, but I am not convinced that entities standing in these relations must be sentences, or sentence-like. According to the possible worlds analysis, propositions have logical structure but nothing corresponding to linguistic structure. Field argues that we need a more fine-grained conception of proposition, one that would support the internal linguistic representation hypothesis, but the analogy with numbers does not, by itself, support this point. I think, however, that the analogy does point the way to a strategy for answering the question of what conception of proposition is required for an adequate account of propositional attitudes. Just as the empirical relations that fix the reference of physical magnitude terms determines which features of numbers are physically significant and which are not, so the empirical relations which a functional theory uses to explain propositional attitude concepts will determine which features of abstract propositions are significant, and so what conception of proposition is appropriate.

Before looking at propositional attitudes and mental representation, I want to consider some simpler relations between persons and propositions, relations that I think can be understood by analogy with physical magnitudes. The analogy suggests that to define a relation between a person or a physical object and a proposition is to define a class of properties with a structure that makes it possible to pick one of the properties out of the class by specifying a proposition. I will give three examples of relations that I think can be understood in this way. They are all artificial and over-simple examples, but I hope they will make the point that it is at least possible to define relations between persons and propositions that are unproblematic from the point of view of the problem of intentionality and do not require or support a hypothesis of internal linguistic representation.

First example: Consider a concept of *need* defined as follows: an organism *needs it to be the case that P* (at a certain time) if and only if the organism would survive (beyond that time) only if *P*. The concept might be generalized: it is not essential that the thing to which needs of this kind are ascribed be an organism; anything for which a notion of survival, or an analogue of the notion of survival, could be specified will be something which might be within the domain of this relation. The organism or object need not represent the propositions that define its needs, and no one would be tempted to ascribe any mysterious nonnatural states to things in need, in this sense. But this simple relation does have some of the properties that philosophers have found puzzling about intentional relations. One can need food (strictly, given my artificial definition, need it to be the case that one eats food) without there being any particular food that one needs. And an unfortunate organism may need something (may need it to be the case that it has something) which does not exist. I take the fact that the simple need relation has such properties to show, not that this relation is intentional, but rather that these properties are not restricted to intentional relations and are not, in themselves, problematic from a naturalistic point of view.

Second example: Suppose we have an organism, physical object, or system of physical objects whose behavior is explainable on the assumption that certain of its states are equilibrium states. When the object or system is in equilibrium, it tends to remain there, while when it is in disequilibrium it tends to change in ways that bring it into equilibrium. The equilibrium state might be an internal state of the object or system, or it might be a relation between it and its environment. The object might move toward equilibrium either by undergoing an internal change or by causing its environment to change in the relevant way. Such objects and systems are, of course, familiar. Feedback mechanisms such as thermostats are examples, but so are simpler systems, about which it would be farfetched to think in teleological terms, such as a closed volume of gas in which the kinetic energy of the different parts tends to equalize. We might define a general relation between objects and propositions in order to talk about such a system: call it *tendency-to-bring-about*. It will be true that x *tends-to-bring-about* that P if and only if P is a logical or causal consequence of x being in its equilibrium state. Again, the relation has some of the allegedly problematic properties of intentional relations, but there is no mystery about how ordinary physical objects and systems can be related to propositions in this way.

My third and last example of a naturalistic propositional relation, suggested by an analysis in a paper by Dennis Stampe, brings us closer to a relation that looks like a relation of representation.[16] Consider an object which has intrinsic states that tend, under normal or optimal conditions, to correlate with its environment in some systematic way, and where the object tends to be in the state it is in *because* the environment is the way it is. For example, the length of a column of mercury in a thermometer tends to vary systematically with the temperature of the surrounding air; the pattern of light and dark on the ground on a sunny day may correlate with the shape of the tree that is between it and the sun; a pattern of radio waves emitted by a transmitter may tend to correlate with the pattern of sounds made in the vicinity of a microphone; the number of rings on a cross section of a tree trunk may correlate with the age of the tree.

To characterize precisely the kind of situation we are considering, one would have to specify three things: first, the relevant set of alternative states of the object doing the representing; second, a one-one function taking these states into the corresponding states of the world; third, the normal or optimal conditions, or what Stampe called *fidelity conditions*. If a is a variable ranging over the relevant states of the object and f is the function, then the relation that must hold between the object and its environment is as follows: for any a, if fidelity conditions obtain, then the object is in state a if and only if the environment is in state $f(a)$. Furthermore, the explanation for the correlation must be that the world's being in state $f(a)$ tends, under the relevant conditions, to cause the object to be in state a.

We could all think of examples of objects of this kind which are very reliable indicators of their environments, but we can also imagine cases for which conditions are often not normal or optimal because of distorting influences of one kind or another. In such cases, even though it is true that under the fidelity conditions, the object will be in state a if and only if its environment is in state $f(a)$, it might be often true in fact that the correlation failed to hold: that is, that the object was in state a while the environment was in some state different from $f(a)$.

Given such an object or system, reliable or not, we might define a relation, which I will call *indication*, between the object and propositions as follows: the object *indicates* that P if and only if, for some a in the relevant set of alternative states of the object, first the object is in state a, and second, the proposition that the environment is in state $f(a)$ entails that P. So, for example, if a tree trunk has 78 rings, then it indicates that the tree is 78 years old, and also that the tree is between 70 and 80 years old. This is true even if, because of a disease that infected the tree, or because of unusual climatic conditions, the number of rings fails to reflect the tree's real age.

I have not defined a general relation of indication; I have just given a schema for defining such a relation for particular kinds of objects against a particular theoretical background of the kind sketched. To make such a relation precise, one would have to spell out the fidelity conditions and characterize the relevant alternative states. But there clearly are objects and systems, both natural and constructed, which have the right properties, and this presents no problem from a physicalistic or naturalistic point of view.

Relations of indication of this kind, unlike the two earlier kinds of relations between objects and propositions that I discussed, do seem to me to be relations that it is reasonable to call representational. Stampe, in fact, argued in the paper cited that a notion like indication can provide a general naturalistic account of the concept of representation. It is certainly appropriate, and common, to use the notion of *information* to describe cases in which a notion of indication could be defined. It seems natural to say that when an object indicates that P, it contains or conveys the information that P. So we might expect notions something like indication to play a role in a naturalistic explanation of paradigm intentional mental states such as belief and attitudes pro and con.

Before going on to look at intentional mental states, let me make a few general comments about the kind of propositional states that I have been discussing. First, note that while I have suggested that my examples—at least the first two—are not intentional in the sense of representational, they are obviously all intentional in a different sense of the word, the sense sometimes called "intensional with an s." Sentences of the form x needs it to be the case that P, for example, will create opaque contexts within the sentence that replaces P. All of my example relations were defined in terms of causal connection and counterfactual dependence—notions which are intentional in this related but different sense. Philosophers have, of course, found this broader kind of intentionality problematic as well, but the problems it presents are different. While some philosophers might reject, or try to explain away, causal connection and counterfactual conditionals, none would argue that intentionality, in this sense, marks a boundary between the mental and the physical. Some philosophers might argue that concepts of causal connection and counterfactual dependence have their origins in the structure we impose on the world, and not in the world itself, but even if this is so, it is the physical world to which we apply concepts which are intentional in this sense.

Second, note that the examples I discussed include both forward-looking and backward-looking propositional relations. That is, in one case a state of an object was defined in terms of what it tended to cause, while in another case a state of an object was defined in terms of what tended to cause it. (The other example—the first—is not really either of these: in this case a state of an object was defined in terms of what would tend to cause the object to be in some different fixed state.) I will argue that we need to use both forward-looking and backward-looking propositional states in order to explain intentional mental states.

Finally, let me summarize the general point that I am trying to make with the examples of propositional states of physical objects. The claim which the examples are intended to illustrate and support is that there can be relations between objects (or persons) and propositions which are unproblematic from a naturalistic point of view. If the claim is right, then we have a rebuttal to a general argument of Hartry Field's against the possibility of using a functional analysis of mental states to solve the problem of intentionality. As I understand it, Field's argument in broad outline is this: all that a functionalist theory of mental states does is to reduce claims about *mental* relations between persons and propositions to claims about the existence of unspecified *physical* relations between persons and propositions. It does nothing to show how it is possible for there to be physical relations between persons and propositions. But this question—how is it possible for a person to be physically related to a proposition—is the problem of intentionality. For this reason, Field concludes, "functionalism does not either solve or dissolve [the problem of intentionality]."[17] My examples are an attempt to respond to this argument by pointing to unproblematic physical relations between objects or persons and propositions.[18]

Of course Field is right that functionalism itself—the thesis that mental states are states of an organism or mechanism which are individuated by their function in the working of the organism or mechanism—does not, by itself, solve our problem. We need to say what the relevant functional states are, and to explain them in terms of unproblematic propositional relations of the kind I have been discussing. I will conclude this chapter by looking at a familiar functionalist strategy for explaining intentional mental states, at some problems with it, some ways of responding to the problems, and some consequences of the strategy concerning the structure of propositions.

The strategy I have in mind is the one suggested by the pragmatic picture of mental acts and attitudes. Belief and desire, the strategy suggests, are correlative dispositional states of a potentially rational agent. To desire that P is to be disposed to act in ways that would tend to bring it about that P in a world in which one's beliefs, whatever they are, were true. To believe that P is to be disposed to act in ways that would tend to satisfy one's desires, whatever they are, in a world in which P (together with one's other beliefs) were true.[19]

Could this, or some more sophisticated variant of it, be an adequate explanation of the nature of belief and desire—one that points the way to a general explanation of intentional mental states? The kind of propositional relations used to explain belief and desire are like one of the examples that I claimed was an unproblematic propositional relation: the tendency-to-bring-about relation. But even if we accept that such relations as that are unproblematic, there remain some difficulties with this strategy for solving the problem of intentionality. First (a problem I will just mention), the account is obviously a gross oversimplification. We need to be sure that the qualifications and distinctions needed to make it more realistic will not smuggle in unexplained notions that are as problematic as what we are trying to explain. Second, and more serious I think, is a problem that has often been noted. The dependence of the explanation of each of the two intentional notions on the other, which is such a striking feature of the pragmatic strategy, presents a threat of vicious circularity. Is this theory simply a shell game that hides the problem of intentionality under belief while it explains desire, and under desire while it explains belief? I think there is a problem of circularity, but it will be important to look carefully at just why there is a problem, and at just what it is. I will argue that the circularity shows, not that the pragmatic analysis is mistaken, but only that it needs to be supplemented in order to provide a solution to our problem.

One reason—not, I think, a good one—for worrying about vicious circularity in the pragmatic analysis is a verificationist worry. Because of the mutual dependence of the analyses of belief and desire, it is clear that distinct and apparently incompatible hypotheses about the beliefs and desires of an agent might both be compatible with the same behavioral data—even with all possible behavioral data. One can vary one's hypothesis about an agent's beliefs without varying the predicted behavior so long as one makes compensating changes in one's hypothesis about the agent's desires. Therefore, it might be argued, there can be no fact of the matter about which of such alternative hypotheses is correct, and so no fact of the matter about what an agent believes or wants.

If the pragmatic analysis had a behavioristic or verificationist motivation—if it were an attempt to reduce unobserved inner states to patterns of behavior—then I think this argument would show that the analysis had failed. But this is not the problem which the analysis is attempting to solve. Belief and desire are problematic, not because they are inner states which are not directly observable, but because they are intentional; the analysis is an attempt to explain the intentional in terms of the nonintentional, not an attempt to explain the unobservable in terms of the observable. So we can, without undercutting the job that the analysis is attempting to do, understand dispositional properties such as belief and desire as real causal properties of persons, and not simply as patterns of actual and possible behavior.[20]

Imagine a machine whose inner states are inaccessible to us and which moves in certain complicated ways. On the basis of its behavior, we formulate a hypothesis that its movements result from two separate but interacting mechanisms inside. Someone else formulates a rival hypothesis with different interacting mechanisms which produce exactly the same behavior under all possible circumstances. Obviously we could not tell, simply by observing behavior, which hypothesis was correct. Perhaps we could not tell at all. But there would still be a fact of the matter about how the machine worked. There could be a fact of the matter, even if the mechanisms hypothesized were defined in abstract functional terms—in terms of their role in producing the behavior.

The pragmatic analysis, with dispositional states understood as real causal properties, treats a rational agent as something analogous to such a machine. In ascribing beliefs and desires to a person, we not only make conditional predictions about how the person will behave; we also commit ourselves to claims about the kind of mechanisms which explain why a person behaves the way he does. The mutual dependence of belief, desire, and action is a reflection of the fact that the hypothesized explanation says more than the conditional predictions which it entails. This fact makes it harder than it might be to verify claims about beliefs and desires, but in itself it presents no conceptual problem to the analysis as an explanation of intentionality.

But there is, I think, a conceptual problem: a fatal relativity in the propositional relations defined by the pragmatic analysis which shows that this analysis cannot, by itself, solve the problem of intentionality. Let me use an example to bring out the problem.

Mary is angry at Fred, her neighbor. She wants him to suffer, and believes that he will suffer if she plays her cello badly at three o'clock in the morning. So she does play her cello badly at three o'clock in the morning. That, at least, is one hypothesis for explaining why Mary did what she did. Here is another: Mary wants *Albert* to suffer, and believes that *Albert* will suffer if she plays her cello at three in the morning. *That* is why she did what she did. Now one might find the second hypothesis less plausible—even perverse—since Mary has no reason to want Albert to suffer; she has never met or heard of him. And she has no reason to believe that playing her cello badly will cause him to suffer, since he lives 3,000 miles away. Suppose the defender of the perverse hypothesis, when pressed about the implausibilities in his explanation, elaborates his hypothesis by saying that Mary believes Albert, rather than Fred, to be her neighbor, believes that Albert, rather than Fred, insulted her, believes that Albert's name is "Fred." In fact, all the attitudes that a sensible observer would say Mary takes toward Fred, the defender of the perverse hypothesis says that Mary takes toward Albert. The *only* difference between the two proposals, let us suppose, is that in the perverse hypothesis, Albert is everywhere substituted for Fred. The two hypotheses will, of course, predict exactly the same behavior, but there is also a stronger equivalence between them. Not only do belief and desire interact to produce the same actions, according to the two hypotheses, but also there is an exact correspondence between the beliefs hypothesized and the desires hypothesized by the two competing accounts. So not only are the two accounts equivalent with respect to the behavioral phenomena, they are also equivalent with respect to the mechanisms they postulate to explain the phenomena. The shift from Fred to Albert looks, from the point of view of the pragmatic analysis, like an innocent shift in the conventional units used to describe Mary's attitudes and relate them to each other, and not a shift in the claims made about the attitudes themselves.

The same point will hold for any such substitution, not only of individuals for individuals, but of properties for properties, or whole propositions for whole propositions. All that is required is that certain internal structure be preserved. And we need not substitute *persons* for persons: we might take Mary's attitudes toward Fred to be attitudes toward a mathematical point, or a class of events in her brain, without affecting the substance of the explanation of her behavior.[21] The *content* of belief and desire cancels out on the pragmatic analysis. Even if that analysis does give us an account of the structure of explanations of rational action, by itself it gives us no account at all of how beliefs and desires can represent the world.

It is obvious from our example what got left out. Our mental states represent what they represent not only because of the behavior they tend to cause, but also because of the events and states that tend to cause them. The reason that Mary's emotions and beliefs are directed at Fred, and not at Albert, is that Fred, and not Albert, caused Mary to be angry, and to have the beliefs that Mary has which the sensible hypothesis says are beliefs about Fred. That's not quite right. Fred might be the innocent victim of a misunderstanding, or of a malicious practical joke played by Albert. But it is clear, as has been emphasized by most recent work in the theory of reference, that the fact that Mary's attitudes are attitudes toward Fred is to be explained, somehow, in terms of Fred's causal role in producing Mary's attitudes. The total relativity of content that is a feature of the pragmatic analysis is the result of ignoring this essential element of mental representation.[22]

The pragmatic analysis tries to explain mental representation entirely in terms of forward-looking propositional relations such as the tendency-to-bring-about relation. The relativity of content that results forces us to recognize that belief is a backward-looking propositional state. What I want to suggest is that belief is a version of the propositional relation I called *indication*. We believe that P just because we are in a state that, under optimal conditions, we are in only if P, and under optimal conditions, we are in that state because P, or because of something that entails P. But a causal account of belief—an account that treats belief as a kind of indication—cannot, I think, *replace* the pragmatic analysis, it can only supplement it. For an account of belief must explain, not only how belief can represent the world, but also what distinguishes *belief* from other kinds of representational states. Consider the retinal images that form on the eye. That is a kind of indication; the state of the retina can be described in terms of a relation between a person and a proposition. And if a bald head is shiny enough to reflect some features of its environment, then the states of that head might be described in terms of a kind of indication—in terms of a relation between the person owning the head and a proposition. But no one would be tempted to call such states belief states. The reason is, I think, that they are not connected in the appropriate way with tendencies to produce action.

If belief is a dispositional state of the kind postulated by the pragmatic analysis, and also a kind of indication, then we have a fixed point with which to break into the circle that is responsible for the relativity of content. Beliefs have determinate content because of their presumed causal connections with the world. Beliefs are *beliefs* rather than some other representational state, because of their connection, through desire, with action. Desires have determinate content because of their dual connection with belief and action. Both the forward-looking and the backward-looking aspects of these mental states are essential to the explanation of how they can represent the world.

Might such an account be right? It is, I think, intuitively clear that however often we may fail to act according to our beliefs, there is a presumption that we do. Where people don't do what is appropriate, given their beliefs, we expect there to be some explanation for this; we may appeal, for example, to incapacity, absentmindedness, or self-deception. It is also intuitively clear, I think, that there is a presumption that people's beliefs will correlate with, and be caused by, their environments. Where beliefs are false, or only accidentally true, we also expect some explanation for the deviation from the norm: either an abnormality in the environment, as in optical illusions or other kinds of misleading evidence, or an abnormality in the internal belief-forming mechanisms, as in wishful thinking or misremembering. These intuitions suggest that we do have the conceptions of normal or optimal conditions which make it possible to understand belief as a kind of indication, and belief and desire together as a kind of tendency-to-bring-about, and so might make it possible to explain the intentionality of such states in naturalistic terms.

I have tried to describe a strategy for analyzing intentional mental states in a way that is motivated by the pragmatic picture, and that solves the problem of explaining how mental states can represent the world. I recognize that what I have offered is only a strategy—only the bare outlines of an account of intentional mental states. But there is enough in this outline of a strategy to allow us to draw some philosophical conclusions about the notions of mental representation and propositional content which are implicit in any way of carrying it out.

First, let me make some remarks about the causal dimension of the causal-pragmatic strategy and causal theories of reference. The strategy suggests that if reference is a causal relation, it is because belief and intention are causal relations, and because reference is to be explained in terms of the intentions and beliefs of speakers. The argument from the relativity of content was an attempt to show that, at least within the framework of the pragmatic picture, belief and desire *must* be considered partly in causal terms. If this is right, then this framework implies that the claim that some kind of causal theory of reference is correct is not a thesis about how language happens to work, but a thesis about how it has to work if reference is to be a device for representing the world.

The hypothesis that belief should be explained in terms of indication does not directly imply any particular causal account of reference. The indication account of belief explains representation in terms of what *would* cause the believer to be in a certain state under certain possibly counterfactual conditions rather than in terms of what does in fact cause the believer to be in that state. In any case, one would need an explanation of reference in terms of belief and intention in order to make the connection. But the indication account of belief shares with causal theories of reference the rejection of the idea, which I think is implicit in earlier accounts of reference, that representation is an internal matter: that one's words and thoughts represent in virtue of the intrinsic properties of speakers and thinkers. Both kinds of accounts argue instead that what we mean, and what we believe, is in part constituted by facts about the environment in which our thoughts and linguistic acts occur, the facts that help to explain why we have the thoughts and say the things we do.

The theses that names refer in virtue of causal connections with things, and that the meanings of certain common nouns "ain't in the head," were initially defended with thought experiments about particular examples rather than with general arguments about the nature of representation, and I think this has led some observers to draw the wrong conclusions from them. I want to comment on two assumptions that have been made about causal theories of reference: that a causal theory of reference requires an atomistic account of representation and that a causal theory of reference applies only to a limited range of expressions or concepts. Both, I think, are mistaken.

Donald Davidson contrasts

> ... two approaches to theory of meaning, the building-block method, which starts with the simple and builds up, and the holistic method, which starts with the complex (sentences, at any rate) and abstracts out the parts. ...
>
> The two approaches are, I think, naturally associated with two views of proper names. With the building-block approach goes the causal theory of proper names. ...
>
> The other view holds that interpreting the sentences (and hence,

by abstraction, the names) used by a speaker depends solely on the present dispositions of the speaker (or a community of speakers) and so the causal history of names is strictly irrelevant.[23]

I think that both of Davidson's contrasts are useful, but I object to the way they are associated. There is no reason why a theory of meaning, or an account of the source of intentionality, cannot be both holistic, explaining representation on the level of propositions, or perhaps even larger representational units, and also causal, explaining representation in terms of causal relations between the agent or a community of agents and the world. An explanation of representation in terms of indication is an example of a kind of account which combines these two approaches.

The most striking of the examples used to defend causal theories of reference have involved proper names and common nouns denoting natural kinds, and some philosophers have assumed that only such expressions should be explained in causal terms. Nathan Salmon, for example, contrasts *directly referential* terms with those that are *descriptional*. He suggests that Putnam's thesis that "meanings ain't in the head" applies only to the former kind of term. For the latter, "whose senses *do* consist solely of general properties, grasping the sense of the term is a wholly internal psychological state."[24] Purely general terms, Salmon assumes, are descriptional in this sense, and so one can represent them in virtue of being in a purely internal psychological state. Salmon takes Putnam's twin earth argument to show that natural kind terms such as "water" and "tiger" are not purely general, but he seems to assume that other terms, perhaps qualitative predicates such as "yellow," are immune to such arguments. This seems to me a mistake. If representation is essentially a causal relation, then no predicate, and no mental state, can represent in virtue of the intrinsic psychological properties of the person who is using the predicate, or who is in the mental state. Purely general properties may still be properties of things in the world, and representing such properties requires interaction with such things.

Second, I want to comment on the consequences that the strategy I have outlined has for the relation between thought and language. The strategy points toward an explanation of attitude and content which makes no essential reference to language. If the strategy can be carried out, then we will have a foundation for the kind of semantic theory that explains the meaning and content of linguistic expressions in terms of the intentions and conventions of language users, and which explains what it is to understand a language in terms of the capacities of speakers and hearers to use the language to serve their needs and desires. But although linguistic representation is not essential to the kind of account the strategy points to, it is essential that there be some form of internal representation in any creature that is correctly said to have beliefs and desires. I emphasized, in discussing the threat of circularity in the pragmatic analysis, that this account, as I understand it, is not behavioristic in the sense that it identifies mental states with patterns of behavior. In attributing beliefs and desires, we are attributing certain kinds of internal causal properties which have a structure that tends to reflect the world in ways that make it appropriate to call them representations. These representations could conceivably take the form of sentences of a language of thought written in the belief center of the brain, but they also could take the form of pictures, maps, charts or graphs, or (most plausibly) a diversity of redundant forms, none of which are very much like any of the forms which our public representations take.

The pragmatic picture and the possible worlds definition of proposition does not then deny that beliefs are internally represented. But it remains neutral on the form that those representations must take. It should be emphasized that the possible worlds conception of proposition does not present an account of the form in which propositions are represented which is a rival to a linguistic account. Accepting this account of propositions does not, for example, commit one to a psychological hypothesis that our minds represent a space of possible worlds point by point, with individual representations of individual worlds. The aim of the definition is to give an account of the structure of what is represented while leaving open questions about the means by which this is accomplished.

One could stretch the concept of language to include all the possible forms of representation, and in this way reconcile the kind of account I am promoting with the thesis that internal *linguistic* representation is essential to mental representation. Some of Gilbert Harman's remarks, in his book *Thought*, seem to be suggesting this kind of reconciliation. On the one hand, Harman accepts a functionalist account of intentional mental states similar to that suggested by the pragmatic picture. "Mental states and processes," he argues, ". . . are constituted by their function or role in the relevant program. To understand desire, belief and reasoning is to understand how desires, beliefs and instances of reasoning function in a human psychology."[25] But on the other hand, he argues that "we can simply take mental states to *be* instances or 'tokens' of appropriate sentences of a language of thought."[26] Harman's motivation for taking the functional states that are states of belief and desire as tokens of sentences is that such states, in order to play their functional role, must have a structure which parallels the structure of sentences.

In particular, the contents of attitudes must be things which can stand in logical relations such as entailment and incompatibility, which can be negated and conjoined and disjoined with each other, which can be *about* things, which can be singular or general. Are not sentences things that have just the right properties, and so can they not provide a useful model for the contents of propositional attitudes? We do, after all, use sentences to express the contents of mental states, and as Harman remarks, "this connection between states and sentences is no accident."[27] One might argue that to talk of a language of thought is to do no more than to talk of a means of representation appropriate to explanations of rational behavior in accordance with the pragmatic picture.

Even if linguistic representation is construed broadly so that any reasonably complex system of internal representation constitutes a language of thought, there remains an important difference between the pragmatic and linguistic pictures. According to the kind of account I have outlined, the *form* in which beliefs and desires are represented is not essential to their content. Two different agents might have the same beliefs even if the forms in which the beliefs are represented are radically different. The conceptual separation between form and content is, I think, the central feature which distinguishes the conception of thought implicit in the pragmatic picture from the one implicit in the linguistic picture.

The aim of the possible worlds definition of proposition is to assign to the *contents* of representations just the structure that is motivated by the pragmatic account of the functional role of representations. Propositions, defined this way, *are* like sentences in some ways: for example, they stand in entailment relations, can be related as contradictories or contraries. But they do not have constituents which correspond to the semantically simple constituents of sentences, and do not have an analogue of grammatical structure. If our internal representations have such structure, this is, the pragmatic account implies, not a matter of *what* is represented but of *how* it is represented.

It is essential to rational activities such as deliberation and investigation that the participants represent alternative possibilities, and it is essential to the role of beliefs and desires in the explanation of action that the contents of those attitudes distinguish between the alternative possibilities. The particular ways in which alternative possibilities are represented, or the particular means by which distinctions between them are made, are not essential to such activities and explanations, even if it is essential that the possibilities be represented, and the distinctions be made, in some way or other.

The conceptual separation between form and content is reflected in the identity conditions for propositions which the causal-pragmatic analysis implies. Whatever propositions are taken to be, and however we make precise the propositional relations of indication and tendency-to-bring-about in terms of which the analysis explains belief and desire, it is clear from the general schemas for the definitions of those relations that the following will be true: if the relation holds between an individual and a proposition x, and if x is necessarily equivalent to proposition y, then the relation holds between the individual and y. This implies that the thesis that necessarily equivalent propositions are identical—the main substantive consequence of the possible worlds analysis of propositional content—is a thesis that is tied to, and motivated by, the causal-pragmatic explanation of intentionality. This does not show that the identity conditions are right, or solve the problem of equivalence that these identity conditions create, but it does show that they, and the possible worlds analysis of proposition that goes with them, have a deeper philosophical motivation than has sometimes been supposed. If this definition had been proposed simply as a technical apparatus meant to systematize brute intuitions about the structure and identity conditions for objects of belief, then the examples of necessary truths and other nontrivial equivalences would show that the definition had missed the mark. The proper response would be to replace the technical apparatus with one that could make finer discriminations between the contents of attitudes and expressions. But since we have an argument to show that the identity conditions are right, as well as examples that seem to show that they are wrong, the proper response is not so clear.

The problem is, I think, that the alleged counterexamples are not just counterexamples to a particular analysis, but cases which are problematic in themselves. We lack a satisfactory understanding, from any point of view, of what it is to believe that P while disbelieving that Q, where the 'P' and the 'Q' stand for necessarily equivalent expressions. One can understand easily enough what it is to *assent* to a statement while dissenting from an equivalent one, but belief cannot be explained in terms of assent, among other reasons because one can assent to a statement without understanding it correctly. In order for a person's assent to a statement to show that he believes what it says (and not just that he believes that whatever it says is true), he must know what it says. What is unclear is how to explain *knowing what a statement says* in a way that does not have the consequence that a person knows what both of two necessarily equivalent statements say only if he knows that they are equivalent.

Could we escape the problem of equivalence by individuating propositions, not by genuine possibilities, but by epistemic possibilities—what the agent takes to be possible? This would avoid imposing implausible identity conditions on propositions, but unfortunately, it would also introduce intentional notions into the explanation, compromising the strategy for solving the problem of intentionality. If belief and desire are to be explained in terms of naturalistic relations such as indication and tendency-to-bring-about, then the possibilities used to individuate propositions must be the ones that are relevant to these relations, and these clearly must be genuine, and not merely epistemic possibilities.

The problem of equivalence is part of a broader problem concerning deductive reasoning. The problem is to explain how it is possible for the conclusion of a deductive argument to contain any information not already contained in the premises and, as a special case of this, how it is possible for a necessary truth to contain any information at all. An answer to this question is needed to explain how drawing deductive inferences can be a way of increasing one's knowledge, and how knowledge of necessary truths can be knowledge at all. The problem does not arise from any easily identifiable philosophical dogma which might be given up to avoid it. It is true that it was empiricists who explicitly drew the conclusion that necessary truths and deductive inferences were empty of content, forced to this conclusion, apparently, by the doctrine that all knowledge has its source in sense experience, together with the belief that mathematical truths are not confirmed or refuted by sense experience. But the conclusion really derives not from any substantive assumption about the source of knowledge, but from the abstract concept of content or information. The difficulty is, I think, that any way of conceiving of necessary truths as having content is at the same time a way of conceiving of them as contingent—as one way things could have been among others. This is, I think, because we do think of content and information in terms of alternative possibilities. Whether the source of my information is my senses, authority, or a faculty of intellectual intuition with access to a Platonic realm of abstract entities, its deliverances are not news unless they might have been different.

The problem of deduction may ultimately be a reason for rejecting our intuitive notion of content, and the possible worlds definition of proposition which expresses it, but before making this move, we should have an alternative conception, and an alternative strategy for solving the problem of intentionality. In the next chapter I will consider some alternative ways of explaining the notion of mental representation. Then in chapters 4 and 5 I will return to the problem of equivalence, and to the question of how one can have inconsistent beliefs or fail to believe the consequences of one's beliefs. I shall try to show that there is at least the possibility of reconciling the apparent facts of deductive ignorance and inquiry with the pragmatic picture, and with the conception of content which I am defending.

Chapter 2

The Linguistic Picture

I argued in chapter 1 that it is theoretically possible to solve the problem of intentionality—to give a naturalistic explanation of intentional mental states—without exploiting linguistic or semantic concepts. I want now to argue for something stronger: that it is *not* possible to solve the problem in the way suggested by the linguistic picture: by reducing intentional relations to semantic relations and then giving a naturalistic explanation of semantic relations. I have no general impossibility argument, but I will explore one detailed proposal for solving the problem in this way, and I will also look more briefly at a second, very different suggestion. The proposal I will discuss in detail was developed by Hartry Field in his paper "Mental Representation." It is a particularly clear and explicit version of the strategy suggested by the linguistic picture; I hope my criticisms of it will bring out some of the limitations of the general approach that it represents.

Field argues that one can give "a materialistically adequate account of the belief relation"[1] in the spirit of the linguistic picture even if belief is taken to be a relation between a person and a proposition, and propositions are construed as sets of possible worlds. (Field does not himself accept that construal, but assumes it for purposes of exposition in the initial sketch of his account.) His strategy begins with an analysis of belief which reduces the intentionality of belief to the intentionality of a semantic relation. To believe a certain *proposition* is to stand in an associated relation (which Field calls belief*) to some sentence, where the sentence expresses, or "means" the proposition.

> X believes that *p* if and only if there is a sentence S such that X believes* S and S means that *p*.[2]

The sentence S might be a sentence of a natural language, or it might be a sentence of some language of thought in which attitudes are encoded in the mind or the brain.

What this analysis does is to divide the initial problem into two subproblems:

subproblem (*a*): the problem of explaining what it is for a person to believe* a sentence (of his or her language).
subproblem (*b*): the problem of explaining what it is for a sentence to mean that *p*.[3]

Subproblem (a), Field suggests, should not present much difficulty; at least the believe* relation should not be problematic from the point of view of the problem of intentionality since it is not itself an intentional relation. Sentence tokens are physical objects or events, so there is no problem in principle with explaining a relation between a person and a sentence as a physical relation. Field suggests that the relation should be analyzed in terms of the way the subject is disposed to use the sentence in reasoning and deliberation, but says very little about the form that such an analysis might take. It is less clear to me than it is to Field that one could give an adequate dispositional account of sentential attitudes without making reference to the meanings of the sentences,[4] but that is not the point I want to press here. I will grant, for the purpose of the argument, that one can isolate intentionality in the relation of meaning or expressing that holds between sentence and proposition, and thus can reduce the problem of intentionality to the second of Field's subproblems, the problem of giving a naturalistic explanation of this relation. I will argue that Field does not give us reason to believe that this problem can be solved.

Field's strategy for solving subproblem (b) exploits the kind of theory of truth developed by Tarski, supplemented with a causal theory of primitive denotation (denotation of primitive expressions). He argues that using these resources, we can give a materialistically acceptable analysis of a relation between the sentences of the language that the theory interprets and the propositions they express. This claim follows from the following three theses, the first two of which Field had argued for in an earlier paper.[5]

(1) While Tarski did not succeed in giving a method for reducing the concept truth (for some specific language) to nonsemantical notions, he did succeed in showing how to reduce truth to *primitive denotation*. (Primitive denotation is the semantic relation holding between the primitive descriptive expressions of the language and their referents.)

(2) Primitive denotation can be explained as a causal relation, and thus as a materialistically acceptable concept.

(3) *"The problem of giving a materialistically adequate account of truth-at-a-possible-world is no more difficult than the task of giving a materialistically adequate account of truth-in-the-actual-world; fundamentally these apparently distinct problems are one and the same."*[6]

The third thesis I will not dispute or discuss, but I will try to give some reasons for doubting that either thesis (1) or thesis (2) is true. I will start with (1).

The main burden of Field's earlier paper, "Tarski's Theory of Truth," is to make a negative point: that Tarski did *not* succeed in giving a materialistically adequate characterization of truth, but *only* reduced that notion to other semantical notions. The argument for the negative point seems to me both sound and important, but I think it can be generalized to show something stronger: that Tarski's theory does not even succeed in reducing the problem of giving a materialistically acceptable account of primitive denotation. So while I accept the negative part of thesis (1), I will argue that the positive part is wrong. And it is the positive part that Field needs for his strategy for solving the problem of intentionality.

I will begin by summarizing the argument for the negative claim. Field argues that a Tarski truth characterization can be construed as a reduction with two parts: first, the recursive semantic rules reduce the concept of truth to that of primitive denotation. Second, the reduction is completed by defining primitive denotation by enumeration. For example, the definition of the primitive denotation relation for singular terms of German would have something like the following form:

> x denotes-in-German y if and only if x is "Frankreich" and y is France, or x is "Deutschland" and y is Germany, or . . .

But, Field argues, a definition or characterization by enumeration does not provide an adequate reduction. To give a scientific reduction of primitive denotation to nonsemantic terms, we need to do more than characterize the *extension* of the denotation relation; what is required is the characterization of the nonsemantic, and materialistically acceptable, *relations* (two-place *properties*) between words and things in virtue of which the former denote the latter.

Field uses an analogy to show that mere extensional equivalence is not a sufficient standard of reduction. Suppose, before the physical basis of the chemical concept of *valence* was understood, scientists had proposed reducing this notion to physical notions by giving the following characterization of valence:

> $(\forall E)(\forall n)(E$ has valence $n \equiv E$ is potassium and n is $+1$, or . . . E is sulphur and n is $-2)$[7]

This characterization obviously contributes not at all to a reduction of chemistry to physics. If no more revealing explanation of valence in physical terms were forthcoming, then scientists would be forced to admit either that valence was an illegitimate concept with no real application, or that the hypothesis of physicalism was false—that there are irreducible chemical properties.

I think the analogy is a good one, and I am persuaded that a definition of primitive denotation by enumeration makes no contribution to a naturalistic explanation of intentionality. But are the recursive rules which reduce satisfaction and truth to primitive denotation any better off? I don't think so, for they are essentially just definitions by enumeration too, for various classes of complex sentences. They establish an extensional equivalence between ascriptions of truth to sentences and ascriptions of primitive denotation to the ultimate constituents of the sentences, but they do not tell us any more about the basis for those ascriptions than does a definition of primitive denotation by enumeration.

The point can be illustrated with a very simple artificial language—one with names, monadic predicates, and truth-functional connectives, but no quantifiers.[8] What would the reduction of truth to primitive denotation for such a language look like? Something like this:

> A sentence is *true-in-L* if and only if it is a member of the smallest set meeting the following three conditions: (1) If F is a predicate and a is a name, and $d(a) \varepsilon d(F)$, then Fa is a member of the set. (2) If Q and R are members of the set, then $(Q\&R)$ is a member of the set. (3) If Q is a sentence that is not a member of the set, then $\sim Q$ is a member of the set.

This definition makes it possible to replace any semantical statement ascribing truth-in-L to a sentence of L with a statement extensionally equivalent to it which uses no semantic notions other than the primitive denotation function, d. But it does not contain any information about the physical properties of complex sentences which explain why they have the truth values they have. One sign of this lack is that the truth characterization does not generalize in any predictable way to cover additions to the language. As Field points out, the extensional and nonexplanatory character of the definition by enumeration of primitive denotation is reflected in the fact that if a new item were added to the primitive descriptive vocabulary of the language one would have to add a new clause to the definition, and nothing in the original definition would give a clue about what that clause should be. The situation would be exactly the same if a new connective or operator were added to the language. Nothing in the original truth definition gives us a clue about how to augment the rules to give truth conditions for sentences containing the new logical expression.

Field's point about primitive denotation was that the materialist seeking a reduction of primitive denotation was motivated by questions such as this: What are the physical properties of the shape "Frankreich" and the physical relations between relevant instances of it and France which constitute the fact that "Frankreich" denotes France? Obviously, an exhaustive list of name-denotation pairs which contains the pair <"Frankreich," France> is not responsive to the question. The parallel point about truth is that the materialist seeking a reduction of truth to primitive denotation is motivated by questions such as this: what are the physical properties of the shape "$\smallsmile$," and the physical relations between relevant instances of it and other things in the world which constitute the fact that a sentence of the form $\smallsmile A$ is true whenever the corresponding sentence A is false? A truth definition such as the one given above will be exactly as responsive to this question as the list was to the previous question. Even if the inquirer has a materialistically acceptable explanation of what it is about the simpler sentence A and its relation to the world that makes it true, he gets no help at all from the truth definition in his search for an explanation of the physical basis of the semantic status of the complex sentence.[9]

Consider the valence analogy again. Field notes that we may apply the concept of valence not only to elements, but also to certain stable configurations of elements (radicals). Suppose we have an extensional valence theory which defines *elementary* valence by enumeration, and also contains recursive rules which determine the valences of configurations of elements as a function of the valences of their parts (together with the structure of the configuration). As Field points out, this is obviously not a satisfactory reduction of the chemical notion to physical terms, but suppose we now discover the physical basis for *elementary* valence. Do we automatically have an explanation of the physical basis of valence in general? No, we do not. It is conceivable that the physical explanation of why *elements* combine together in the way predicted by valence theory be quite different from the physical explanation of why radicals combine together, and with elements, in the way predicted by the valence theory. We might have an explanation of the first kind which provided an appropriate reduction of elementary valence, together with an *extensional* reduction of valence in general to elementary valence without yet having any physical explanation of the second kind. It is even conceivable that valence in general be an irreducibly chemical property even if elementary valence is a physical property.

So what does a Tarskian truth characterization accomplish? I am suggesting that it makes no contribution at all to a solution to the problem of intentionality for semantic notions—that is, to providing a naturalistic explanation of what it is for a linguistic expression to represent objects, events and states of affairs. Despite whatever claims Tarski may have made to the contrary, and despite the interpretation which some of Tarski's philosophical contemporaries (such as Carnap and Popper) placed on his work, I think its significance lies elsewhere.

We may contrast two kinds of questions about the semantic status of sentences. First, there are questions about what it is, in general, for a sentence to have certain truth conditions. What physical (or sociological or psychological) facts constitute the fact that sentence S expresses the proposition x? This kind of question asks for a solution to the problem of intentionality. Second, there are questions about how a sentence comes to have the truth conditions which it has. Given that we understand (in naturalistic terms) the relation between S and x that constitutes the fact that S expresses x, can we explain how it is that S and x came to stand in that relation? This kind of question presupposes a solution to the problem of intentionality. Field argues that a Tarskian truth characterization is part of an answer to a question of the first kind. I want to suggest instead that it makes a contribution to an answer to a question of the second kind.

Perhaps I can make the contrast between the two kinds of questions clearer by considering the broad outlines of some answers that have been proposed—answers that I think are on the right track.[10] One might begin an explanation of the nature of the semantic relation between a sentence S and a proposition x by explaining what it is for a *speaker* to mean x by uttering S. Then one might go on to explain what it is for a *sentence* S to mean x in terms of the existence of a convention in a population of speakers that S should be used to mean x.[11] Conventions are to be explained in terms of the pattern of beliefs and intentions of the members of the population.[12] If one had an adequate account of this kind, then one would have a reduction of a principal semantic relation to the mentalistic intentional relations, belief and intention. The final step in the project of answering the first kind of question about semantic relations would be to give a naturalistic explanation of belief and intention along the lines suggested by the causal-pragmatic picture as discussed in chapter 1.

Now, presupposing this kind of account of semantic relations, we may turn to the second kind of question. Given that sentence S's expressing proposition x is constituted by the existence of a certain convention in the relevant population, how is it that that convention arose, and how is it sustained? How do speakers acquire the intentions and beliefs which they must acquire for the convention to continue to exist? Questions of this kind about conventions are often answered in terms of precedent or imitation. That is, the maintenance of a convention will often be explained by the fact that members of the population perceive other members of the population behaving in conformity with the convention, and in this way acquire the relevant beliefs and conditional intentions. But this would not be a plausible explanation of the maintenance of the convention that some specific complex sentence S is used to express the proposition x. For, as linguists and philosophers have long been fond of pointing out, speakers and hearers continually produce and understand new sentences, sentences that have never before been uttered or heard by that speaker or hearer, or by anyone.[13] To explain the rich and flexible set of conventions which constitute the fact that a population speaks and understands a language, one must find a small finite number of basic conventions which it *is* plausible to believe could be sustained by precedent, imitation, and explicit teaching, but which together have a large, possibly infinite set of deductive consequences of the form "S is used to mean x." This, of course, is just what a compositional semantic theory such as a Tarski truth characterization provides. The fact that both the clauses characterizing primitive denotation and the recursive clauses characterizing the values of complex expressions in terms of the values of their parts are just enumeration is exactly what one should expect, and is no threat to the explanatory power of the theory, interpreted in this way. Both kinds of clauses enumerate the basic conventions which speakers learn by precedent, imitation, and explicit teaching. The speakers' powers of deductive reasoning can then explain how they can acquire the beliefs and intentions which constitute the conventional relations between sentences in general and the propositions they express.

Let me turn now to Field's thesis (2): that the primitive denotation relation can be explained as a causal relation. I will argue that Field has given us no good reason to believe that it is possible to give the kind of causal account of primitive denotation which his project requires. Even if (contrary to what I have just argued) Field were right that a Tarskian truth characterization reduces truth to primitive denotation, I think the project could not yield a materialistically acceptable explanation of intentionality, since I do not think the final step in the reduction could be carried out.

The first two moves in Field's project are successive attempts to relocate the problem of intentionality in narrower and more tractable places. The analysis of belief into the belief* relation and the meaning relation shifts the locus of representation from mental states to linguistic objects; then the Tarskian truth characterization tries to shift the locus of semantic representation from sentences in general to simple descriptive expressions. It is at this level, according to Field's account, that representation really takes place. It is at this level that the connection between words and the world is accomplished and explained. For this reason, if Field's project of explaining intentionality is to be completed, the denotation relation must be explained independently not only of mentalistic intentional notions but also of the semantic relations which hold between complex expressions such as sentences and the information they convey. One must be able to say, in causal terms, what it is for one thing to *denote* another without appealing to any use that might be made of the first thing to express or convey information about the second.

What kind of causal account of reference does Field have in mind? The brief and programmatic remarks that he made are "deliberately very vague," as are many discussions of causal theories of reference. Citing Saul Kripke's *Naming and Necessity*, Field wrote:

> According to such theories [as Kripke's] the facts that 'Cicero' denotes Cicero, and that 'muon' applies to muons are to be explained in terms of certain kinds of causal networks between Cicero (muons) and our uses of 'Cicero' ('muon'): causal connections both of a social sort (the passing of the word 'Cicero' down to us from the original version of the name, or the passing of the word 'muon' to laymen from physicists) and of other sorts (the evidential causal connections that give the original users of the name "access" to Cicero and gave physicists "access" to muons.)[14]

If a causal theory of reference along these lines were developed in detail, would it provide the kind of reductive analysis which Field needs to complete his naturalistic explanation of intentionality? I do not think that it would. The problem is that the kinds of causal connection alluded to are themselves described in intentional terms. It is not clear how either the social processes in which names are transmitted or the interactions which give an inquirer evidential access to things can be described without making use of a prior understanding of the intentions of speakers, and of the transmission of information. Certainly Kripke made no attempt to give a reduction of reference to nonintentional terms.[15]

Field's solution to the problem of intentionality is *atomistic* in the sense that it holds that the most basic kind of representation relation—the kind from which all other representational relations derive—is a relation between linguistic atoms—the semantically simple expressions—and elements of the world. The name-object and predicate-property relations come first; the sentence-proposition relation is derivative. One may contrast this kind of account with one that tries to explain basic semantic representation on the level of sentences and propositions, and then to explain the representational properties of simpler expressions in terms of their role in determining the representational properties of the sentences in which they are parts. The issue between atomistic and nonatomistic explanations of intentionality does not turn on the question of whether representation should be explained in causal terms. In discussing the pragmatic strategy for solving the problem, I argued that representation is a causal notion, but the kind of causal relation that I appealed to (the notion of indication) was a relation between a person and a proposition. A theory that explains representational relations in terms of this kind of causal notion holds that representation of an object is always essentially representation of it as being a certain way. According to this account, one cannot separate the question, "How does a name denote an object?" from the question, "How does a sentence containing a name say something about the object named?" If this is right, then one cannot, without circularity, reduce the second question to the first.

Frege's slogan, "only in the context of a sentence does a word stand for anything," can be taken to sum up the thesis that intentional semantic relations are to be explained on the level of sentence and proposition rather than on the level of simple expressions and their referents. Michael Dummett reads Frege this way: "For Frege, the sense of a word or of any expression not a sentence can be understood only as consisting in the contribution which it makes to determining the sense of any sentence in which it may occur. . . . If this is so, then, on pain of circularity, the general notion of the sense possessed by a sentence must be capable of being explained without reference to the notions of the senses of constituent words of expressions."[16] But as Dummett points out, there is also a sense in which the sense (or reference) of a simple expression is primary. If the question is, "What is it for an expression to have a sense, or to represent?" the one answers the question first for sentences, and then for other expressions in terms of the answer for sentences. But if the question is, "How does a speaker know what the sense, or representational character, of an expression is?" then one answers the question first for simple expressions, and second for sentences in terms of the answer for simple expressions. A compositional semantic theory in the Fregean tradition, of which Tarskian truth characterizations are of course prime examples, is a contribution to answering both of these questions. Given that we understand what kind of thing the sense of a sentence is, it tells us what kinds of things the senses of simpler expressions are. And given that we understand what kind of thing the sense of a sentence is, it tells us how we come to know the senses of particular sentences by knowing the senses of their parts. But such a theory does not give us the explanation that both of these questions presuppose: the explanation of what it is for a sentence to have a sense, to express a proposition, to represent a world.

Field's response to the problem of intentionality is, I have argued, an atomistic one, and partly for this reason will not work. Might one give a more holistic explanation of intentionality which was still in accord with the linguistic picture? That is, might one accept that the most basic semantic relation is the relation between a sentence and its truth conditions, while still explaining semantic relations independently of mentalistic intentional notions? I will describe and discuss one strategy of this kind. Although the project I will outline is inspired by some of Donald Davidson's writings, I will not ascribe it to him, since Davidson has explicitly denied that his account of the foundations of a theory of meaning is an attempt to explain semantic notions in nonintentional terms,[17] and since he does not identify the problem that a theory of meaning is designed to solve with the problem of intentionality. Nevertheless, I think some of Davidson's ideas about the role of a theory of truth in a theory of interpretation are suggestive of a strategy for solving the problem of intentionality in the spirit of the linguistic picture. In outlining this strategy, I will borrow some of Davidson's ideas and terminology. In particular, I will call the kind of theory whose outlines I will sketch a theory of interpretation.[18]

The domain of phenomena which a theory of interpretation is designed to explain consists of the utterances of a community of speakers. The claim that a group of individuals is a community of speakers and the selected actions are utterances is the claim that the actions can be explained according to the pattern to be described; specifically, that the class of actions identified as utterances conform to two hypotheses.

The first hypothesis is that the utterances speakers produce are selected from a class of possible utterances which can be characterized in the following way: the possible acts of utterance are complex actions made up of a small number of simple actions (normally the production of certain sounds or shapes) combined according to recursive rules. The first task of the theory is to enumerate the basic sounds or shapes, and the recursive rules for combining them into complex utterances— sentences—from among which actual utterances are to be selected.

The second hypothesis is that speakers tend to utter certain sentences and not others, and that which ones they choose to utter depends, in a systematic way, not just on the intrinsic properties of sentences and relations between sentences, but also on the way the world is. The main task of the theory of interpretation is to give a systematic procedure for dividing the sentences into two classes, the division to be dependent on the way the world is. On the basis of a small finite number of postulates establishing correlations between the basic sound or shape types and things and properties, together with recursive rules classifying complex utterance types on the basis of these correlations, the theory defines a class of *true* sentences. The empirical claim of the theory is that the actual utterances will normally be drawn from this class.

The leading idea of theory of interpretation—and this is a thesis that Davidson defends—is that it is an *a priori* truth that speakers tend to speak the truth. This is so because the claim that a sentence has certain truth conditions is the claim that the sentence tends to be uttered only when those conditions are satisfied.

The account I have sketched is, of course, a gross oversimplification in many ways. People do utter ungrammatical sentences and do say things that are false. Speakers register the acceptance of or assent to sentences in other ways than by uttering them. And, as we have long been taught, people do many things with words besides trying to say what is true. A realistic theory of the kind I have described would have to identify a subclass of utterances which are *assertive utterances*. It would have to identify an action of assent or acceptance (of a sentence) such that the assertive utterance of the sentence was one, but not the only, criterion of assent or acceptance. It would have to explain the representational properties of nonassertive speech acts in terms of the role of the words in them in determining the status of the assertive utterances containing them. And the theory as a whole would have to be understood as an idealization: as describing norms from which actual speech can be seen to deviate in systematic ways.

Suppose we had a realistic and empirically adequate theory of this kind. Would it provide a way of understanding, in naturalistic terms, the semantic properties of the expressions of some language? I think it would, but one would want to ask a further question. The theory predicts a systematic correlation between acts of accepting sentences as true and certain facts about the way the world is, but it does not suggest any explanation for the correlation. Presumably, the theory should add at least the very general claim that the correlations hold because the relevant facts about the way the world is tend to cause speakers to engage in the actions which constitute the acceptance as true of the correlated sentences. This further claim brings out a parallel between the solution to the problem of intentionality implicit in this kind of theory and the causal-pragmatic solution that I sketched in chapter 1. Both explain representation in terms of a relation between a person and a proposition of the kind I called indication. In both cases, there is a correlation which holds, under normal conditions, or *fidelity conditions*, between the represented state of the world and some state of the person, and in both cases, the correlation is explained by the fact that the state of the world tends to cause the person to be in the corresponding state. The main difference is that in one case the state of the person is a linguistic disposition—the disposition to utter or assent to some sentence—while in the other case the state of the person is a more general dispositional state, a disposition manifested in action. On the former account—theory of interpretation—the correlation between utterances or linguistic acts of assent and the satisfaction of their truth-conditions is used directly to explain the representational character of linguistic expressions. On the latter account—the causal-pragmatic analysis—the connection is indirect: it is the correlation between *beliefs* and the world rather than utterances and the world which is used to explain representation. Because of the fact that rational agents often want to communicate some of their beliefs, and because of the existence in populations of rational agents of patterns of mutual knowledge about what sorts of actions will most effectively and efficiently communicate those beliefs (patterns of mutual knowledge which constitute the fact that those agents are a community of speakers of a certain language), one will also expect a general correlation between assertive utterances and the world. But on the causal-pragmatic account, this derivative correlation plays no direct role in the explanation of the representational character of either mental states or linguistic expressions.

The idea of theory of interpretation, in the extreme form I have presented it, with linguistic action identified and explained in isolation from other kinds of action, has little plausibility. If what was alleged to be speech played no role in a wider range of rational activity, then we would surely conclude that it was not really speech. If what a theory of interpretation identified as the *beliefs* of a speaker were irrelevant to the rational explanation of that speaker's nonlinguistic action, then we would reject the theory, however close the correlation between the sounds or shapes produced and the world. But no one has proposed or defended such a theory in this extreme form. Davidson writes, "of course it should not be thought that a theory of interpretation will stand alone." He suggests that we need a composite theory which "should provide an interpretation of sentences, and at the same time assign beliefs and desires, both of the latter conceived as relating the agent to sentences or utterances. The composite theory would explain all behavior, verbal and otherwise."[19] Davidson makes no claim for the conceptual priority of language or speech, but does claim that language and speech are essential to mental representation. "A creature cannot have thoughts unless it is the interpreter of the speech of another."[20] "We have the concept of belief only from the role of belief in the interpretation of language." Belief is "not intelligible except as an adjustment to the public norm provided by language."[21]

Once one grants that it is essential to the concept of belief that beliefs play the role ascribed to them by the pragmatic picture in the determination of action, it is no longer clear what the motivation is for the centrality of language and speech in the explanation of mental representation. Suppose we find a creature whose sophisticated manipulations of its environment give us reason to ascribe to it functional states of the kind postulated in the causal-pragmatic account of belief and desire, but which engages in no behavior which could be called communication. Maybe it is completely isolated from other creatures of its kind, or maybe its needs are so much in conflict with other creatures in its environment that communication would be of no value to it. Should we conclude, simply on the basis of the fact that the creature is not the interpreter of the speech of another that it does not really have beliefs and desires? That, it seems to me, would be arbitrary. The fact that a creature was not an interpreter of the speech of another might be a purely accidental fact about its environment, having nothing to do with its intrinsic capacities. When creatures fail to communicate in a way we can understand, we lose one valuable source of evidence for deciding whether they have attitudes, interests, and ends, and for deciding what specific attitudes, interests, and ends they have, but the fact that an incommunicative mind is less accessible is not a good reason for concluding that it does not exist.

To say that the concept of mental representation can and should be understood independently of the activity of speech is not, of course, to deny that the contents of some particular attitudes may essentially involve speech: that there are certain particular beliefs and intentions that only language users could have. It is obvious that intentions to speak and beliefs about what was said are attitudes that only one who understands a language could have, but it may also be that intentions and beliefs that are less explicitly about language are possible only because the agent is able to speak and understand a language. Beliefs about some theoretical questions, or even about distant times and places, may be impossible for creatures that are not part of a community of speakers. Richard Grandy argues that this is so:

> In many cases the state that is being portrayed in a belief report can only be fully identified by reference to language. For someone who has never been anywhere near China and speaks no Chinese, the belief that Peking is in China is typically achieved only through the mediation of language. By that I do not mean merely that one learns this fact through language, but that there are virtually no behavioral dispositions that would identify the internal state that do not involve linguistic items. And it is via the meaning of these linguistic items that we fix the content of the belief.[22]

Tyler Burge has used several detailed thought experiments to make a similar point, arguing that "the propositional attitudes of the individuals in a community do not seem to be individuated independently of publicly accessible meaning."[23] Both of these philosophers take the dependence of the contents of specific attitudes on a linguistic community to undercut a language-independent notion of mental representation and an analysis of meaning in terms of beliefs and intentions. But the fact that the subject matter of attitudes can involve language and speech, and the fact that this can be true even when it is not obvious that it is, do not show that propositional attitudes in general are not understandable independently of the use of language.

I have suggested that the centrality that theory of interpretation gives to speech and language in the explanation of mental representation is not well motivated. I also have an empirical reason for doubting that this kind of account of intentionality will work. Even the modest compromise between the linguistic and pragmatic pictures that Davidson seems to be proposing requires a semantics for a natural language that is autonomous in the following sense: one must be able to specify the semantic values of the sentences independently of the beliefs and other attitudes of speakers. But it does not seem plausible that natural languages, or any substantial fragments of them, are autonomous in this sense.

The clearest case of a language with an autonomous semantics would be a context-independent language. The semantic rules for such a language determine the content or truth conditions of all the sentences, independently of the circumstances of their use. A context-dependent language—for example a language with tenses or personal pronouns—might also have an autonomous semantics, in the relevant sense, provided the contextual determinants were nonintentional features of the situation in which sentences are used: for example, who is speaking, and the time and place of utterance. But if the semantic rules determine the content or truth-conditions of sentences as a function of the attitudes of the speaker or other participants in the conversation, then the semantics is not autonomous in the relevant sense. So, for example, if the referents of demonstratives and other referring expressions or the determination of the domain of quantifiers are a function of the mutual beliefs of speaker and addressees, then the semantics is not autonomous.

The more pervasive such context-dependence is, the less promising is a theory which understands beliefs and intentions in terms of relations between persons and *sentences*, since the truth-conditions of sentences can be understood only as a function of the beliefs and intentions of speakers. If (as seems plausible to me) what an adequate semantic theory for natural language does, in general, is to determine the truth-conditions of sentences as a function of the shared common background beliefs or assumptions of the speaker and his audience, and if truth-conditions for particular sentences often vary with variations in this shared common background, then the correlation between utterances and the fulfillment of their truth-conditions with which theory of interpretation begins cannot be identified without some prior understanding of the attitudes of speakers.

One response to the problem caused by this kind of context-dependence might be to shift the burden of the explanation of representation from natural language to a more context-independent inner language of thought into which speakers translate natural language. This would be to return to a version of the linguistic picture more like the one developed by Hartry Field. But this move would not be compatible with the main motivating idea of the theory of interpretation, which is that intentionality is essentially a social phenomenon: belief, as a private mental attitude "is not intelligible except as an adjustment to the public norm provided by language."[24] If this is the motivation for holding that language is essential to thought, then the language must be a language actually used by members of communities of speakers.

I have discussed two quite different ways of developing an account of intentionality in the spirit of the linguistic picture, accounts which give language a prominent place in the explanation of mental representation for quite different reasons. One kind of development of the linguistic picture—the one represented here by Hartry Field's account—focuses on linguistic *structure*. Mental representations—the contents of attitudes—are sentence-like because their structure mirrors the structure of sentences. They represent what they represent because they consist of name-like mental events, objects or states arranged in an analogous way. The second kind of development of the linguistic picture—the one represented here by theory of interpretation—focuses on linguistic *function*: mental representations are sentence-like because they are reflections or internalizations of the social activity in which sentences are used—the activity of communication. The pragmatic picture that I have been using to motivate the possible worlds analysis of propositional content rejects both reasons for assigning language an essential role in the explanation of mental representation. It holds that the semantic structure of sentences reflects the means by which propositions are determined, and not the structure of propositions themselves. And it holds that it is conceivable that beings might inquire, deliberate, calculate and speculate without being able to share the fruits of their thought with fellow beings.

Even if my painting of the pragmatic picture is persuasive, one might still have qualms about the possible worlds definition of propositional content, since one might have qualms about possible worlds. In the next chapter, I will address those qualms, arguing that, properly understood, possible worlds are not so difficult to believe in as many have taken them to be.

Chapter 3
Possible Worlds

According to Leibniz, the universe—the actual world—is one of an infinite number of possible worlds existing in the mind of God. God created the universe by actualizing one of those possible worlds—the best one. It is a striking image, this picture of an infinite swarm of total universes, each by its natural inclination for existence striving for a position that can be occupied by only one, with God, in his infinite wisdom and benevolence, settling the competition by selecting the most worthy candidate. But in these enlightened times, we find it difficult to take this metaphysical myth any more seriously than the other less abstract creation stories told by our primitive ancestors. Even the more recent expurgated versions of the story, leaving out God and the notoriously chauvinistic thesis that our world is better than all the rest, are generally regarded, at best, as fanciful metaphors for a more sober reality. J. L. Mackie, for example, writes, ". . . talk of possible worlds . . . cries out for further analysis. There *are* no possible worlds except the actual one; so what are we up to when we talk about them?"[1] Larry Powers puts the point more bluntly: "The whole idea of possible worlds (perhaps laid out in space like raisins in a pudding) seems ludicrous."[2]

These expressions of skepticism and calls for further analysis are of course not directed at Leibniz but at recent uses of parts of his metaphysical myth to motivate and give content to formal semantics for modal logics. In both formal and philosophical discussions of modality, the concept of a possible world has shown itself to have considerable heuristic power. But, critics have argued, a heuristic device should not be confused with an explanation. If analyses of modal concepts (or the concept of a proposition) in terms of possible worlds are to be more than heuristic aids in mapping the relationships among the formulae of a modal logic, the concept of a possible world itself must be explained and justified.

Although it is commonly taken to be an obvious truth that there really are no such things as possible worlds—that the myth, whether illuminating or misleading, explanatory or obfuscating, is nevertheless a myth—this common opinion can be challenged. That is, one might respond to the possible worlds skeptic not by explaining the metaphor but by taking the story to be the literal truth. David Lewis responds in this way, and he cites common opinion and ordinary language on his side:

> I believe there are possible worlds other than the one we happen to inhabit. If an argument is wanted, it is this: It is uncontroversially true that things might have been otherwise than they are. I believe, and so do you, that things could have been different in countless ways. But what does this mean? Ordinary language permits the paraphrase: there are many ways things could have been besides the way that they actually are. On the face of it, this sentence is an existential quantification. It says that there exist many entities of a certain description, to wit, 'ways things could have been', I believe permissible paraphrases of what I believe; taking the paraphrase at its face value, I therefore believe in the existence of entities which might be called 'ways things could have been.' I prefer to call them 'possible worlds'.[3]

Lewis does not intend this as a knockdown argument. It is only a presumption that the sentences of ordinary language be taken at face value, and the presumption can be defeated if the naive reading of the sentences leads to problems which can be avoided by an alternative analysis. The aim of the argument is to shift the burden to the skeptic who, if he is to defeat the argument, must point to the problems which commitment to possible worlds creates, and the alternative analysis which avoids those problems. Lewis does not think the skeptic can do either.

The rhetorical force of Lewis's argument is in the suggestion that possible worlds are really not such alien entities as the metaphysical flavor of this name seems to imply. The argument suggests not that ordinary language and our common beliefs commit us to a weighty metaphysical theory, but rather that what appears to be a weighty metaphysical theory is really just some ordinary beliefs by another name. Believing in possible worlds is like speaking prose. We have been doing it all our lives.

But for this to be convincing, the shift from "ways things might have been" to "possible worlds" must be an innocent terminological substitution, and I do not believe that, as Lewis develops the concept of a possible world, it is. To argue this point I will state four theses about possible worlds, all defended by Lewis. Together they constitute a doctrine which I will call extreme realism about possible worlds. It is this doctrine against which the skeptic is reacting, and against which, I shall argue, he is justified in reacting. I believe the doctrine is false, but I also believe that one need not accept or reject the theses as a package. The main burden of my argument will be to show the independence of the more plausible parts of the package, and so to defend the coherence of a more moderate form of realism about possible worlds—one that might be justified by our common modal opinions and defended as a foundation for a theory about the activities of rational agents.

Here are Lewis's four theses:

1. *Possible worlds exist.* Other possible worlds are just as real as the actual world. They may not actually exist, since to actually exist is to exist in the actual world, but they do, nevertheless, exist.

2. *Other possible worlds are things of the same sort as the actual world*—"I and all my surroundings."[4] They differ "not in kind, but only in what goes on at them. Our actual world is only one world among others. We call it alone actual not because it differs in kind from all the rest, but because it is the world we inhabit."[5]

3. *The indexical analysis of the adjective 'actual' is the correct analysis.* "The inhabitants of other worlds may truly call their own world actual if they mean by 'actual' what we do; for the meaning we give to 'actual' is such that it refers at any world *i* to that world *i* itself. 'Actual' is indexical, like 'I' or 'here' or 'now': it depends for its reference on the circumstances of utterance, to wit, the world where the utterance is located."[6]

4. *Possible worlds cannot be reduced to something more basic.* "Possible worlds are what they are and not another thing." It would be a mistake to identify them with some allegedly more respectable entity, for example a set of sentences of some language. Possible worlds are "respectable entities in their own right."[7]

The first thesis, by itself, is compatible with Lewis's soothing claim that believing in possible worlds is doing no more than believing that things might have been different in various ways. What is claimed to exist are things which ordinary language calls "ways things might have been," things that truth is defined relative to, things that our modal idioms may be understood as quantifiers over. But the first thesis says nothing about the nature of the entities that play these roles. It is the second thesis which gives realism about possible worlds its metaphysical bite, since it implies that possible worlds are not shadowy ways things could be, but concrete particulars, or at least entities which are made up of concrete particulars and events. The actual world is "I and my surroundings." Other possible worlds are more things like that. Even a philosopher who had no qualms about abstract objects like numbers, properties, states and kinds might balk at this proliferation of fullblooded universes which seem less real to us than our own only because we have never been there.

The argument Lewis gives for thesis (1), identifying possible worlds with ways things might have been, seems even to be incompatible with his explanation of possible worlds as more things of the same kind as I and all my surroundings. If possible worlds are ways things might have been, then the actual world ought to be *the way things are* rather than *I and all my surroundings*. *The way things are* is a property or a state of the world, not the world itself. The statement that the world is the way it is is true in a sense, but not when read as an identity statement (compare: "the way the world is is the world"). This is important, since if properties can exist uninstantiated, then *the way the world is* could exist even if a world that is that way did not. One could accept thesis (1)—that there really are many ways that things could have been—while denying that there exists anything else that is like the actual world.

Does the force of thesis (2) rest, then, on a simple equivocation between "the actual world" in the sense that is roughly captured in the paraphrase "I and all my surroundings" and the sense in which it is equivalent to "the way things are"? In part, I think, but it also has a deeper motivation. One might argue from thesis (3)—the indexical analysis of actuality—to the conclusion that the essential difference between our world and the others is that we are here and not there.

Thesis (3) seems to imply that the actuality of the actual world—the attribute in virtue of which it is actual—is a world-relative attribute. It is an attribute which our world has relative to itself but which all other worlds have relative to themselves too. But the moderate realist conception of possible worlds seems to conflict with this world-relativity, or contingency, of the property of actuality; if possible worlds are abstract "ways things could have been," then there is something distinctive about one of them, which constitutes its actuality: it is the one which corresponds to the world itself. Lewis argues that any "moderate version of modal realism comes to grief in the end" for this reason. Referring to abstract "ways things could have been" as "ersatz worlds," he argues that, on the moderate realist account, "the actualized ersatz world is special, since it alone represents the one concrete world. *And it is special not just from its own standpoint, but from the standpoint of any world.* So it is noncontingently special, since contingency is variation from world to world. But it is part of the theory that the actualized ersatz world is the special one. So it seems to turn out to be a noncontingent matter which of the ersatz worlds is actualized."[8]

The mistake in this argument, I think, is in the italicized statement. It *is* a special fact about "the actual world" (the way things are) that it alone corresponds to the one concrete world. But this is a contingent fact, which means that from the standpoint of other worlds, it is not a fact. From the standpoint of a counterfactual possible world, that world has the special property of being the one and only "way things could have been" that corresponds to the concrete world.

But does this not mean that, looking at things from an objective, absolute standpoint, merely possible people and their surroundings are just as real as we and ours? Only if one identifies the objective, or absolute standpoint with a neutral standpoint outside of all possible worlds. But there is no such standpoint. The objective, absolute point of view is the view from within the actual world, and it is part of the concept of actuality that this should be so. We can grant that fictional characters are as right, from their points of view, to affirm their full-blooded reality as we are to affirm ours. But their point of view is fictional, and so what is right from it makes no difference as far as reality is concerned.

My point is that the *semantic* thesis that the indexical analysis of "actual" is correct can be separated from the metaphysical thesis that the actuality of the actual world is nothing more than a relation between it and things existing in it. Just as one could accept the indexical analysis of personal pronouns and be a solipsist, or accept the indexical analysis of tenses and believe that the past exists only as memory and the future only as anticipation, one can accept the indexical analysis of actuality while excluding from one's ontology any universes that *are* the way things might have been.

Let me see if I can use the analogy between the present time and the actual world (an analogy that Lewis obviously has in mind) to make my point a little clearer. Pretend for the moment that we accept an Augustinian thesis about time, the one expressed in the following quotation:

> At any rate it is now quite clear that neither the future nor the past really exist. Nor is it right to say there are three times, past, present, and future. Perhaps it would be more correct to say: there are three times, a present of things past, a present of things present, a present of things future. For these three exist in the mind, and I find them nowhere else: the present of things past is memory, the present of things present is sight, the present of things future is expectation. If we are allowed to speak thus, I see and admit that there are three times, that three times truly are.

By all means continue to say that there are three times, past, present, and future; for, though it is incorrect, custom allows it. By all means say it. I do not mind, I neither argue nor object: provided that you understand what you are saying and do not think future or past now exist. There are few things that we phrase properly; most things we phrase badly; but what we are trying to say is understood.[9]

Now suppose we are trying to give a semantic analysis of tenses. Is our pretended metaphysical belief about time compatible with the standard semantic account—the one that says, for example, that at any time t a future tense statement is true at t just in case the corresponding present tense statement is true at some t' later than t? I think it is, *provided we understand the times in terms of which our past and future tense statements are interpreted as things which exist in the present*. That is exactly how Augustine does understand them.

Just as we needed to distinguish two senses of "possible world," so the Augustinian theory needs to distinguish two senses of time. There is the sense in which "neither the future nor the past really exist," and the sense in which, "if we are allowed to speak thus," we can correctly say "that three times truly are." The future and the past (in the latter sense) exist in the present (former sense), which is to say that they exist. So they are available as resources for the interpretation of tensed statements.

Only the present really exists (we are supposing). So the word "now" picks out the time that is uniquely real (that is uniquely realized). But, one might object, do not speakers in the past, and in the future, who say "only the present really exists" refer to their own times, and do they not speak the truth? Yes, they *did*, or *will*, refer to their own times, and they *did*, or *will*, speak the truth. But the fact remains (according to our hypothesized metaphysics) that their times do not exist *now*, which is to say that they do not exist at all (except as memory or anticipation). The fact that those times were or will be real does not show that they *are* real.

I do not want to defend the Augustinian theory of time, or even a less idealistic version that substitutes traces and potentialities for memory and anticipation. My only point is that Augustine and his metaphysical opponents who believe that other times are as real as our own might share the same semantics for tenses. The correctness of the standard semantics for tenses and temporal indexicals is not, in itself, a refutation of a theory that denies the reality of other times.

The thesis that the actual world alone is real is superficially analogous to the Augustinian thesis that the present alone is real—that all else, or all that appears to be else, is an aspect of the present. But the

Augustinian thesis has content, and can be coherently denied, because it says something substantive about what alone is real. In effect, it says that the actual world is a moment of time. But the thesis that the actual world alone is real has content only if "the actual world" means something other than the totality of everything there is, and I do not believe that it does. The thesis that there is no room in reality for other things than the actual world is not, like the Augustinian thesis, based on a restrictive theory of what there is room for in reality, but rather in the metaphysically neutral belief that "the actual world" is just another name for reality.

The extreme realist will, of course, deny this. He must hold that the indexical "actual" picks out, not the whole of reality, but only a part of it. But what part? How do I draw the boundaries around that part of reality which is appropriately related to me to be part of my actual world? I do not think the extreme realist can give a satisfactory answer to this question. Presumably, any part of reality that is spatially or causally connected with something in the actual world is itself part of the actual world. No one thinks that other possible worlds are literally "out there" in space (like raisins in a pudding), or that we might communicate with merely possible beings. But if other possible worlds are causally disconnected from us, how do we know anything about them? If the truth or falsity of our modal claims depends on the existence of things and events which are causally disconnected from us, then even the simplest claims about what is possible are unverifiable speculations.

My point is not a verificationist one. I am not bothered by the fact, freely admitted by Lewis, that there may be some modal facts—facts about what is possible—which we can never know. My worry is that I do not see how, on Lewis's account, there can be any other kind of modal fact. I do not see how we could ever have any reason to believe that a proposition we know to be false was nevertheless one that might have been true. As Lewis says in the argument quoted above, "I believe, and so do you, that things could have been different in countless ways." But we also believe that this belief is a reasonable one, and not a speculation about what is going on in some place so far away that it is not even part of our universe. It is the reasonableness of modal beliefs which I think Lewis's extreme realism cannot account for.

In the course of defending his version of modal realism, Lewis makes some general remarks about his conception of the methodology of metaphysics. The particular problem with extreme realism that I have just pointed to derives, I think, from a limitation in that methodology. Let me quote some of Lewis's remarks:

> One comes to philosophy already endowed with a stock of opinions.

It is not the business of philosophy either to undermine or to justify
those preexisting opinions, to any great extent, but only to try to
discover ways of expanding them into an orderly system. A me-
taphysician's analysis . . . succeeds to the extent that (1) it is systematic, and (2) it respects those of our pre-philosophical opinions
to which we are firmly attached. Insofar as it does both better than
any alternative we have thought of, we give it credence. . . .

So it is throughout metaphysics; and so it is with my doctrine
of realism about possible worlds. . . . Realism about possible worlds
is an attempt, the only successful attempt I know of, to systematize
preexisting modal opinions.[10]

There is much in this conception of metaphysics that seems to me
right, but I think we must ask more of our philosophical theories. They
must not only systematize preanalytic opinions, but also help to explain
the source of those opinions and their role in our practical activities.
We want to know not only what it is to believe that things might have
been different in various particular ways, but also why those beliefs
make a difference to inhabitants of the actual world. We want to know
why it is reasonable to have such beliefs, and why it is reasonable to
use them in the way we do. Even if extreme realism were to succeed
in providing an elegant systematization of modal opinions, it would,
I think, preclude a plausible explanation of the practical significance
which we believe those opinions to have.

The moderate realism whose coherence I am trying to defend accepts
theses (1) and (3), and rejects thesis (2). What about thesis (4)? If we
identify possible worlds with ways things might have been, can we
still hold that they are "respectable entities in their own right," irreducible to anything more fundamental? Some may believe that even
if a moderate realism about possible worlds is coherent, one buys the
added plausibility which it has over extreme realism only at the cost
of incurring the obligation to give some further analysis or explanation
of the concept of a possible world. If there were possible worlds, in
the sense of other things like me and my total environment, then they
could perhaps be referred to and quantified over even if not much
more could be said about them than that they are other things like our
actual universe. As concrete objects, they can stand alone, if they stand
at all. One would need no justification for including them in one's
theory of reality other than that they are there. But the moderate realist
believes that the only possible worlds there are—ways things might
have been—are (like everything that exists at all) elements of our actual
world. They obviously are not concrete objects or situations, but abstract
objects whose existence is inferred or abstracted from the activities of

rational agents. It is thus not implausible to suppose that their existence is in some sense dependent on, and that their natures must be explained in terms of, those activities. Thus Mackie, discussing possible worlds analyses of conditionals, writes, "possible situations, or possible worlds, just because they are not actual (or may not be actual) do not stand on their own, do not exist independently. . . . People can consider possibilities; but the possibilities exist only as the contents of such considerings . . . 'possible situations'. . . cry out for some further analysis. This analysis must be given in terms of what people do."[11]

The claim that possible worlds are dependent on actual human activities and the demand that possible worlds be explained in terms of such activities are vague, but their general intent and motivation are clear enough. I shall try to respond to this concern by locating claims about possible worlds in a theory of rational activities. But I want to resist a more specific demand with the same motivation: this is the demand, which Robert Adams argues must be met if we are to escape commitment to extreme realism, that "if there are any true statements in which there are said to be nonactual possible worlds, they must be reducible to statements in which the only things there are said to be are things which are in the actual world, and which are not identical with nonactual possibles."[12] Unless the reminder that by "possible world" we mean nothing more than "way things might have been" counts as such a reduction, I do not see why this should be necessary.

Two problems need to be separated: the first is the general worry that the notion of a possible world is a very obscure notion. How can explanations in terms of possible worlds help us to understand anything unless we are told what possible worlds are—and told in terms which are independent of the notions which possible worlds are intended to explain? The second problem is the specific problem that believing in possible worlds and in the indexical analysis of actuality seems to commit one to extreme realism, which is obviously false. Now to point to the difference between a way our world might have been and a world which *is* the way our world might have been, and to make clear that the possible worlds whose existence the theory is committed to are the former kind of thing and not the latter, is to do nothing to solve the first problem; in fact, it may make it more acute since it uses a modal auxiliary to explain what a possible world is. But this simple distinction does, I think, dissolve the second problem, which was the motivation for Adams's demand for an analysis.

Not only is an eliminative reduction of possible worlds not necessary to solve the second problem, it also may not be sufficient to solve the first. I shall argue that the particular reduction that Adams proposes— a reduction of possible worlds to propositions—by itself says nothing that answers the critic who finds the concept of a possible world obscure. His reduction says no more, and in fact says less, about propositions and possible worlds than the reverse analysis that I am defending—the analysis of propositions in terms of possible worlds.

Adams's analysis is this:

> Let us say that a *world-story* is a maximal consistent set of propositions. That is, it is a set which has as its members one member of every pair of mutually contradictory propositions, and which is such that it is possible for all of its members to be true together. The notion of a possible world can be given a contextual analysis in terms of world-stories.[13]

For a proposition to be true in some or all possible worlds is for it to be a member of some or all world-stories. Other statements that seem to be about possible worlds are to be replaced in a similar way by statements about world-stories.

There are three undefined notions used in Adams's reduction of possible worlds: *proposition, consistent,* and *contradictory.* What are propositions? Adams leaves this question open for further discussion; he suggests that it might be answered in various different ways. Little is said about them except that they are to be thought of as language-independent abstract objects, presumably the potential objects of speech acts and propositional attitudes. And it is, of course, assumed that they have truth-values.

What is consistency? The notion used in the definition of world-story is a property of *sets* of propositions. Intuitively, a set of propositions is consistent if it is possible for all its members to be true together. We cannot, of course, explain this intuitive idea in terms of the existence of a possible world in which all of them are true. Presumably, consistency will be a primitive notion, but we must be sure that the world-story theory includes some constraints on it which ensure that it has the right properties. Two assumptions that are necessary, and that should be uncontroversial, are the following:

(W1)   The set of all true propositions is consistent.

(W2)   Any subset of a consistent set is consistent.

What is a contradictory? This relation between proposition might be defined in terms of consistency as follows: A and B are contradictories if and only if $\{A, B\}$ is not consistent, and for every consistent set of propositions Γ either $\Gamma \cup \{A\}$ or $\Gamma \cup \{B\}$ is consistent. The theory tacitly assumes:

(W3)   every proposition has a contradictory.

These definitions and postulates yield a minimal theory of propositions. It is minimal in that it imposes no structure on the propositions except what is required to define the standard propositional relations such as compatibility, implication, and equivalence, and to ensure that these relations have the right properties. Implication, for example, can be defined in a familiar way: *A implies B* if and only if a set consisting of *A* and a contradictory of *B* is not consistent. (W1) and (W2) ensure that implication, defined this way, has the right properties. For example, it is transitive, reflexive, and preserves truth.

This minimal theory is not, however, sufficient to justify what Adams calls "the intuitively very plausible thesis that possibility is holistic rather than atomistic, in the sense that what is possible is possible only as part of a possible completely determinate world."[14] The assumptions we have made so far do not imply that every consistent set of propositions is a subset of a world story,[15] so to ensure that the theory satisfies the principal thesis that motivates it, we must add the following as an additional postulate.

(W4)   Every consistent set is a subset of a maximal consistent set.

It will be useful to compare this reduction of possible worlds to propositions with the competing reduction of propositions to possible worlds. What is at stake in choosing which of these two notions to define in terms of the other? Adams refers to the "not unfamiliar trade-off between non-actual possibles and intensions (such as propositions); given either, we may be able to construct the other, or do the work that was supposed to be done by talking about the other."[16] But the two proposals are not equivalent. Part of what distinguishes them is an elusive question of conceptual priority, but there are also more substantive differences, both in the structure imposed on propositions and possible worlds and in the questions left to be answered by further developments of the respective theories.

One might think that a reduction of possible worlds to propositions was more appropriate than the reverse since propositions are more familiar entities than possible worlds, and analysis should explain the less familiar in terms of the more familiar. However problematic propositions may be, we can still point to particular examples of them (like the proposition that Gerald Ford became President of the United States in 1974), and to facts about them with which we are familiar (for example, that the above-mentioned proposition is believed by Richard Nixon, and that it entails that Gerald Ford became either the President or the Vice President in 1974). Possible worlds, on the other hand, are a philosopher's invention and are further removed from the phenomena of speech and thought. So they are more in need of analysis.

I think this reasoning is based on a mistaken assumption about the point and content of a philosophical analysis. An analysis makes a claim about a relation among concepts which, if accepted, can be informative in either direction, or in both directions. It may be as helpful in explaining an obscure concept to reduce other things to it as to reduce it to other things. This would not be true if an analysis were like a stipulative definition of a previously meaningless sign, but normally all the terms involved in a philosophical analysis are terms that we understand, to some extent, prior to the analysis.

What is more important than familiarity for choosing the order of an analysis is the question of structure. Normally, one would expect to analyze the more highly structured set of entities in terms of a less highly structured one so that the analysis might help to explain the structure. Propositions are highly structured. One proposition can be stronger or weaker than another, or equivalent to it, compatible or incompatible with it, related to it as contrary or contradictory. These relations give rise to questions about the identity conditions for propositions, about closure conditions for the set of all propositions, about whether some propositions are constructed out of others. Possible worlds, on the other hand, are relatively unstructured. One may, for some purposes, want to define relations between possible worlds, like resemblance in some respect or other, or accessibility of some kind, but such relations are not essential to the concept of a possible world in the way that relations like entailment and compatibility are essential to the concept of a proposition. A minimal theory of propositions and possible worlds needs an account of the propositional relations, but it can get along without an account of relations between possible worlds.

Both of the theories that I am comparing impose structure on the set of propositions, but in the minimal world-story theory that structure derives from a primitive and unexplained concept of consistency. In contrast, the possible worlds analysis of proposition yields definitions of consistency and the other propositional relations in terms of elementary set-theoretic relations between the sets of possible worlds determined by the propositions. Whether one accepts these definitions as explanations of the propositional relations may depend on whether, in the end, one accepts the concept of a possible world as having intuitive content and an independent role to play in a theory; but even if possible worlds are totally opaque postulated entities, the possible worlds analysis of propositions still imposes a structure on the set of propositions which can be tested against intuitions about propositions, and against theoretical assumptions about the role of propositions in a theory of mental states and linguistic actions.

If we set aside questions of conceptual priority—of which concepts and principles should be primitive and which defined or derived—what are the differences between the two theories we are comparing? The world-story theory is weaker, leaving open questions which are settled by the possible worlds analysis of propositions. The following two theses are consequences of the possible worlds analysis but not of the world-story theory; the first is a closure condition; the second concerns identity conditions.

(W5)   For every set of propositions Γ there is a proposition A such that Γ implies A, and A implies every member of Γ.

(W6)   Equivalent propositions are identical.

Are these consequences of the possible worlds analysis welcome or not? Thesis (W5) seems reasonable on almost any theory of propositions and propositional attitudes. What it says is that for every set of propositions, there is a proposition which says that every proposition in the set is true. Whatever propositions are, if there are propositions at all then there are sets of them, and for any set of propositions, it is something determinately true or false that all the members of the set are true. If one is willing to talk of propositions at all, one will surely conclude that that something is a proposition. It may not be possible to express all such propositions since it may not be possible, in any actual language, to refer to all such sets; it may not be humanly possible to grasp them. But if this is so, it is surely a contingent human limitation which should not restrict the range of potential objects of propositional attitudes. So I will assume that the world-story theorist will want to add thesis (W5) to his theory.

Thesis (W6) I have discussed already, and I will return to it below. As we have seen, it has some intuitively problematic consequences, but it is also a thesis for which we have an independent argument. If the world-story theorist accepts the pragmatic picture, then he will want (W6) in his theory as well. It is compatible with the minimal theory, so he can add it as a further postulate.

If (W5) and (W6) are added as postulates to the world-story theory, then it becomes equivalent to the possible worlds analysis with respect to the structure it imposes on the set of propositions. For every set of world-stories, there will be a unique proposition that is a member of just the world-stories in the set. This means that every function from possible worlds (or world-stories) into truth-values will correspond to a unique primitive proposition which is true just where the function takes the value true, and false just where the function takes the value false. It seems that the sole difference that remains between the two theories is that one takes as primitive what the other defines. And even this difference will be eliminated if we make one more change in response to a question about the further development of the world-story theory.

The next question for the world-story theorist is this: can he say more about his fundamental concept, the concept of a proposition? In particular, are there some *basic* propositions out of which all the rest can be constructed? The usual way to answer this kind of question is to model basic propositions on the atomic sentences of a first order language; propositions are constructed out of individuals and primitive properties and relations in the same way that sentences are constructed out of names and predicates. But this strategy requires building further structure into the theory. There is another way to answer the question which needs no further assumption. We can deduce from what has already been built into the world-story theory that there is a set of propositions of which all propositions are truth-functions: this is the set of strongest contingent propositions—those propositions which are members of just one world-story. It is thus a harmless change, a matter of giving the theory a more economical formulation, to take these to be the basic propositions. (This change does not foreclose the possibility of a further reduction of what are here called basic propositions to propositions even more basic. Any alternative reduction can be expressed as a further reduction of this kind; this is why this move is harmless.) We can then define propositions generally as sets of basic propositions (or, for a neater formulation, call the basic elements *propositional elements* and let their unit sets be the basic propositions. Then all propositions will be things of the same kind.) A nonbasic proposition will be true just in case one of its members is true. This reduction has the added advantage that it allows us to define the previously primitive property of consistency, and to derive all of the postulates. With these primitive notions and assumptions eliminated, the world-story theory looks as good as the theory that takes possible worlds as primitive and defines propositions. This is, of course, because it is exactly the same theory.

I have gone through this exercise of changing the world-story theory into the possible worlds analysis of proposition in order to make the following point: first, the minimal world-story theory with which I began is indeed a minimal theory, a theory that assumes nothing about propositions except what is required to capture the principal intuition of the theory: that something is possible only as part of a possible completely determinate situation. But second, every step in the metamorphosis of this minimal theory into the possible worlds analysis is motivated either by uncontroversial assumptions about propositions (such as that truth-functions of propositions are propositions) or by the pragmatic picture of propositional attitudes, or by theory-neutral considerations of economy. If this is right, then the possible worlds analysis is not just one theory which gives propositions the identity conditions which are motivated by the pragmatic picture. More than this, it is the whole content of that analysis to impose the minimal structure on propositions which is appropriate to a theory which is guided by this conception of propositional attitudes. Anyone who believes that there are objects of propositional attitudes and who accepts the assumptions about the formal properties of the set of these objects, must accept that there are things which have all the properties that the possible worlds theory attributes to possible worlds, and that propositions can be reduced to these things.

Is the form of realism about possible worlds that I have been defending really realism? It is in the sense that it holds that statements about what is possible are to be explained in terms of quantification over possible worlds, and that some such statements are true. It is in the sense that it claims that the concept of a possible world is a basic concept in a correct account of the way we represent the world in our propositional acts and attitudes. But on the other hand, the moderate realism I want to defend need not take possible worlds to be among the ultimate furniture of the world. Possible worlds are primitive notions of the theory, not because of their ontological status, but because it is useful to theorize at a certain level of abstraction, a level that brings out what is common in a certain range of otherwise diverse activities. The concept of possible worlds that I am defending is not a metaphysical conception, although one application of the notion is to provide a framework for metaphysical theorizing. The concept is a formal or functional notion, like the notion of an *individual* presupposed by the semantics for extensional quantification theory. An individual is not a particular kind of thing; it is a particular role that things of any kind may occupy: the role of subject of predication. To accept the semantics for quantification theory is not to accept any particular metaphysics of individuals, even though one may use the resources of that semantic theory to help clarify one's metaphysical commitments.

Similarly, a possible world is not a particular kind of thing or place. The theory leaves the *nature* of possible worlds as open as extensional semantics leaves the nature of individuals. A possible world is what truth is relative to, what people distinguish between in their rational activities. To believe in possible worlds is to believe only that those activities have a certain structure, the structure which possible worlds theory helps to bring out.

Let me develop the analogy between domains of possible worlds and domains of individuals to try to make my point clearer. One may think of quantification theory as a framework for representing, once and for all, one's total ontological commitment. To do this is to assume that there is one big domain of discourse—the domain of what there is—which gives the intended interpretation of quantification theory. To be, then, is to be a value of a bound variable, under this interpretation. But one can reject this metaphysical interpretation and still accept the referential semantics for quantification theory. One can deny that there is a domain of all there is, of which all the domains of discourse in particular contexts are subdomains. One can deny that it makes sense to ask ontological questions outside of a particular context.

Analogously, one may choose to put a metaphysical interpretation on the concept of a possible world, assuming that there is one domain of all metaphysically possible worlds from which the restricted domains relevant to interpreting different kinds of possibility and necessity are drawn. But one may also reject that interpretation, and the coherence of the metaphysical questions which it raises, without rejecting a realistic understanding of possible worlds semantics. One may say that in particular contexts of inquiry, deliberation and conversation, participants distinguish between alternative possibilities, and that they should do so is definitive of those activities. It does not follow from this that there is a domain from which all participants in inquiry, deliberation and conversation must take the alternative possibilities that they distinguish between.

Chapter 4
Belief and Belief Attribution

Any account of mental representation must explain the parallels between the objects or contents of speech acts and the objects or contents of propositional attitudes. Sentences are used both to say how things are and to attribute beliefs. As Jerry Fodor says, "it could hardly be an accident that the declarative sentences of English constitute the (syntactic) objects of verbs like 'believe.' "[1] Proponents of both the linguistic and the pragmatic pictures of propositional attitudes can agree that the object of saying, at least when the speaker says what he believes, is the same as the object of believing, but they give quite a different explanation of why this is so. On the pragmatic picture, saying is like believing because saying is normally the expression of belief. A speech act is an act performed with certain beliefs and intentions, and its content is derived from the contents of the beliefs and intentions of the speaker, or more generally from the beliefs and intentions of the group of speakers who constitute the speech community. On the linguistic picture, the parallel is explained by the assumption that the object of belief is the same as, or is modeled on, what is *uttered* in a speech act. The initial idea is that to believe that P is to be disposed to *say P*. A more sophisticated development of the idea might say something like this: to believe that P is to be in a state that is relevantly similar to the state that I would be in if I were to say the following: P.[2] Both kinds of account can explain why it is possible to attribute beliefs using the same form of words that one uses to make statements, but on the linguistic account the parallels run deeper. On the linguistic account, the structure of a state of belief is something very much like the structure of a set of statements. On the alternative account, belief *attributions* parallel statements, but the mental state of the person in virtue of which the attribution is true will be something with a completely different form. In this chapter I will look at some examples and arguments in the light of these contrasting accounts of the relation between belief states and the belief attributions that describe them. I will consider what we may lose and what we may gain by locating semantic complexity in the means by which propositions are determined and the ways that belief states are described, and not in the propositions and belief states themselves.

Gilbert Harman has argued that we lose some generalizations about the objects of propositional attitudes by treating the structure by which a proposition is determined as something that cannot be recovered from the proposition itself. He writes:

> Consider the logical relations between beliefs. If the belief that *snow is white and grass is green* is true, then the belief that *snow is white* is true. . . . Clearly a generalization is possible: whenever a belief that *P & Q* is true, the corresponding belief that *P* is true. Some such general statement is appropriate. We cannot simply list the relevant instances since there are an infinite number of them. But the relevant generalization presupposes that certain beliefs have the structure of conjunction.[3]

Jerry Fodor has given a similar argument, emphasizing that generalizations about the logical relations between beliefs are essentially involved in the explanations of behavior in terms of beliefs and desires. Belief-desire explanations, Fodor argues, require that propositional attitudes "are typically *non*-arbitrarily related in respect of their content." For example, the explanation of Mary's cello playing in terms of her desire to make Fred suffer and her belief that he will suffer if she plays her cello depends on the entailment relation between the set of propositions {*Fred will suffer if Mary plays her cello, Mary plays her cello*} and the proposition *Fred will suffer*. This relation, Fodor seems to assume, requires that, for example, the first of these propositions be represented as a *conditional* proposition.[4]

To see the fallacy in these arguments, consider this parody of Harman's: If $7 - 2$ is an odd number, then 7 is; if $4 - 2$ is an odd number then 4 is. Clearly a generalization is possible: if $x - 2$ is odd, then so is x. But this presupposes that certain numbers have the structure of differences between numbers.

What is presupposed is of course something weaker than this: namely that certain numbers can be determined by computing the difference between other numbers. In the same way, what is presupposed by Harman's generalization is that some propositions can be determined by performing the operation of conjunction on other propositions. But this does not imply that the operation of conjunction is a constituent of the proposition determined, or that a proposition determined in this way can be analyzed into conjuncts in a unique way. Belief-desire explanations do presuppose that propositions stand in logical relations such as entailment, and one can generalize about entailment relations by describing propositions in terms of the way they are or might be determined. But as the possible worlds analysis of propositions makes clear, the assumption that propositions stand in logical relations does not imply that they have linguistic structure or logical form.

The analogy between numbers and propositions is an appropriate one, given the possible worlds analysis. Just as one number can be the value of many different complex numerical expressions, so one proposition can be the value of many different complex linguistic expressions. Inferring that Socrates (or the sense of his name) is a constituent of the proposition that Socrates is wise from the fact that the individual (or sense) plays a role in the determination of the proposition is like inferring that the number 7 is a constituent of the number $(7-2)$ from the fact that the latter number is here determined as a function of the former. But is this analogy plausible? Doesn't Socrates stand in some more intimate relation to the proposition that he is wise than 7 does to $(7-2)$? Isn't that proposition *about* Socrates? More generally, we do commonly characterize propositions in terms of the way they are determined—as singular or general propositions, conditional propositions, subject-predicate or relational propositions. Don't these characterizations suggest that propositions themselves are constructed out of individuals and general concepts, antecedents and consequents, subjects, predicates and relations?

We need not concede that propositions are complex in this way in order to account for such characterizations as characterizations of propositions themselves. The numerical analogy is useful here: the number 38, however expressed, is an even number; this fact can be stated by saying that for a certain function (multiplication by 2) there is an argument (a natural number) for which the function takes the value 38. In the same way, one might give an account of aboutness by specifying a class of propositional functions (functions from individuals to propositions) and say that a proposition x is about individual a just in case x is the value of one of the functions for the argument a. (I do not know how to give an account of this kind that is adequate. One cannot define the relation of aboutness in terms of *all* propositional functions, since for any proposition and any individual, there will be functions that take that individual into that proposition.)

There is this difference between the numerical and the semantic examples: there are many ways to represent the number 38 other than as a function of 2 (for example as $37 + 1$), but we may have no way of expressing the proposition that Socrates is wise except by referring to Socrates, and so representing the proposition as a function of Socrates. For this reason, the relation between Socrates and the proposition that he is wise may be more like the relation between the number π and the number $3\pi - 2$ than it is like the relation between the number 2 and the number 38. But in neither case do we need to say that the one number is a constituent of the other.

One might argue that even if attributing semantic structure, or logical form, to the objects of belief is not necessary for generalizing about the relationships between them, still, it is part of our common sense conception of belief that its objects have such structure. Stephen Stich, for example, assumes "that commonsense psychology takes beliefs to be structured states (some of) whose components are concepts, and that the concepts composing a particular belief are at least roughly correlated with the words we would use to express the contents of the belief."[5] I will argue that this assumption is not an essential part of commonsense psychology and that we can better account for the way we ordinarily attribute belief if we assume that the objects of belief do not have such structure.

Consider the problem of the attribution of beliefs to animals. Do animals such as dogs really have beliefs? Stich thinks that we have strong reasons for both the positive and the negative answers to this question. The case for the positive answer appeals to the naturalness of common sense psychological explanations of animal behavior in terms of beliefs and desires. The case for the negative answer is based on the difficulty of characterizing precisely the contents of animal beliefs. In making this case Stich exploits his assumption that the objects of belief are structured objects made up of concepts. Here is his example:

> ... consider trusty Fido who sees his master bury a meaty bone in the backyard. Fido goes out the door and begins pawing at the very spot where the bone is buried. On the belief-desire account, Fido believes that there is a meaty bone buried in the yard, and wants to get it. ... [But] it surely cannot be quite right to say that Fido believes there is a meaty bone buried in the yard. After all, Fido does not even have the concept of a bone, much less the concept of a meaty bone or a yard. He may be able to recognize bones tolerably well, provided they are typical examples and presented under conditions that are not too outlandish. But this is hardly enough to establish that he has the concept of a bone, or any belief or desires about bones. For Fido does not, it seems safe to assume, have any beliefs about the origin and general anatomical function of bones. ... Worse yet, Fido does not know the difference between real bones and a variety of actual or imagined ersatz bones (made of realistic looking plastic, perhaps, and partially covered with textured soy protein suitably flavoured). ... Given Fido's *conceptual and cognitive poverty* in matters concerned with bones, it is surely wrong to ascribe to him any beliefs about a *bone*."[6]

This argument is difficult to answer if we regard propositions as linguistic items or as quasi-linguistic complexes stored in the mind or the brain. The problem, on this assumption, would be to translate as accurately as possible the dog's mental language into English, or to find English expressions for the concepts that are the constituents of the content of its propositional attitudes. If one operates with a conception of proposition that raises these questions, then it is plausible to conclude that despite the naturalness of belief attributions and belief-desire explanations to them, dogs do not *really* have beliefs at all, since it is not very plausible to hypothesize such linguistic or conceptual structures.

But the problem looks quite different if one begins with the possible worlds conception of proposition. When we ascribe attitudes to the animal, what we presuppose is simply that it has *some* mechanism for representing and distinguishing between alternative situations. It may be a very crude one, recognizing only gross differences, and containing no representation at all of possible situations radically different from the way things actually are. The conceptual space necessary to account for its capacities and dispositions might consist of just a few relevantly different "ways things might be." But *our* language, with its complex structure and capacity to make more subtle discriminations and describe more distant possibilities, may be used to distinguish between the few alternative possibilities represented by the dog without thereby attributing our concepts to it. Because propositions do not mirror the structure of sentences that express them, it is possible to use sophisticated, semantically complex sentences to ascribe attitudes to creatures with very limited cognitive capacities.

Even if propositions do not have concepts as constituents, we may still be tempted to say that our attributions only approximate the real contents of the animal's attitudes. Both Fido and his master believe that there is a bone buried in the yard, but do they really believe exactly the same thing? The master's belief implies that what is buried in the yard is a *real* bone, and not an ersatz one such as Stich describes. Fido does not believe this, it seems, for he does not distinguish the actual situation from a similar counterfactual situation with an ersatz bone substituted for the real one. But if we think of a proposition as a way of dividing a given set of alternative possible ways things might have been into two parts, then we can say that, in one sense, the master's belief is exactly the same as the dog's. They both divide the set of alternative possible ways things might have been that is relevant to explaining Fido's capacities and dispositions in exactly the same way. Since propositions are functions, the identity conditions are relative to a given domain of arguments. Two expressions may determine the same proposition relative to one set of possible states of the world, but distinct propositions relative to a larger set. One might want to say that the propositions determined are *really* identical only if the functions take the same value for *all* possible worlds, but as I have argued, the possible worlds analysis does not commit one to accepting that there is such a set. One who is skeptical about metaphysical necessity and possibility, or about context-independent identity conditions for propositions, can still accept this analysis.

The problem of the precise identification of content is particularly dramatic in examples of animal belief, but on the linguistic picture of content, there will be similar problems even if one sticks to ordinary beliefs of ordinary people. Just as Fido's belief that there is a meaty bone buried in the yard seems different from his master's, so the beliefs of laymen seem different from those of experts; the beliefs of children seem different from those of adults; the beliefs of those with some perceptual, cognitive or linguistic peculiarity will seem different from those of more normal people. Belief, knowledge and understanding seem to be holistic, to be matters of degree, to grow and change in ways that are difficult to reconcile with a realistic conception of mental representation as a relation to a determinate sentence-like object. If one begins with a sentential conception of belief, one is likely to end in skepticism, not just about animal belief but about belief in general. To illustrate this point, I will discuss a number of examples that philosophers have used to raise problems about belief and belief attribution.

First an example of Daniel Dennett's: suppose a child of six tells us that his daddy is a doctor. Under what conditions should we say that he understands what he says?

> Must the child be able to produce paraphrases, or expand on the subject by saying that his father cures sick people? Or is it enough if the child knows that Daddy's being a doctor precludes his being a butcher, a baker, a candlestick maker? Does the child know what a doctor is if he lacks the concept of a fake doctor, a quack, an unlicensed practitioner? Surely the child's understanding of what it is to be a doctor (as well as what it is to be a father, etc.) will grow through the years, and hence his understanding of the sentence 'Daddy is a doctor' will grow.

If the child does not yet fully understand the content of his own statement, can the statement correctly express the content of his knowledge? "One is inclined to say that he only 'sort of' knows this, or 'half' knows this. If the proposition is to be the thing known, we have to allow for quasi-knowledge of propositions. Yet one might argue that when the child only half knows the proposition there is still something—something somehow 'less'—that he fully or really knows." Dennett concludes that if knowledge and understanding admit of degrees in this way, "this bodes ill for *things* known, for facts or propositions, or whatever."[7]

The general point that Dennett is making is that the capacities and dispositions that constitute a person's knowledge do not divide up neatly into discrete items of information—into propositions. But one of the virtues of the possible worlds analysis is that it does not require such a division. One can describe very naturally the situation in which one is tempted to say that a person only 'sort of' knows something, and one can explain very naturally how a person's understanding of a proposition can grow. The child who says his daddy is a doctor understands what he says, and knows it is true, to some extent, because he can divide a certain, perhaps limited, range of alternative possibilities in the right way and locate the actual world on the right side of the line he draws. As his understanding of what it is for Daddy to be a doctor grows, his capacity will extend to a larger set of alternative possibilities or, rather, the extension of this capacity will *be* the growth of his understanding.

My second example is one of several cases, invented by Stich, of people whose perceptual capacities are abnormal. Suppose a man— call him George—calls most red things "red," but also applies this label to certain specific shades of green and blue. This peculiarity of George's is not simply a *linguistic* mistake; he systematically confuses those shades of blue and green with certain shades of red. Suppose, finally, that he is not aware of his condition. George sincerely assents to the statement "Beefeater jackets are red." Does he *believe* that beef-eater jackets are red? Most people, Stich suggests, would be inclined to say that he does, but would be somewhat hesitant. And if we vary the example, making George's perceptual abnormality more extreme, we can get a case in which many people would be reluctant to attribute the belief to George, despite his sincere assent. Stich uses this example, and variations of it, to argue that the correctness of belief attributions is a matter of degree and is dependent on context. The correctness of my attribution of belief to George depends, Stich proposes, on a *similarity* relation between the content of George's belief and that of the belief *I* would express by saying that beefeater jackets are red.[8]

The indeterminacy and context-dependence in such examples can be accounted for by the possible worlds analysis of content and the pragmatic-causal strategy for explaining propositional attitudes. One source of indeterminacy is the one we have already discussed. The identity of content is defined relative to a domain of relevant alternative possibilities, and the possibilities in which beefeater jackets are green or blue (of the relevant shades) may or may not be relevant. Imagine a context in which what is at issue is whether beefeater jackets are red or gold. In such a context, we might say that George not only believes but knows, despite his perceptual limitations, that beefeater jackets are red. But there is also an additional more interesting potential source of indeterminacy that is relevant here. Suppose, as I suggested in chapter 1, we were to explain belief as a kind of *indication*. Roughly, to believe that P is to be in a certain kind of state that *under normal conditions* I would be in only if P: But what are the relevant normal conditions, or fidelity conditions as Dennis Stampe calls them? Two kinds of answers are possible, one yielding a more individualistic conception of belief, one a more social conception. Both answers require that external conditions be right in order for fidelity conditions to obtain: lighting conditions are normal, there are no hidden mirrors or distorting atmospheric conditions. But the two answers differ on what George's perceptual capacities must be like in order for fidelity conditions to obtain. On the first answer, fidelity conditions relevant to George's perceptual beliefs require that George's perceptual system be functioning as *it* normally does. George must not, for example, be drugged or asleep. But what is normal for George is not what would be normal for most of us. On the second answer, fidelity conditions relevant to George's perceptual beliefs require that George's perceptual system function normally—the way a normal person's perceptual system functions. On the second answer, George's perceptual beliefs depend on what is normal for members of his community or species, and not just on the way George interacts perceptually with his environment.

If we explain fidelity conditions in the first way, then we may conclude that George does not really believe that beefeater jackets are red. Perhaps what he really believes is that they are either red or one of certain shades of green or blue. But if we explain fidelity conditions in the second way, then we will conclude that George does believe exactly what we believe. For when George is perceiving something red (or something blue or green of the appropriate shade) he is in a state that, *if conditions were normal*, would be caused only by red things.

Which kind of account of fidelity conditions is more appropriate? For this example, the second seems more natural, but for other examples, the first may be better. The decision will depend partly on context— for example on the reason one is asking about George's beliefs—and partly on the nature and extent of the abnormality. If George's perceptual system were more radically different from our own, it might be difficult to talk in a determinate way about what would be true if George were in the state he is in fact in, but with a normal perceptual system. If George's perceptual system had a different organization, rather than just a local defect, then the state he was in might not be one he *could* be in if his perceptual system were normal. In this case, we would have to give the first kind of account of fidelity conditions.

The third example I want to comment on in this context is Tyler Burge's notorious arthritis example.[9] First let me sketch the example. Arthritis is an inflammation of the joints. Inflammation of tendons or muscles, whatever its cause or nature, is not arthritis. But some people don't know this. Take Mabel, for example, who has arthritis and also has many beliefs about arthritis. One of them is that she has recently developed arthritis in her thigh, a place where no one could develop arthritis. This is the actual situation, according to Burge's story. Now compare the actual situation with the counterfactual situation in which Mabel's inner states and dispositions are just as they actually are, and in which the physical facts about inflammations of the joints, muscles and tendons are also the same as they actually are. What is different in the counterfactual situation is the way certain words are used, not by Mabel but by other people. The word "arthritis," in this counterfactual situation, is properly used to refer to a wider class of rheumatoid ailments, including the one that is afflicting Mabel's thigh.

Mabel does not, of course, have *arthritis* of the thigh in the counterfactual situation since her medical condition is exactly the same there as it is in the actual situation. Anyway, it is impossible to have arthritis in the thigh. But the condition that she calls "arthritis" in the counterfactual situation is one that she does have, and the belief that she would express there by saying "I have arthritis in my thigh" is a true belief. It follows that Mabel's belief in the actual world is different from her belief in the counterfactual world despite the fact that both her inner states and her causal interactions with her environment are exactly the same in both worlds.

Burge uses this example to argue for the social character of belief. What a person believes may depend in part on facts about conventions and practices of members of the believer's linguistic community, even when those facts do not directly affect the believer. I think that this general point is right, and I think the causal-pragmatic strategy can account for it. In the same way that fidelity conditions relevant to explaining one person's perceptual beliefs may depend on the perceptual capacities which are normal in a community, the fidelity conditions which are relevant to beliefs formed by a process that involves language may depend on the linguistic capacities that are normal in the believer's linguistic community. Mabel, in the actual world, suffers from a mild linguistic abnormality (an incomplete, partly mistaken understanding of the way the word "arthritis" is used). Just as George would say "Beefeater jackets are red" even if they were green (of a certain shade), so Mabel might say "Arthritis is a common affliction among older people" even if older people suffered only from certain other related ailments. Very roughly, according to an explanation of belief in terms of indication, Mabel's beliefs are about *arthritis* only if they are (under fidelity conditions) sensitive to facts about arthritis. As things are, Mabel's beliefs expressed with the term "arthritis" are sensitive to facts about the more general kind of affliction, but because of Mabel's small linguistic mistake, fidelity conditions do not obtain. But in the counterfactual situation, the same states of Mabel count as normal states since there she makes no linguistic mistake. Fidelity conditions are different, and so the contents of some of her beliefs are different.[10]

I want now to consider some examples of attributions of tacit beliefs or presuppositions—beliefs ascribed even though the believer has never expressed or consciously thought about them. Here is an example discussed by Stich: "It would not be counterintuitive to assert that Bertrand Russell believed (indeed knew) that Big Ben was larger than Frege's left earlobe, even if, as is almost certainly the case, Russell would have had to infer that belief from other beliefs were the question ever to have arisen." Common usage is tolerant of such belief attributions, Stich says, but they are not literally correct. ". . . Our folk theory can comfortably concede that perhaps Russell didn't actually believe Big Ben is larger than Frege's earlobe, though he certainly would have come to believe it, had he been asked."[11] This is the only plausible thing to say if we think of beliefs as sentence-like representations of propositions. No one could have stored away in his memory bank representations of all of the trivial and obvious facts that most of us take for granted. The mind is just not big enough. But I don't think it is plausible to say that all such apparent beliefs are only potential beliefs, for they may play an actual psychological role in the believer's actions and reasoning even if the believer never entertains the proposition.

If we explain beliefs in accordance with the pragmatic picture, then it will be clear that we should conclude that Russell literally believed that Big Ben was larger than Frege's left earlobe. It might be more appropriate in some contexts to describe his attitude as presupposing that proposition, or as taking it for granted, but it was available to play the same role as his beliefs in the explanation of his behavior. We should also accept the consequence that Russell, and even we people with more ordinary minds, may have an infinite number of independent beliefs, but we should not conclude from this that he might be in a belief state with an infinite number of components. The pragmatic picture and the possible worlds analysis suggest that a state of knowledge or belief should not be thought of as something with propositions as components at all. Attitudes are primarily attitudes to possible states of the world and not to the propositions that distinguish between those states. A belief state can be represented as a set of possible worlds. Individual beliefs are properties of such a belief state: to believe that P is for the proposition that P to be true in all the possible worlds in the belief state.[12] If one conceives of beliefs in this way, they look like something negative: to believe that P is simply to be in a belief state which lacks any possible world in which P is false. To be more opinionated than one ought to be is to have too many beliefs, but having too many beliefs is the same as not recognizing enough possibilities, and according to the possible worlds conception of a state of belief, it is the latter characterization that is the more fundamental. This makes it easier to see how a person can have beliefs by default, or through a lack of imagination. And there is no difficulty, on this conception, in the idea of a finite believer with a large or even an infinite number of separate beliefs. One might reply that there are surely an infinite number of possible worlds compatible with anyone's belief state. But a believer's representation of a space of possible worlds need not distinguish between them all. Just as a finite perceiver may see a space which in fact consists of an infinite number of points, so a finite believer may represent a space of possible worlds which in fact consists of an infinite number of possible worlds.

More interesting than the case of propositions believed but too obvious to be noticed are those propositions taken for granted only because they are not noticed. With riddles and puzzles as well as with many more serious intellectual problems, often all one needs to see that a certain solution is correct is to think of it—to see it as one of the possibilities. Difficult problems are sometimes difficult only because the alternative solutions from among which one is trying to select the correct one does not include the correct one. One has beliefs, or presuppositions, which exclude the correct answer. To understand this very important kind of intellectual problem, it is essential that propositions believed, or taken for granted, be given the negative character which the possible worlds analysis suggests.

Propositions taken for granted only because they never occurred to the agent, if they are beliefs, are counterexamples to any analysis of belief in terms of a disposition to assent to the proposition when asked about it. One may believe that a proposition is false in the sense that one is disposed to act in ways that will be successful if the proposition is false, while at the same time be disposed to come to believe that the proposition is true immediately on recognizing it as a possibility. In such cases, one is disposed to assent to a proposition that one takes for granted is false.[13]

The conception of beliefs as negative properties of a belief state also allows for a simple and natural account of what is going on when one reconstructs an argument in order to explain a process of reasoning. Suppose I see a footprint in the sand and immediately infer that a person has been walking by here within the past few hours. Someone might explain my inference by constructing a deductively valid argument, adding to the explicit premise—the perceptual belief that there is a certain sort of impression in the sand—some suppressed premises: standing beliefs such as that such impressions are made only by human feet, and that any footprints made more than a few hours ago would have been washed away by now. In order for such a reconstructed argument to be a correct explanation of my reasoning, how must the suppressed premises have entered into the process by which my conclusion was reached? It is common, in discussing such explanations, to deny that for the reconstruction to be right the agent need have gone through any process, conscious or unconscious, which reflects the steps of the argument as reconstructed.[14] But on the other hand, the argument is intended to be more than just one argument that the agent could have used to justify his conclusion. It is intended to explain, in some sense, how the agent actually did reach his conclusion. But it is not always clear how both of these things can be true. This kind of explanation by reconstruction seems to face a dilemma: either it imposes on the agent implausible unconscious processes, or else it is not really an explanation at all but just an imaginative model of how the inference might have been made.

The conception of belief I am defending escapes the dilemma and makes clear the commitments of this kind of explanation. According to this conception, a complicated reconstruction with many suppressed premises may still be a literal description of a simple situation. If the explanation is correct, then the inital belief state (before the agent acquired the perceptual belief) will be one relative to which the premise entails the conclusion. That is, for all possible worlds compatible with the initial belief state in which the premise is true, the conclusion is also true. So the inference can be direct: no process of bringing standing beliefs out of storage and adding them to the explicit premises is required. What role, then, do the suppressed premises play? They are properties of the initial belief state—properties which show that that belief state is one relative to which the explicit premise entails the conclusion. All that is necessary for the reconstructed argument to be a correct account is for the initial belief state to be one containing no possible worlds in which the premises listed are false.

One might object that if my account is right then one could always correctly reconstruct any rational argument by giving just one suppressed premise: the material conditional with the conjunction of the explicit premises as antecedent and the conclusion as consequent. On my account, such a reconstruction would always be a correct description of an immediate inference, but it would not normally be explanatory. For the reconstructed argument to be explanatory, the suppressed premises must be such that it is independently plausible that the agent be in an initial belief state characterized by those premises.

The linguistic picture of mental representation is motivated in part by the parallels between the expressions with which speech acts are performed and the expressions with which attitudes are attributed. Common sense psychology, it is argued, assumes that the objects of attitudes are in many ways like sentences. They have truth-values, stand in logical relations like entailment and compatibility, are sometimes *about* individuals, can be conjoined, negated, and otherwise combined to determine other propositions. Harman and Fodor, among others, conclude from these parallels that the objects of propositional attitudes *are* sentences, or sentences under analysis, or sentence-analogues. On the other hand, it is also generally agreed that commonsense psychology assumes that beliefs play a role in the determination of rational action. Philosophers such as Stich and Dennett have emphasized the difficulty of characterizing realistically the rational dispositions and capacities of an agent in terms of lists of sentence-like items. They conclude that these capacities and dispositions have a holistic character which perhaps can be described only imperfectly in terms of propositional content. The possible worlds analysis of content seeks to resolve the tension which is revealed in the clash between these two emphases. Enough structure is imposed on propositions by the analysis to explain their sentence-like properties, but the structure is also flexible enough, and different enough from the structure of a set of sentences, to permit realistic description of the capacities and dispositions of rational agents in terms of relations to propositions. To argue for this I have pointed to three differences between propositions, analyzed in terms of possible worlds, and sentences. First, propositions do not have constituents in the ordinary sense. Semantic complexity lies in the means of determining a proposition and not in the proposition itself. Second, identity conditions for propositions, and relations between propositions like entailment and compatibility, hold relative to a domain of possible worlds. Commitment to propositions does not require commitment to a context-independent conception of proposition. Third, according to the possible worlds analysis, a system of beliefs need not be thought of as a list of sentence-like items. Propositions are not components but characteristics of a belief state, ways of distinguishing between the possible worlds that define a belief state.

A critic is bound to remind me at this point that the very features ascribed to propositions that I have been calling advantages of the possible worlds analysis are responsible for a serious problem for which we have yet to suggest a solution: the problem of equivalence, and the larger problem of deduction behind it. He might point out that I have defended the appropriateness of this analysis mostly with examples of the beliefs of dogs and children, of beliefs that are too trivial to be noticed, inferences that are direct and immediate. Even if the analysis of propositions and propositional attitudes that I am defending were to give an adequate account of rational activities at this end of the intellectual spectrum, if it failed to allow for any account at all of mathematical beliefs, nontrivial belief in necessary truths and false-hoods, and nonimmediate deductive reasoning, it would surely be un-satisfactory. So I must try to show that the existence of mathematical inquiry and deductive ignorance is compatible with the possible worlds analysis of proposition.

Let us look more closely at the problem of equivalence. The problem is that the possible worlds analysis seems to have the following par-adoxical consequence: if a person believes that P, then if P is necessarily equivalent to Q, he believes that Q. Now let me make the use-mention distinctions ignored in this way of putting the consequence. The expres-sions "that P" and "that Q" are schemas for sentential complements which denote propositions. The statement "P is necessarily equivalent to Q," however, is a schema for a claim about the relation between two *expressions*. Hence here the letters P and Q stand in for expressions that denote things that express the proposition that P. Now once this is recognized, it should be clear that it is not part of the allegedly paradoxical consequence that a person must know or believe that P is equivalent to Q whenever P *is* equivalent to Q. When a person believes that P but fails to realize that the *sentence* P is equivalent to the sentence Q, he may fail to realize that one of the propositions he believes is expressed by that sentence. In this case, he will still believe that Q, but will not himself put it that way. And it may be misleading for others to put it that way in attributing the belief to him. Because items of belief and doubt lack grammatical structure, while the formulations asserted and assented to by an agent in expressing his beliefs and doubts have such a structure, there is an inevitable gap between prop-ositions and their expressions. Whenever the structure of sentences is complicated, there will be a nontrivial question about the relation be-tween sentences and the propositions they express, and so there will be room for reasonable doubt about what proposition is expressed by a given sentence. This will happen on any account of propositions which treats them as anything other than sentences or close copies of sentences.

Now if mathematical truths are all necessary, then on the possible worlds analysis there is no room for doubt about the truth of the propositions themselves. There are, it seems, only two mathematical propositions, the necessarily true one and the necessarily false one, and we all know that the first is true and the second false. But the functions that determine which of the two propositions is expressed by a given mathematical statement are just the kind that are sufficiently complex to give rise to reasonable doubt about which proposition is expressed by a statement. Hence it seems reasonable to take the objects of belief and doubt in mathematics to be propositions about the relation between statements and what they say.[15]

I said above that when the agent believes that P, but fails to realize that P is equivalent to Q, it would be *misleading* to say that he believes that Q. But in fact it seems worse than this. Suppose O'Leary believes that two plus two is four, but fails to realize that "Two plus two is four" is necessarily equivalent to "There are an infinite number of primes." If O'Leary sincerely dissents from the latter statement, then surely it is simply *false*, and not just misleading, to say that O'Leary believes that there are an infinite number of primes. How can *this* fact be reconciled with the possible worlds definition of proposition?

Two questions need to be distinguished. First, when inquirers seem to be mistaken or ignorant about necessary truths and deductive relationships, what is the nature of the information they are mistaken or ignorant about? Second, what statements attributing beliefs or doubt about what seem to be necessary truths and deductive relationships are true? The former question is about the nature of the subject matter of mathematical inquiry; the latter is in part about the semantics for the sentences which express and attribute those beliefs. My suggestion concerns the first question. It implies that the information O'Leary lacks when he fails to see that there are an infinite number of primes is information about the relationship between the sentence "There are an infinite number of primes" and the one necessarily true proposition. But I do not and need not infer from this that the statement "O'Leary believes that there are an infinite number of primes" is merely misleading. It is clear that whatever the nature of O'Leary's mathematical beliefs and doubts, the way we *attribute* those beliefs is to say such things as "O'Leary believes that two plus two is four, but not that there are an infinite number of primes." To account for this fact, we need a semantics for belief sentences which explains how sentential complements such as "that two plus two is four" and "that there are an infinite number of primes" can be used to attribute to O'Leary the beliefs and doubts that he has. Such a semantic theory of belief attribution, if it is to accord with my suggestion about the nature of mathematical belief and doubt, will have to recognize more complexity and more context-dependence than is usually recognized in the relationship between the sentential complements of sentences attributing beliefs and the contents of the beliefs attributed. Such a theory will not be simple, but I think it is necessary to account for the phenomena.[16]

The suggestion that the contents of mathematical attitudes are propositions about the relation between expressions and the one necessary proposition is *prima facie* more plausible in some cases than in others. To take an easy case, if I do not recognize some complicated truth-functional compound to be a tautology, and so doubt whether what it says is true, this can naturally be explained as doubt or error about what the sentence says. For example, one who has not yet figured out whether a formula such as "$((P \supset ((Q \supset P) \supset Q)) \supset (P \supset Q))$" is a tautology is like one who has not yet processed some syntactically complex sentence of a natural language. The information which he lacks seems, intuitively, to be metalinguistic information—information about the formula. The information is quite specific to the notation in which the formula is expressed. But in other cases, it seems less plausible to take the subject matter of a· mathematical proposition to be the semantic structure of a sentence. For example, geometrical propositions seem to be about the structure of a space, and not about the structure of sentences describing the space. For these cases we might take the objects that beliefs and doubt are about to be a common structure shared by many, but not all, of the formulations which express the necessarily true proposition. This is still to take mathematical propositions to be about linguistic expressions in some sense, but they may be about relatively abstract features of expressions, features shared by sentences in different languages, and by sentences with different grammatical structures. A common abstract semantic structure would be a kind of intermediate entity between the particular sentences of mathematics and the single, unstructured necessary proposition. In this kind of case, doubt about a mathematical statement would be doubt about whether the statements having a certain structure express the necessarily true proposition.

It is not, I think, entirely artificial to treat mathematical propositions as propositions about expressions, or about structures which expressions exhibit. If one looks at the kind of actions that might be explained by mathematical beliefs, and at the abilities that constitute mathematical knowledge, one finds that they are actions and abilities that essentially involve operating with some kind of notation—for example, calculating and constructing proofs. So it is appropriate, according to the pragmatic picture, which in the general case motivates a separation of propositions from linguistic expressions and semantic structure, to treat mathematical propositions as essentially involving expressions and semantic structure by having them as its subject matter.

Even if it is plausible to take the subject matter of mathematical propositions to involve language or linguistic structure, it is less clear that this is plausible for belief in other kinds of necessary truths or falsehoods. Consider Mabel's belief that she has arthritis in her thigh, for example. The proposition that Mabel has arthritis in her thigh is necessarily false, so on the possible worlds account of proposition, she can't really believe that proposition. But her belief does not seem to be a metalinguistic one—a belief about the relation between her words and the world. Let's take a closer look at the example.

Consider three possible worlds: (a) the actual world, in which Mabel has some kind of inflammation in her thigh; (b) the counterfactual world described by Burge in which Mabel's physical condition is the same, but the word "arthritis" is generally used to refer to a broader class of ailments, including the one afflicting Mabel's thigh; (c) a possible world in which Mabel has no problem with her thigh. According to Burge's story, what does Mabel think the world is like? Obviously, of these three worlds, (b) best describes the world as Mabel thinks it is, and if she were to assert "I have arthritis in my thigh" she would be trying to say that world (b) is actual. That is, the proposition she is trying to assert is the one that is true in (b) and false in (a) and (c). Is this proposition metalinguistic? Is it a proposition about the meanings or proper uses of words? It is not clear how to answer these questions since on the possible worlds analysis propositions are not complexes of concepts, and so the subject matter of a proposition is not something one can read off of its form. One might give a rough account of what a proposition is about in terms of the differences between the possible worlds in which it is true and the possible worlds in which it is false. On this sort of account, the proposition is partly about language, since the difference between (a) and (b) is a linguistic difference, but it is partly about nonlinguistic facts since the difference between (b) and (c) is independent of language. From Mabel's point of view, it is the second difference that is the main one. When she says "I have arthritis in my thigh," she is not intending to distinguish (b) from (a). She takes for granted that the world is either (b) or (c)—that "arthritis" has a certain meaning—and says that it is (b).

My suggestion provides a way of reconciling the possible worlds analysis with two obvious facts: that there is a plurality of mathematical truths and that there can be nontrivial belief in necessary truths and falsehoods. But it will not by itself provide a general solution to the problem of deduction. The reason it is not the whole solution is that it fails to explain how a deductive inquiry—an investigation into the deductive relationships between propositions—differs from an empirical investigation. The suggestion implies that whenever a person fails to know some mathematical truth, there is a nonactual possible world compatible with his knowledge in which the mathematical statement says something different than it says in this world. Learning that the mathematical statement is true is coming to know that *that* world is not the actual world. But this does not seem to locate the source of mathematical ignorance in the right place.

Take a simple case of calculation: I did not know before I performed some calculations that $689 \times 43 = 29,627$. But it is surely not plausible to explain my ignorance with an epistemically possible world in which one of the numerals, "689" or "43," denotes a different number, or in which the multiplication sign represents a different operation. If my ignorance were a matter of not knowing which numbers were involved, or which operation to perform on them, it is not clear how performing a calculation could remove it.

The feeling that my suggestion, as an attempt to explain mathematical ignorance, mislocates the source of that ignorance is supported by the following argument:[17] consider a particular axiomatic formulation of first order logic with which, suppose, I am familiar. While it is a contingent fact that each axiom *sentence* expresses a necessary truth (however the descriptive terms are interpreted), this is a contingent truth which I know to be a fact. It may also be only contingently true that the rules of inference of the system when applied to sentences which express necessary truths always yield sentences which express necessary truths, but this fact too is known to me. Now consider any sentence of the system in question which happens to be a theorem. It is only a contingent truth that that sentence expresses a necessary truth, but this contingent fact follows deductively from propositions that I know to be true. Hence if my knowledge is deductively closed, as seems to be implied by the conception of states of knowledge and belief that I have been defending, it follows that I know of every theorem sentence of the system in question that it expresses a necessary truth. But of course I know no such thing.

This argument does not show that the suggestion I have made for interpreting mathematical propositions is wrong. It shows only that it cannot, by itself, solve the problem of deduction. There are two theses apparently implied by my account of propositions and propositional attitudes which seem to lead to a conflict between that account and the facts of mathematical ignorance and inquiry: first, necessarily equivalent propositions are identical; second, a person believes any proposition which is a deductive consequence of a set of propositions, each one of which he believes. The first thesis follows from the analysis of propositions I have been defending. The second thesis seems to be implied by the account of a belief state which I have used to motivate that analysis. The suggestion I made is an attempt to reconcile the first thesis with the phenomena. What the argument I gave shows is that this suggestion does not succeed in avoiding the unpalatable consequences of the second thesis. I shall argue that the second thesis is false, and that the rejection of this thesis can be reconciled with the causal-pragmatic strategy for explaining belief. But before doing this, I must look more carefully at the concept of belief, or rather at a more general propositional attitude concept which I will call acceptance.

Chapter 5

The Problem of Deduction

Our main concern is not with the explanation of rational action generally but with the particular cluster of rational activities which are directed toward answering the questions about the way the world is. Engaging in inquiry is of course itself a form of rational behavior and the pragmatic picture implies that such behavior should be explained according to the same belief-desire pattern as the naive, unreflective behavior of dogs and children. But in order to treat the special problems that arise in explaining those actions which explicitly concern the evaluation and modification of the agent's beliefs, we need a more specialized apparatus designed to describe that specific kind of activity. We need to be able to talk about an agent's beliefs about his beliefs, about the form in which his beliefs are expressed, and about the ways in which his beliefs may change in response to his experience.

The concept of *acceptance* will be a central concept in the account of inquiry developed here. Acceptance, as I shall use this term, is a broader concept than belief; it is a generic propositional attitude concept with such notions as presupposing, presuming, postulating, positing, assuming and supposing as well as believing falling under it. Acceptance is a technical term: claims I make about acceptance are not intended as part of an analysis of a term from common usage. But I do want to claim that this technical term picks out a natural class of propositional attitudes about which one can usefully generalize. Belief is obviously the most fundamental acceptance concept, but various methodological postures that one may take toward a proposition in the course of an inquiry or conversation are sufficiently like belief in some respects to justify treating them together with it.

To accept a proposition is to treat it as a true proposition in one way or another—to ignore, for the moment at least, the possibility that it is false. One may do this for different reasons, more or less tentatively, more or less self-consciously, with more or less justification, and with more or less feeling of commitment. As a rough criterion, one may say that a propositional attitude concept is an acceptance concept if the attitude is said to be *correct* whenever the proposition is true. Belief is an acceptance concept because a correct belief is a true belief. Correct here contrasts with justified. To say that a belief was correct is not to say it was adequately supported; to say that an assumption was correct is to say nothing about whether the assumption should have been made. Correct beliefs, assumptions, suppositions and presumptions are beliefs, assumptions, suppositions and presumptions the contents of which are true. A correct desire or hope, however, is not one that will in fact be satisfied, nor is a judgment that P is highly probable said to be correct because P turns out to be true. Thus this criterion distinguishes acceptance concepts from so-called pro attitudes like wishes and wants, from mixed emotive-cognitive attitudes like hope and fear, and from attitudes of partial belief or acceptance as represented by subjective probabilities.

Within this class of propositional attitudes there is considerable diversity. To accept a proposition is to act, in certain respects, as if one believed it, but there are several ways in which acceptance, in the intended sense, may differ from belief, and in which acceptance concepts may differ from each other. First, acceptance may have a social dimension. In a cooperative inquiry, a dialogue or a debate, what *we* accept may be more important than what *I* accept. It is our common beliefs and assumptions, or what we take to be our common beliefs and assumptions, that will set the boundaries of our discussion and determine its direction. No matter how convinced you are that something is true, if it is what I am disputing, then you beg the question by accepting it in the context of our argument.[1]

Second, acceptance may be more passive or more active. As noted in the last chapter, some propositions may be taken for granted or presupposed by a person only because the possibility of their being false has never occurred to him, while others are explicitly accepted after reflection or investigation. Some people may be reluctant to apply the term "belief" to tacit presuppositions, but they are among the propositions accepted.

Third, a person may accept a proposition for the moment without the expectation that he will continue to accept it for very long. If a person expects a particular one of his *beliefs* to be overturned, he has already begun to lose it, but an assumption he makes may be quite explicitly temporary, and he may presume that something is true even when expecting to be contradicted.

Fourth, what a person accepts can be compartmentalized in a way in which what he believes cannot be. A person may accept something in one context, while rejecting it or suspending judgment in another. There need be no conflict that must be resolved when the difference is noticed, and he need not change his mind when he moves from one context to the other. But something is wrong if I have separate incompatible sets of beliefs for different circumstances. I cannot reasonably believe what I disbelieved yesterday without thinking that yesterday's belief was mistaken.

Finally, acceptance may be the product of methodological decision rather than subjective commitment. One may accept something for the sake of the argument, although one cannot believe things for this reason. The judge may direct the members of the jury to accept something, although he cannot reasonably direct them to believe it. In these ways, acceptance may diverge from belief, although belief is a kind of acceptance.

Ignoring for the moment the important differences between different kinds of acceptance, think of an inquirer as a person in an initial *acceptance state* preparing to perform some actions which are intended to lead to a change in that state. Following the strategy discussed in the last chapter, I will define an acceptance state not as a set of propositions accepted, but as a nonempty set of possible situations—the possibilities that remain open for an agent in the acceptance state. The set of propositions accepted contain just those propositions that are true in all of these possible situations. This way of defining belief and acceptance states has the advantages previously discussed: it imposes on the set of propositions accepted a structure that is motivated by the pragmatic-causal picture; it allows for a natural account of unconscious beliefs, tacit presuppositions and enthymematic reasoning. But it has the disagreeable consequence that the set of propositions accepted relative to an acceptance state is always consistent and deductively closed, which seems to imply that an inquirer never has inconsistent beliefs and always accepts all the consequences of any set of propositions every member of which he accepts. And this consequence is not just a rationality condition imposed on a set of propositions accepted, but a condition that follows from the definition of an acceptance state. So one cannot soften the disagreeable consequence by calling it an ideal which ordinary acceptance states strive for. If acceptance is to be defined in this way then acceptance states, however far from the ideal, must meet the consistency and closure conditions. Thus the model of acceptance that I will develop faces the problem of deduction in a particularly acute form.

To discuss the problem of deduction, I will distinguish three deductive conditions on the set of propositions determined by an acceptance state, all of which must hold if acceptance states are to be defined in terms of possible situations in the way I have suggested. Then I will argue that each of the conditions, applied to belief, is motivated by the pragmatic picture. Finally, I will try to show how they can be reconciled with the phenomena.

The three conditions are as follows:

1. If P is a member of a set of accepted propositions, and P entails Q, then Q is a member of that set.

2. If P and Q are each members of a set of accepted propositions, then $P\&Q$ is a member of that set.

3. If P is a member of a set of accepted propositions, then not-P is not a member of that set.

Beliefs, according to the pragmatic picture, are conditional dispositions to act. A rational agent is, in general and by definition, disposed to act appropriately, where what is appropriate is defined relative to his beliefs and desires. To say that an agent believes that P is to say something like this: the actions that are appropriate for that agent—those he is disposed to perform—are those that will tend to serve his interests and desires in situations in which P is true. But this is not quite right for the following reason: it would be too strong to require that appropriate actions tend to serve the agent's ends in *any* possible situation in which one of his individual beliefs is true. Suppose I believe, as I do, that someone will be elected President of the United States in 1988. One way in which that proposition could be realized is for *me* to be the one elected, but I know that that is not the way my belief will come true. For my actions to be appropriate, given that I have this belief, it is surely not required that I take account of that possibility, since it is excluded by other of my beliefs. The actions that are appropriate for an agent who believes that P depend not only on what he wants but also on what else he believes. So it is necessary to define appropriateness relative to a total set of beliefs, or a belief state. And all that matters about such a belief state, as far as the appropriateness of actions or the agent's dispositions to act are concerned, are the entailments of the belief state. So there is no basis, on the dispositional account, for excluding from the set of an agent's beliefs any propositions that are entailed by his beliefs. That is, there is no basis, given the pragmatic account of belief, for defining the set of propositions believed, relative to a belief state, in a way that conflicts with the first deductive condition.

If one accepts this, then the argument for the second deductive condition is straightforward. If a person is in a belief state that entails both P and Q, then he is in a belief state that entails the conjunction of P and Q. If a person is, in general, disposed to act in ways that would tend to be successful if P (together with his other beliefs) were true, and is also disposed to act in ways that would be successful if Q

(together with his other beliefs) were true, then he is disposed to act in ways that would be successful if $P\&Q$ (together with his other beliefs) were true. But while the second deductive condition is a reasonable one, given the pragmatic account, to impose on the propositions determined by a belief state, it is not a reasonable condition to impose on the totality of an agent's beliefs. It is compatible with the pragmatic account that the rational dispositions that a person has at one time should arise from several different belief states. A person may be disposed, in one kind of context, or with respect to one kind of action, to behave in ways that are correctly explained by one belief state, and at the same time be disposed in another kind of context or with respect to another kind of action to behave in ways that would be explained by a different belief state. This need not be a matter of shifting from one state to another or vacillating between states; the agent might, at the same time, be in two stable belief states, be in two different dispositional states which are displayed in different kinds of situations. If what it means to say that an agent believes that P at a certain time is that some one of the belief states the agent is in at that time entails that P, then even if every set of propositions defined by a belief state conforms to the second deductive condition, the total set of propositions believed by an agent might not conform to that condition.[2]

The same distinction can be made with respect to the third deductive condition—the consistency condition. Applied to the set of propositions determined by a single belief state, it must hold. This is clear since the only set of propositions conforming to the first two conditions but violating the third is the set of all propositions, and no belief state in which all propositions were believed could distinguish any actions as appropriate or inappropriate. But if an agent can be in distinct belief states at the same time in the way suggested above, then there is no reason why these belief states cannot be incompatible. In such a case an agent would believe both a proposition and its contradictory, but would not therefore believe everything. It would still be possible in such a situation to explain the agent's actions as rational actions according to the usual pattern.

I noted above, in distinguishing belief from acceptance in general, that acceptance may be compartmentalized in a way that belief cannot. Now I am suggesting that an agent may at one time be in separate, even incompatible belief states. But there is no conflict here. The earlier point was not that an agent's beliefs *are* always integrated into a single state, but rather that they ought to be. A person's beliefs are defective if they do not fit together into a single coherent system. An agent who recognizes the consequences of the conjunction of separate beliefs must either accept the consequences or abandon one of the original beliefs.

An agent who discovers a conflict between his separate beliefs must modify them in some way. One cannot agree to disagree with oneself.

There are, then, two ways in which the second and third deductive conditions apply to belief. First, they are *defining* conditions of the concept of a belief state. Second, they are *rationality* conditions on the set of all beliefs that an agent has at one time. They are rationality conditions on an agent's beliefs because, ideally, an agent's beliefs should be integrated into a single system.

In calling the closure and consistency conditions rationality conditions, I do not mean to imply that an agent whose beliefs fail to conform to them is irrational but only that his beliefs diverge from an ideal of perfect rationality. The ideal is perhaps one that is never met, but that is an imperfection in rational agents, not in the model of rationality. The fact that the ideal is unrealistic does not threaten the adequacy of the theory because one can still use the theory to describe coherently the dispositions of agents whose beliefs diverge from the ideal, and to explain their actions as rational actions.

I also want to emphasize that it is not implied that conforming to the rationality conditions is an easy or a mechanical task. If the contents of beliefs were like sentences and belief were something like assent, then it would be a simple matter of noting and remembering what one is doing to put a belief that P and a belief that Q together into a belief that $P\&Q$. But on our account, beliefs are behavioral dispositions. Separate belief states are dispositions which are displayed in different kinds of situations. To integrate such belief states is to change one's dispositions so that the actions one is disposed to perform in the two kinds of situations are appropriate relative to the same belief state—the same conception of the way the world is. To change one's rational dispositions in this way may require only a routine calculation, or it may be a challenging and creative intellectual task. It is this kind of task, I want to suggest, that deductive inquiry is designed to accomplish.

There are two complementary parts to the strategy I am suggesting for treating the problem of deduction. The first, discussed at the end of the last chapter, begins with the observation that it may be a nontrivial problem to see what proposition is expressed by a given sentence. The apparent failure to see that a proposition is necessarily true, or that propositions are necessarily equivalent, is to be explained as the failure to see what propositions are expressed by the expressions in question. Relative to any propositional expression one can determine two propositions: there is the proposition that is expressed, according to the standard rules, and there is the proposition that relates the expression to what it expresses. If sentence s expresses (according to the standard rules) proposition P, then the second proposition in question is the proposition that *s* expresses *P*. In cases of ignorance of necessity and equivalence, I am suggesting, it is the second proposition that is the object of doubt and investigation.

The second part of the strategy begins with the observation that it may be a nontrivial problem to put separate beliefs together into a single coherent system of belief. All of my actions may be rational in that they are directed toward desired ends and guided by coherent conceptions of the way things are even if there is no single conception of the way things are that guides them all. There may be propositions which I would believe if I put together my separate systems of belief, but which, as things stand, hold in none of them. These are the propositions whose truth might be discovered by a purely deductive inquiry.

Is this a plausible strategy for explaining deduction? Given the very general conception of content and information that we are using, I think it can be seen as a natural, even inevitable, strategy. There are two questions posed by the problem of deduction: first, what is the nature of the information conveyed in a statement about deductive relationships? Second, how do we acquire this information? The first part of the strategy responds to the first question; the second part responds to the second question.

According to the conception of content that lies behind the possible worlds analysis of propositions and propositional attitudes, content requires contingency. To learn something, to acquire information, is to rule out possibilities. To understand the information conveyed in a communication is to know what possibilities would be excluded by its truth. Now if one asks, what real possibilities are excluded when one learns that a necessary truth is true, the answer is clear: they will not normally be situations in which extralinguistic facts are different than they actually are, but they will be possible situations where the rules for determining the truth value of the statement yield a different result from the result they actually yield.

For some examples of necessary truths, pointing this out would be sufficient to reconcile necessity with the possibility of ignorance. If someone is ignorant of the fact that all ophthamologists are eye doctors, this is probably because he is ignorant of the meaning of one of the words in that statement. The relevant possible situations which his knowledge fails to exclude are ones in which the *sentence* "all ophthamologists are eye doctors" means something different from what it actually means. If a person is ignorant of the fact that Hesperus is Phosphorus, it is because his knowledge fails to exclude a possible situation in which, because causal connections between names and objects are different, one of those names refers to a different planet, and so the statement, "Hesperus is Phosphorus" says something different than it actually says. In both of these cases, there is clearly a piece of factual information which the person ignorant of the truth of a necessary truth is missing. Empirical inquiry, about language or about astronomy, is what is needed to straighten the situation out. But in the case of ignorance of mathematical truths and deductive relationships, there are no such pieces of missing factual information in terms of which the ignorance can be explained, and that is why, even given the answer to the first question, there remains a puzzle about the second. Deductive inquiry is concerned neither with lexicography nor with causal connections between names and things in the world. The information which one receives when one learns about deductive relationships does not seem to come from outside of oneself at all. It seems to be information which, in some sense, one has had all along. What one does is to transform it into a usable form, and that, it seems plausible to suppose, is a matter of putting it together with the rest of one's information.

If this conception of deductive inquiry is to fit the facts, then even to account for straightforward mechanical deductive problems one will have to postulate a large number of concurrent but separate belief states. According to the pragmatic picture, many separate belief states means many separate dispositions, each with its own domain of display. This can be plausible only where there is a natural way to match up separate beliefs with actions—where there is some basis independent of what the agent happens to do for saying which of his many belief states is relevant to explaining which of his actions. If the belief that P is to be kept distinct from the belief that Q, there must be some actions appropriate to the belief that P and some actions appropriate to the belief that Q which are different from the actions that are appropriate to the belief that $P\&Q$. This is, I think, exactly the situation in mathematics. The answer to the first question about deductive knowledge suggested that the subject matter of mathematical propositions is notation or structures exhibited in notation. The actions that are made appropriate by belief in distinctively mathematical propositions are actions of manipulating notation: calculating in particular ways and making moves in the construction of proofs. Because mathematical beliefs concern expressions, it is easy to find actions that manifest belief in particular propositions without manifesting belief in other stronger propositions which have them as consequences. To take a simple case of calculation, a person may display his belief that four plus three equals seven by performing certain operations on numerals that contain four and three as digits—for example by writing down "7" as the first step in adding sixty-four to twenty-three. A person who is competent at doing sums but not particularly quick or intuitive could manifest his separate beliefs that four plus three equals seven and that six plus two equals eight in calculating the sum of sixty-four and twenty-three, but he would show that before doing the calculation, he did not have the belief that sixty-four plus twenty-three is eighty-seven. That last belief results only after the two simpler arithmetic beliefs were put together against a background of more general beliefs and presuppositions about arithmetic operations.[3]

The thesis that acquiring deductive knowledge is putting one's separate belief states together will not, by itself, throw much light on the process of deductive inquiry. It says nothing about how one goes about answering questions about deductive relationships; the focus is not on the means of deductive inquiry, but on its end, and even the end is described only in very abstract terms. But our concern is not with the special features of deductive inquiry. The problem this thesis is intended to solve is the problem of finding a way to describe deductive inquiry as a special case of inquiry in general, a way which brings out the common features which the search for mathematical knowledge shares with the search for knowledge about the world. We need a framework in which one can give analyses of such concepts as knowledge, explanation, inference, and justification which allows for their application to both mathematics and empirical investigation.

The goal of inquiry, in both cases, is the acquisition of knowledge, and this is most naturally thought of as the receiving of information from outside. The simple conception of the inquirer adjusting his beliefs in response to new data, or filling in further details in his picture of the world as a result of interaction with it obviously fits empirical contexts more comfortably than mathematical ones. But the account of deduction as the integration of the separate belief states of a single agent provides a way to apply this conception to deductive inquiry as well. Inquiry in general is a matter of adjusting one's beliefs in response to new information, but in the case of deductive inquiry, the information that initiates the change is new, not to the agent, but only to one of his belief states. By dividing the agent into separate centers of rationality, we make it possible to see the processing of the information an agent already has as a phenomenon with the same structure as the reception of new information.

Whether this kind of account of deduction will work remains to be seen. One needs to look carefully at more detailed and challenging examples of mathematical questions, and at particular problems in the epistemology of mathematics. But I will assume that it gives us a way around the problem of deductive ignorance and inquiry—that it at least shows that the existence of deductive ignorance and inquiry is not an immediate refutation of the assumptions I am making about propositions, propositional attitudes, and inquiry.

Even if the deductive constraints on acceptance can be reconciled with the existence of deductive inquiry in the way I have suggested, there are other objections to them which must be answered. First, there are apparent counterexamples to the first deductive condition—that a person accepts any proposition that is entailed by any single proposition that he accepts. It is not obvious how the suggestion that a person's beliefs can be divided among separate belief states is relevant to explaining counterexamples to this principle. Second, there are examples and arguments that purport to show that the deductive principles are not acceptable even as rationality conditions. Sometimes, it has been suggested, one may reasonably accept each member of a set of propositions while not accepting their conjunction, even when one sees all the relevant deductive connections. I will discuss several such examples, some of them familiar in the literature, and try to show how the deductive constraints on acceptance can be defended against them.

I will begin with two counterexamples to the first deductive condition, as applied to belief. (1) William III of England believed, in 1700, that England could avoid a war with France. But avoiding a war with France entails avoiding a nuclear war with France. Did William III believe England could avoid a nuclear war? It would surely be strange to say that he did. (2) The absentminded detective believes that the butler did it. There is no direct evidence of his guilt, but the detective has made what he thought was an exhaustive list of the possible suspects, investigated them one by one, and eliminated everyone except the butler. The problem is that he completely forgot about the chauffeur, who had both motive and opportunity. Would it be correct to say that the detective believes that the chauffeur did not do it? He does believe that no one other than the butler did it—that was essential to his reasoning—and this entails that the chauffeur did not do it. But it would be misleading to say that the detective had this belief, since that seems to suggest that the chauffeur was one of the suspects eliminated from his list.

Even if it is strange or misleading, I am not sure whether it would be literally incorrect to say that William III and the absentminded detective had these beliefs. It is not that the king was in doubt about nuclear war or that the detective suspended judgment on the chauffeur's guilt. If these propositions were not believed, they were at least tacitly presupposed, and so they were propositions which were accepted in some sense. One way or another, the king and the detective ignored the possibility that the propositions in question were false. So the examples do not threaten the principle that one must *accept* the deductive consequences of any proposition one accepts, even if they do refute the principle as applied to a more specific kind of acceptance such as belief. The examples do not suggest that acceptance states should be defined in a different way, but at most that different acceptance concepts may be used to categorize the propositions entailed by a single acceptance state.

Perhaps for it to be true that x believes that P, it is necessary that x understand the proposition that P, or that x have entertained the proposition that P. If so, then it is too simple to identify the propositions believed with the entailments of a belief state. One would have to say that the beliefs were the entailments of a belief state which met certain further conditions. One might, for example, define the *active* beliefs of an agent as those propositions which are entailed by a belief state, but not entailed by the weaker acceptance state which determines the tacit presuppositions. This would ensure that an agent's beliefs would include only propositions which distinguish between possibilities that he recognizes.

Compare some other propositional attitudes where it is clearer that this kind of move is necessary. The first analogy is with wanting. If a rational man *wants* it to be the case that P, and recognizes that P entails Q, must he want it to be the case that Q? If wanting it to be the case that P is wanting one of the possible worlds in which P is true to be the actual world, then it would seem that the consequence condition should hold for wanting. One cannot rationally want P to be true without Q, since that is a logical impossibility, and there are no possible worlds, desirable or undesirable, in which logical impossibilities are realized. But there are persuasive counterexamples to the consequence condition on rational wants. Suppose I am sick. I want to get well. But getting well entails having been sick, and I do not want to have been sick. Suppose there was a murder. I want to know who committed the murder. But my knowing who committed the murder entails that the murder was committed, and I never wanted the murder to have been committed. One can reconcile these examples with a qualified consequence condition by noting that wanting something is preferring it to certain relevant alternatives, the relevant alternatives being those possibilities that the agent believes will be realized if he does not get what he wants. Some propositions which are entailed by propositions that one wants to be true in this sense are also entailed by the relevant alternatives. It is not that I want these propositions to be true—it is just that I accept that they will be true whether I get what I want or not. Given that there was a murder, I would rather know who committed it than not know. The question of whether or not I look with favor on the fact that there was a murder—whether I am glad that it happened or wish that it had not—does not arise in that context. To raise *that* question, one needs to expand the set of relevant alternatives, to compare the actual situation with possible situations in which the murder never took place.

The qualified consequence condition for rational wants motivated by these considerations is this: the propositions one wants to be true (relative to a set of relevant alternative possibilities) includes all the consequences of any proposition one wants to be true *which distinguish between the relevant alternatives.*

The second analogy is with epistemic concepts such as knowledge and justified belief. Suppose all justification is local in the sense that it takes place against a background of beliefs and presuppositions which themselves need not be justified, at least in that context. Then justified belief, and perhaps knowledge, will conform only to a qualified consequence condition such as the one discussed above for rational wants. Here is an example, taken from an article by Fred Dretske, which tends to support such a conclusion. You are at the zoo next to the zebra cage with your son. The zebras are in plain view and the sign on the cage says "zebra." Your son asks you what they are, and you tell him. Do you *know* that they are zebras? Of course. But that they are zebras entails that they are not mules cleverly disguised by the zoo authorities to look like zebras. Do you know that they are not mules cleverly disguised in this way? Dretske suggests that you do not. The hypothesis that they are mules may not be very plausible; it is surely reasonable to ignore the possibility that they are. But you must admit that if they were disguised mules, things would look exactly as they in fact look. The kinds of reasons you have for ignoring this hypothesis—general considerations of plausibility—do not seem sufficient to give you knowledge.[4]

The example is, of course, a typical Cartesian skeptic's example. Given the assumption that a person knows all the known consequences of anything known, the example supports the conclusion that you do not *really* know that the animals you see are zebras. But Dretske suggests abandoning the consequence condition instead of the knowledge claim. This is not the place to discuss the adequacy of this response to the skeptic. The point I want to make here is just that this kind of context-dependent conception of justification and knowledge which rejects the consequence condition for propositions known or justifiably believed is compatible with the possible worlds analysis of states of knowledge and belief. In fact, the possible worlds framework allows for a natural formulation of such a conception.

Let me now consider some examples and arguments, drawn from the work of Henry Kyburg, which go against the second deductive condition, the conjunction principle. First, the notorious lottery paradox. I have ticket number seven in a fair lottery with a million tickets.

"Consider the hypothesis 'ticket number seven will not win. . . .' There is only one chance in a million that the hypothesis is false. Surely . . . this is reason enough to accept the hypothesis." The same reasoning applies to each of the other tickets, and so I should accept every hypothesis of the form "ticket i will not win." But I cannot consistently accept the conjunction of all these hypotheses since I know that some ticket will win.[5]

The weak point in this argument, I think, is the assumption that a probability of .999999 is sufficient for acceptance. Why should a probability of .999999 be a reason for doing anything more than believing the hypothesis to degree .999999? The practical difference between accepting a hypothesis and believing it to degree $1-\epsilon$ may, in some cases, become negligible as ϵ diminishes, but there does seem to be a significant difference in this case. If the price of the ticket is low enough, and the value of the prize is great enough, it is rational for me to buy a ticket even if I will benefit from the purchase only if I win. But my purchase is rational, on this assumption, only if I leave open the possibility that I might win. The day that the winning ticket is announced, I learn that ticket number seven did not win. My attitude toward the hypothesis that ticket seven would not win changes. I do not come to accept that a proposition I already accepted was true—that would be no change at all. Rather, I learn that a hypothesis I was almost sure of is indeed true.

One could easily enough define a concept of acceptance which identified it with a high subjective or epistemic probability (probability greater than some specified number between one-half and one), but it is not clear what the point of doing so would be. Once a subjective or epistemic probability value is assigned to a proposition, there is nothing more to be said about its epistemic status. Bayesian decision theory gives a complete account of how probability values, including high ones, ought to guide behavior, in both the context of inquiry and the application of belief outside of this context. So what could be the point of selecting an interval near the top of the probability scale and conferring on the propositions whose probability falls in that interval the honorific title "accepted"? Unless acceptance has some consequences, unless the way one classifies the propositions as accepted, rejected, or judgment suspended makes a difference to how the agent behaves, or ought to behave, it is difficult to see how the concept of acceptance can have the interest and importance for inquiry that it seems to have.

If the conjunction principle governs the concept of acceptance, then it is clear that one can say something, at least, about the consequences of acceptance: to accept a proposition is to permit oneself to put that proposition together with any others that one accepts, and draw any consequences that may follow. Reasoning in this way from accepted premises to their deductive consequences (P, also Q, therefore R) does seem perfectly straightforward. Someone may object to one of the premises, or to the validity of the argument, but one could not intelligibly agree that the premises are each acceptable and the argument valid, while objecting to the acceptability of the conclusion. But given a probabilistic rule of acceptance (accept P if and only if the probability of P is at least as great as some fixed number between one-half and one), just knowing that P has the status *accepted* would give you no license to put it together with anything else. One would have to know, among other things, the probability on which the proposition achieved that status.

Another paradox, closely related to the lottery paradox, is the paradox of the preface. In the preface to his historical narrative, the author admits that he has undoubtedly made some mistakes—that some of the statements he made in his narrative are false. He is not confessing to insincerity—he continues to *believe* everything he wrote—he is just confessing to fallibility. It does not take excessive modesty to believe that *some* of one's many beliefs or sincere assertions are false. This is only reasonable. Yet to believe this is to believe each member of a set of propositions that are recognized to be inconsistent. If these propositions were conjoined and their consequences accepted, the result would be to accept the truth of every proposition.

The paradox of the preface and the lottery paradox are alike in that both may be used to support the conclusion that a person may sometimes be justified in accepting all the members of a recognizably inconsistent set of propositions. But the two paradoxes are different in at least one important respect. The assumption that high probability is sufficient for acceptance is essential to the argument of the lottery paradox. One response to that paradox—the one I endorsed—is to reject that assumption. But the paradox of the preface does not depend on that assumption and cannot be answered in the same way. It cannot plausibly be denied that the author *accepts* the truth of each of the statements made in his narrative, nor can it be denied that he accepts that at least one of those statements is false. But it also seems plausible to say that the author accepts, or at least commits himself to, any conjunction of the statements in the narrative. In presenting his narrative, the author is aiming at a coherent total story. It is, in fact, a methodological constraint on a historian's construction of his narrative (as on a scientist's interpretation of his results) that the propositions he accepts fit together into a coherent story. Unless one can freely conjoin propositions, it is difficult to see how considerations of coherence can play the methodological role which they obviously play in inductive procedure.

So the historian does not intend his confession of fallibility to prevent the reader from putting together the different statements made in telling his story. He intends only that the reader recognize that the story as a whole is undoubtedly wrong in some of its details. But the fact remains that the author denies in his preface something that is entailed by what he asserts in his narrative, and the reader is obviously not supposed to conjoin these contradictory accepted propositions. So I agree with Kyburg in rejecting a global conjunction rule for accepted propositions, even as a rationality condition. This is not because high probability is sufficient for acceptance; it is rather because sometimes it is reasonable to *accept* something that one knows or believes is false.

When is it reasonable to accept something one believes is false? When one believes that it is *essentially* true, or close to the truth—as close as one can get, or as close as one needs to get for the purposes at hand. It is not obvious how one judges a false proposition, or a whole story, to be roughly or essentially correct, or even what one is judging when one does, but it is obvious that people do make such judgments and that they play a role in their decisions about what to accept. Sometimes these decisions are based on practical considerations. Accepting a certain false proposition may greatly simplify an inquiry, or even make possible an inquiry not otherwise possible, while at the same time it is known that the difference between what is accepted and the truth will have no significant effect on the answer to the particular question being asked. When a scientist makes idealizing assumptions, he is accepting something for this kind of reason. Particles or planets may be treated as point masses, the atmosphere may be assumed to be a vacuum, consumers or governments may be thought of as rational. Of course in other inquiries these same assumptions might greatly distort the results, but the scientist might be in a position to know that in his inquiry they would not. The scientist does not, of course, *believe* the propositions he accepts, but he acts, in a limited context, as if he believed them in order to further his inquiry.

Even if an inquiry has no practical motivation—even if one's aim is just to tell a story right—a divergence between acceptance and belief may be reasonable. The historian in the example believes that his narrative is *mostly* right, and the doubts he does have about it are based on general considerations of fallibility. What more effective way does he have to say just what he is *sure* of than to tell the story as best he can, and then add, in the preface, that it is probably only roughly true. Here his motive for accepting what he does not believe is that doing so is an efficient means of telling what he does believe.

I am suggesting that one may accept, for various reasons, what one does not believe, but one may not, of course, believe what one does not believe or reasonably believe what one believes is false. The explanation of the preface phenomenon that I am suggesting requires that we say that the historian does not, without qualification, *believe* that the story he accepts is correct; nor does he believe, without qualification, all of the individual statements he makes in telling the story. We must say this to reconcile the phenomenon with a conjunction condition as a rationality condition for belief. But isn't this what we do want to say? The historian, when he wrote his preface, was not just making some additional statements for the reader to believe along with those in his narrative; he was taking something back. It is a conjunction condition for belief, together with a consistency condition, which explains why the reader takes the preface as a hedge or a qualification to the text.

Kyburg has a more general reason for rejecting the conjunction principle as a rationality condition on belief: he believes that it leads to a distorted picture of the process of inductive inquiry. He points out that any system of acceptance rules that includes the strong deductive conditions will require that there be "essentially only *one* hypothesis that we may induce from given evidence. Anything else we are allowed to induce will turn out to be merely an implicate of the evidence and that one strongest hypothesis."[6] "This approach . . . suggests that as scientists or even as people we do not induce hypothesis by hypothesis, but that induction consists in principle of inducing at each stage of inquiry . . . a single monumentally complex conjunctive statement."[7] "It is preposterous to suppose that all our inductive knowledge has to be embodiable in a single fat statement."[8]

Kyburg is of course right that if rational belief conforms to the strong deductive conditions, then an ideal state of rational belief could be represented by a single proposition—a proposition that is itself believed and which entails all propositions believed by someone in that ideal state. It is because of this fact that it is possible to represent any belief state meeting the strong deductive conditions by a single set of possible worlds. But is this so preposterous? Some of the things Kyburg says make this consequence seem more implausible than it is.

First, Kyburg's remarks suggest that he has a linguistic picture of the objects of propositional attitudes in mind. The strongest accepted proposition is described as a "monumentally complex conjunctive statement." But on the possible worlds conception of proposition, the complexity of a statement is in the means of representing a proposition and not in the proposition itself. And the fatter the statement, the thinner the proposition, since a proposition is defined by the possible worlds in which it is true. Some of Kyburg's reservations about the consequences of the conjunction principle may derive from questionable assumptions about the structure of propositions.

Second, it must be kept in mind that a global conjunction rule is a rationality condition for belief, which means that conjunction or integration of separate beliefs is an ideal that believers aim at rather than a feature essential to the set of a person's beliefs. It may be preposterous to suppose that anyone's inductive knowledge or beliefs actually do get embodied in a single very fat (or very thin) proposition, but that by itself does not threaten the normative force of the ideal.

Third, while it is true that any state of belief which conforms to the conjunction principle *can* be represented by a single strongest proposition, it does not follow from this that that representation has any special methodological status. Despite Kyburg's claims to the contrary, the conjunction principle does not prevent people from inducing hypothesis by hypothesis, or require them to reevaluate all of their beliefs every time they receive a new piece of evidence. The description of a rational change of belief as the replacement of one fat conjunctive hypothesis with a different one may seem to suggest that every belief change must be a scientific revolution, but if it does so, then it is a misleading description. Nothing implied by the conjunction principle says that one can't replace one fat conjunctive hypothesis with another one simply by tinkering with one of the conjuncts. Nothing implied by the conjunction principle requires one to ignore the fact that some propositions have nothing to do with one another. Where the evidence for or against one proposition is irrelevant to another and where the actions to which the truth or falsity of the one proposition is relevant are distinct from the actions to which the truth or falsity of the other are relevant, then believing the conjunction of the two propositions is no different from believing them separately. To recognize their independence *is* to conjoin or integrate them in the only way that is required.

Still, I think there is a real problem which Kyburg is pointing to, not a problem with the conjunction principle but a limitation of the possible worlds representation of a belief or acceptance state. The problem can be most clearly seen by considering how one might represent a change in what one accepts—a change brought about by a discovery of information that conflicts with something that one initially accepts. If a belief state is represented by a set of possible situations, then in the case of this kind of change the initial belief state and the new one must be represented by disjoint sets of possibilities. The two sets will have no possibilities in common, even if the change of belief is, intuitively, a very small one. At this level of abstraction, there is no difference between a discovery that one was mistaken about some small isolated factual detail and a scientific revolution or global conversion. In both cases, *all* of the possibilities compatible with one's initial belief state are incompatible with the new one. But surely an adequate account of inquiry must account for such extreme differences.

It might seem that a representation of a belief state as a list of sentence-like propositions would more easily and naturally account for what is preserved in a belief change, and for the difference between minor and major belief changes. And so in terms of such a representation, it might be easier to state and defend rules for revising belief in response to discoveries that conflict with one's initial beliefs, or at least to put constraints on such rules. The following kind of rule of revision, for example, might seem initially plausible: add the new information to the list of propositions believed that constitutes one's initial belief state, and then delete from the list the items which are incompatible with the new information. But there are well-known problems here. There will not, in general, be a unique consistent revision of the list, since the new information may require the deletion of one of a set of items without requiring the deletion of any particular one of them. And one cannot adequately compare the magnitude of a belief change simply by counting the propositions changed, since there will be logical and conceptual relations between them. A list of propositions believed will not be a list of independent pieces of information.

A simple abstract example will illustrate the problem. Suppose two agents, George and Harry, both begin by believing both P and Q, and then discover that P is false. George rejects Q along with P, while Harry retains his belief in Q. Isn't it obvious that George's beliefs change more than Harry's? Not necessarily, for P and Q won't be George and Harry's only initial beliefs. If they recognize the obvious consequences of their beliefs, then both of them will also believe, for example, $P \lor \neg Q$. Harry, to remain consistent, must give up this belief when he learns that P is false, while George need not. Each must choose between his belief that Q and his belief that $P \lor \neg Q$, and it is not obvious that one change is more minimal than the other.

This may seem artificial. One might argue that Q is more basic than $P \lor \neg Q$. The latter is believed only because P is believed, while the former is believed independently. But this may or may not be true. One cannot infer from the logical complexity of $P \lor \neg Q$ that belief in it is epistemically dependent on its parts. If George has some independent reason to believe $P \lor \neg Q$ then it will seem perfectly reasonable to take it, together with the new information that P is false as a reason for rejecting Q.

A belief change in response to conflicting information will always force one to choose between alternative revisions, none of which can be seen, on logical grounds alone, to be preferable to the others. The choice will depend on assumptions about epistemic and causal dependence and independence, on the reasons one has for one's beliefs as well as on the beliefs themselves. Whether we represent belief states by lists of sentences or by sets of possible worlds, we will need to impose additional structure on our notion of a belief state before we can say very much about the way beliefs change or ought to change in response to new information.

The abstract example we used above is reminiscent of the examples used by Nelson Goodman to refute various proposed analyses of counterfactual conditionals.[9] The problem of belief change in response to conflicting information is closely related to Goodman's problem; a solution to one is likely to come together with a solution to the other. It was the main negative lesson of Goodman's early paper on counterfactuals that one cannot analyze this kind of statement using only logical relations such as logical independence, compatibility and entailment, together with unproblematic factual assumptions. Some additional, more substantive relations between propositions were needed. The possible worlds analysis of propositions—an analysis Goodman would have no use for—is obviously not the source of Goodman's problem, or of the related problem about belief change. What this analysis does is to make the problems manifest by representing propositions in terms of their minimal logical structure, thereby removing the illusion that we have some account of the structure of possibilities and of the intuitive notions of dependence and independence, similarity and difference between possibilities, which a solution to the problems will require.

The abstract possible worlds framework treats possible worlds as unstructured points. This is not, of course, because the theory makes a claim that possible worlds are some kind of simple unstructured object, but because the theory seeks to capture what is essential and common to a diverse range of applications. The structure of possibilities may be very different from one context to another, but in any interesting context possible situations will be quite complex, and the way we represent and express propositions as well as the way we respond to new information will depend on the structure of the possible worlds in terms of which the propositions and propositional attitudes states are defined. Possible worlds will normally have spatiotemporal structure, domains of individuals instantiating properties and standing in relations to each other. The facts and states of affairs that constitute a possible world may be more or less independent of each other. In terms of the structure of a possible world, one might characterize various relations of similarity and difference between possible worlds, and in terms of such relations one might say more about rational belief change and more generally about the process of inquiry.

What I want to explore in the remaining chapters is the way methodological policies represented by an inquirer's dispositions to change what he believes interact with his conception of the way the world is. I want to suggest that the influences go both ways: it is obvious that one's conception of the way the world is influences the way one changes one's beliefs, but less obviously, epistemic and methodological policies are projected onto the world, contributing to the inquirer's conception of the way things are. This is a familiar theme from the Humean tradition. Necessary connection is the projection of habits of mind onto the world; objective probability is the projection of certain stable patterns in changing subjective probabilities—degrees of belief. Some philosophers have offered such explanations of the origin of allegedly objective concepts as the diagnosis of a confusion. The projection of methodological policy onto the world, they suggest, is the mislocation of necessary connection and explanatory relations in the world rather than in the mind where they really belong. But the process might instead be regarded as a legitimate process of concept formation—a process that yields concepts with which we can make genuine objective claims about the way the world is. The issue is one of realism about dependencies, connections, and explanatory relations. I will argue for what seems to me to be a realistic interpretation of these notions, but one that recognizes the tension between a pragmatic account of belief and a realistic account of truth.

Let me conclude by describing the picture of inquiry that has emerged from our discussion so far. A state of belief is most perspicuously represented, not by a set of sentences or propositions believed, but by the set of possibilities recognized as ways the world may be. Propositions believed, relative to such a belief state, are propositions true in all possible situations in the set. There is nothing essentially linguistic about belief, according to this picture, although the subject matter of belief may be linguistic expressions, or conceptual structures that essentially involve language, and this may be true even when it is not evident from the surface forms of belief attributions.

The beliefs of a perfectly rational intelligence could be represented by a single belief state of this kind—one coherent conception of the way the world is represented by one set of alternative possibilities. But the beliefs of mere mortals will require a more complicated representation. Mortals may be in many belief states at once, represented by separate spaces of possibilities. The integration of such separate belief states may in some cases be a simple matter of putting two and two together, but it may also be a task that requires nontrivial computation or creative activity. Deductive inquiry, I suggested, is inquiry which is designed to accomplish such tasks.

Belief is not the only attitude that is relevant to the cognitive situation of inquirers. Inquirers make posits, presumptions, assumptions and presuppositions as well. These methodological attitudes may diverge from belief in various ways, giving rise to additional complexity in a representation of an epistemic situation. But, I suggested, the cluster of propositional attitudes which were grouped together under the label *acceptance* share a common structure with belief.

Inquiry is the process of changing such acceptance states, either by interaction with the world or by interaction between different acceptance states. Methodological policies are policies constraining such changes. To have a framework for describing methodological policy, we might assume that acceptance states have two components: a set of alternative possibilities representing the inquirer's current conception of the way the world is, and a change function representing his disposition to change what he accepts in response to new information. This function will take propositions (the potential new information) into new acceptance states. It seems plausible to assume that when the new information is compatible with everything initially accepted, then the new acceptance state will be the intersection of the new information with the initial state. But where the new information conflicts with something initially believed, the new acceptance state will be a disjoint set of possible situations. No constraints can be put on such changes without adding further structure to our representation of an inquirer's epistemic situation, or to our representation of the possible situations.

One should expect the two components of an acceptance state to interact: our current conception of the way the world is constrains our dispositions to change our beliefs in response to new evidence, and those dispositions may contribute to the formation of concepts in terms of which we describe the world. In the next chapter, I want to begin looking at this interaction by considering the relationship between conditionals that express one's disposition to accept the consequent upon coming to believe the antecedent and conditionals that make categorical claims about the world.

Chapter 6

Conditional Belief

It has been suggested by some proponents of the pragmatic account of belief that there are two very different kinds of beliefs. According to Frank Ramsey, and David Armstrong following him,[1] there are on the one hand beliefs about particular matters of fact, which are pictures or maps of reality by which we guide our actions. On the other hand there are general beliefs, which are dispositions to extend or change our maps of reality, " 'habits of inference' which dispose us to move from a belief about some particular matter of fact to a further belief about some particular matter of fact."[2] General beliefs, according to this suggestion, are a step further removed from reality and from action. If ordinary beliefs are conditional dispositions to act, then general beliefs are conditional dispositions to acquire conditional dispositions to act.

There is, I think, something right and something wrong with this suggestion. What is right about it is the recognition that a theory of belief must account not only for static conceptions of the way the world is, but also for the way those conceptions are disposed to change in response to new information. What is wrong is the idea that there are two sharply distinguishable kinds of beliefs, only one of which is belief about the way the world is.

Ramsey distinguished these two kinds of beliefs in part because he did not see how unrestricted universal generalizations could be represented in (partial) maps of reality. I am not sure why there is a problem here, but if there is one I suspect that it derives from taking the map metaphor too literally. A representation of the way the world is need not be restricted to particular matters of fact. According to the pragmatic picture, an agent's mental representation of the way the world is that constitutes his belief state just *is* a complex conditional disposition to act in certain ways. While the map analogy may provide a useful way to characterize such complex dispositions, we must be sure to use a conception of map that is rich and flexible enough to account for all the differences in the potential actions of the relevant agents. If two agents with the same values and desires have different rational dispositions to act, then that difference must be explained either in terms of the different locations of the agents in the world as they conceive it to be,[3] or in terms of a difference in their conceptions of the world. The way we cut up the space of possibilities—the distinctions we make between different alternative possible worlds—is determined by the differences between the dispositional mental states of the relevant agents. Since the beliefs that guide action will include general beliefs, conditional beliefs, and beliefs about causal and explanatory connections as well as beliefs about particular matters of fact, these must be represented in our maps of how things are. They will also, of course, be relevant to guiding the way in which inquirers change what they accept in response to new information.

While the model of a belief state sketched at the end of the last chapter did not distinguish two kinds of belief, it did make a closely related distinction between two components of a belief state: first, a set of possible worlds representing the agent's conception of the way the world is, and second, a change function representing the agent's dispositions to change what he accepts in response to new information. My main concern in this chapter will be with the relation between these two components—with the way that an agent's dispositions to change what he accepts are determined by, or reflected in, his conception of how things are. I will argue that different dispositions to change what one accepts are always grounded in different factual beliefs. This is why the distinction between the two components of a belief state does not amount to a distinction between two kinds of belief.

Normally a difference between two people's dispositions to change their beliefs will be explained by a difference in their ordinary factual beliefs. I am disposed to believe, on hearing the doorbell ring, that the plumber has arrived, while you are not. The reason is that I know that plumber has been called, and you do not. But isn't it at least conceivable that two people might agree in all their beliefs about how things are but disagree about how to respond to new information? This is not conceivable, I will argue, because even if there is no independent way to specify the factual disagreement that explains the difference in methodological policy, we take the latter difference itself to constitute a factual disagreement. Suppose neither of us expects Ted Kennedy to be the Democratic nominee for President in 1984, but we are prepared to discuss that possibility. I am disposed to believe that he will win should I learn that, contrary to what I expect, he seeks and obtains the nomination; you, let us suppose, are not. Probably we disagree about other related things—few factual disagreements are isolated—but even if we do not, this difference itself reflects a disagreement about the way things are—about the way the world is disposed to respond to a possibly counterfactual sequence of events. I believe Kennedy would win if he were nominated, and you do not.

Conditional sentences are used to express our methodological dispositions: I express my disposition to come to believe that the plumber has arrived by saying "if the doorbell rings, that will be the plumber." We also use conditional sentences to make factual claims. I may believe that it is *true* that Kennedy would win if he were nominated, and I may continue to believe this long after the possibility that he be nominated has been foreclosed. These two uses of conditional sentences are obviously closely related, and, I will suggest, the relation between them reflects a connection between methodological policy and factual belief. I want to explore this connection by looking at the relation between the two kinds or uses of conditionals.

The strategy I will explore, which I will call the *projection strategy*, assumes, in general, that natural necessities should be explained as projections of epistemic principles and practices onto the world. Examples of the kind of strategy I have in mind include Hume's explanations of causal beliefs in terms of habits of inference, de Finetti's explanation of objective probability (or the appearance of objective probability) in terms of underlying features of subjective probability functions, and Goodman's attempt to connect practices of inductive inference with the kind of projection required for the formation of dispositional concepts. Specifically, what I want to explore is the idea that understanding conditional belief can help us understand the content of conditional propositions.

What I will have to say about the projection strategy will be tentative and preliminary. I have more to say about the problems that such a project will encounter than I do about how to solve these problems. The main thing I want to do in this chapter is to sketch an account of conditional belief, and to show why conditional belief must diverge from belief in conditional propositions. The upshot is that the explanation of one in terms of the other cannot be as simple and straightforward as one might wish. I will conclude with some vague and impressionistic remarks about how one might spell out the connection between them.

I will assume, to begin with, that an agent's rational dispositions to change what he accepts may be identified with his conditional beliefs, expressed in conditional sentences. To be disposed to accept B on learning A is to accept B conditionally on A, or to accept that if A, then B. This is a relatively innocent assumption as I will understand it. To bring out its innocence I will mention five things that I take it not to imply.

First, I am not assuming that whenever a person is disposed to accept

B on learning *A* he is disposed to *assent* to the corresponding conditional sentence, or that he recognizes that he has the conditional belief. Conditional beliefs, like any other beliefs, may be tacit, unrecognized, inarticulate. Just as I may properly ascribe to Fido the belief that there is a bone buried in the yard without implying that he has the capacity to express his belief, so I may properly ascribe to him the conditional belief that if he digs in a certain place, he will uncover the bone without implying that he has the conceptual or linguistic resources to say so.

Second, even though conditional beliefs, like other beliefs, may be tacit, it is not assumed that every disposition to alter one's beliefs in a particular way is a conditional belief. There may be nonrational belief changes, and nonrational dispositions to change. Suppose, for example, that I am on the brink of a conversion experience, although I don't know it. Suppose that if I were to learn that I had a fatal disease this would trigger the experience, causing me to become a devout believer in God. After the change, neither I nor anyone else would be inclined to say that I inferred that God exists from the fact that I had a fatal disease. No one would say that this was my reason for changing my belief. The new information just caused me to see things in a new light. Despite my disposition to change my beliefs in this way, I did not believe, even tacitly, before the conversion that if I have a fatal disease, God exists.

The line between rational and nonrational dispositions is neither sharp nor easy to draw, but the problem of drawing it is not a special problem concerning *conditional* belief. One can see the same rough intuitive distinction, in general, between more or less rational and more or less irrational or nonrational dispositions to act, and one is less inclined to identify the less rational dispositions with beliefs. For example, if I have a phobia about airplanes, I may act in ways that would be appropriate for someone who believes that airplane travel is dangerous. But I may know that planes are really quite safe, that my fear is irrational. Despite my behavioral tendencies, it would be implausible to say that I believed that airplanes are dangerous. What distinguishes my attitude from clear cases of belief is its relationship to other attitudes that I have, and its susceptibility to change in response to evidence. Nonrational dispositions to change one's beliefs will be distinguished from conditional beliefs in similar ways.

Third, the assumption does not imply that even the perfectly rational agent who accepts *if A then B* will always come to accept *B* upon learning *A*. For *A* may not be all that one learns, and the additional information that comes along with *A* may give one reason to reject the conditional belief which represents the disposition to change one's belief. For example, I may believe that if John comes to the party, Mary will come with him. Then I learn that John comes to the party by seeing him walk in the door alone. Here I learn, not just that John came to the party, but that he came alone, and this gives me reason to change my mind about the conditional belief that if John comes to the party, Mary comes with him. The disposition to accept *B* on learning *A* must be understood as the disposition to accept *B* when *A* is the total new information that one receives. But it will be in general true that so long as the total new information is compatible with the initial acceptance state, the agent will accept *B* whenever he initially accepts *if A then B*, and then learns *A*.

If one is not careful to take account of the total information received, or hypothetically received, one may think that some examples show a divergence between conditional belief and dispositions to change one's beliefs. Someone might, for example, accept that if his employees dislike him, he will never know it. But he is not thereby disposed to come to accept that he will never know that his employees don't like him upon learning that they don't. The problem here is that when we imagine him learning that his employees dislike him, we imagine him learning something else as well: that he learns that his employees dislike him. This additional information is not something inferred from the main fact we imagine him learning; it is something else he learns along with it. So the proposition that his employees dislike him will not be the total information that initiates the imagined belief change. Normally—perhaps always—when we learn *A* we also learn that we have learned it (and that we learned it in some particular way). Perhaps this is essential to belief. If so, then there are some propositions— propositions which are not in part about the believer's own state of belief—which cannot be the total information received. In many contexts one can ignore this additional information because it will be irrelevant, but when the believer's state of mind is part of the relevant subject matter as it is in this example, it cannot be ignored, and may be responsible for the appearance of a divergence between conditional belief and the disposition to change one's beliefs.

Fourth, the assumption is that dispositions to change are conditional beliefs represented by conditional sentences, but not that *all* conditionals that one accepts represent such conditional beliefs. It is clear that some conditionals, for example some counterfactual conditionals, do not play this role. Suppose I accept that if Hitler had decided to invade England in 1940, Germany would have won the war. Then suppose I discover, to my surprise, that Hitler did in fact decide to invade England in 1940 (although he never carried out his plan). Am I now disposed to accept that Germany won the war? No, instead I will give up my belief in the conditional. In this case, my rejection of the antecedent was an essential presupposition of my acceptance of the counterfactual, and so gives me reason to give up the counterfactual rather than to accept its consequent, when I learn that the antecedent is true. But for every counterfactual conditional which does not represent a rational disposition to change one's beliefs, there will be a contrasting conditional, which I will call an *open conditional*, with the same antecedent and consequent which does, or would if accepted. If I accept that if Hitler *did* decide to invade England in 1940, then Germany *did* win the war, then I will be rationally disposed to accept that Germany won the war upon learning that Hitler decided to invade England in 1940. This example fits a pattern of examples, the originals invented by Ernest Adams, which shows that there must be a semantic, and not merely a pragmatic, difference between so-called subjunctive and indicative conditionals. To use Adams's example, we all accept that if Oswald didn't shoot Kennedy then someone else did, since we are disposed to conclude that someone other than Oswald shot Kennedy on learning that Oswald did not. But it would be quite a different matter to accept that if Oswald hadn't shot Kennedy, someone else would have.[4]

Fifth, I will make no assumption, initially, about the logic or truth-conditions of conditionals. I will not assume even that conditional beliefs are necessarily beliefs that some proposition is true. I did suggest above that the differences in dispositions to change beliefs are always grounded in differences in beliefs about the way the world is, which means in a difference in the propositions one believes, but this does not imply that conditional beliefs must always themselves be beliefs about the way the world is.

My strategy will be to use the assumption that accepted open conditional sentences represent dispositions to change one's belief in response to new information to evaluate hypotheses about what such sentences are used to say. The assumption, together with intuitions about methodology—about how it is appropriate to respond to evidence—will give us a basis for finding and defending answers to questions about the meaning of open conditionals, and about the logical relations between conditionals.

There is an initially attractive argument, based on this strategy, leading to the conclusion that the material conditional analysis is the correct analysis of open conditionals: Suppose one initially accepts a material conditional, $A \supset B$, in a context in which it is an open question whether or not A is true or false. If one were then to learn that A were true, one would be logically committed to coming to accept B, assuming that one did not give up the previously accepted material conditional. And since the new information one receives is compatible with the initial beliefs, one would have no reason to change one's belief in that proposition. So in general, if one accepts a material conditional in such a context, one is therefore rationally disposed to accept the consequent on learning the antecedent, which means that given our assumption, one accepts the open conditional.

The converse claim, that one who accepts an open conditional must accept the corresponding material conditional, seems also correct. For suppose I do *not* accept the material conditional, $A \supset B$. Then a possible situation in which A is true and B false will be compatible with what I accept. But then I cannot rationally infer B from A—A cannot be my *reason* for subsequently accepting B since the truth of A can give me no reason for ruling out a possibility in which A is true. So at least in contexts in which A is compatible with what is initially accepted, acceptance of the material conditional is both necessary and sufficient for the acceptance of the corresponding open conditional.

But this conclusion does not imply that the *truth* of the material conditional is necessary and sufficient for the truth of the open conditional. That is, it does not imply that the two kinds of conditional express the same proposition. For first, there may be a divergence between the acceptance conditions of the two kinds of conditionals in contexts in which the antecedent is not compatible with what is initially believed. And second, the conditions under which material conditionals are *rejected* may diverge from conditions under which open conditionals are rejected, even when the antecedent is compatible with what is initially believed. Here are two examples that illustrate these divergences: (1) I believe that the Yankees won the American League pennant in 1927, and thus believe as a logical consequence of this that they won either the American or the National League pennant that year. That is, I accept the material conditional, "the Yankees didn't win the American League pennant in 1927 $\supset$ they won the National League pennant in 1927." But I am of course not disposed to conclude, on learning that I was wrong about the 1927 American League race, that the Yankees were in the other league, and I would not assent to the conditional, "if the Yankees didn't win the American League pennant that year, then they won the National League pennant." (2) I am not sure who will win the American League pennant in 1987, but one thing I am prepared to reject is this: if the Yankees win the pennant in 1987, then the Red Sox will win the World Series in 1987. But the corresponding material conditional may, for all I know, be true. So the conditional and the material conditional cannot say the same thing.

More generally, our strategy suggests that the logic of the open conditional is different from the logic of the material conditional. Given the methodological rule that one should maintain consistency in one's beliefs, it would never be rational to be disposed to accept B and also *not-B* on receiving the same information *A*. So if one accepts the open conditional, *if A then B*, one will be committed to rejecting the opposite conditional, *if A then not-B*. This seems to imply that the principle of conditional noncontradiction (not both *if A then B* and *if A then not-B*) is valid for open conditionals, but it is not valid for the material conditional. The formula $(A \supset B) \mathrel{\&} (A \supset \smallsmile B)$ is true whenever *A* is false.

Should one conclude, then, that an open conditional expresses some proposition stronger than the material conditional? The problem with this suggestion is that it is difficult to see, in some contexts at least, what additional information is conveyed by an open conditional. Suppose neither you nor I know initially whether the British will be coming by sea or by land. You tell me that if they are coming by sea, there will be two lanterns in the church tower, and I believe you. What have I learned? Surely not necessarily any more than that either there will be two lanterns, or the British won't be coming by sea. For, as we have seen, this is all you need to know in order to accept and appropriately assert the open conditional.

To accept what you tell me when you say "two if by sea," I must accept the material conditional, but I need not change my beliefs or rational dispositions in any other way. In particular, I need not myself acquire the disposition to accept that there will be two lanterns in the tower on learning that the British are coming by sea. After accepting what you say, I need not myself be in a position to say "two if by sea." For suppose I know for certain that there is only one lantern in the church tower, although I do not initially have an opinion about how the British are coming. When you tell me that there are two lanterns in the church tower if the British are coming by sea, I infer, by modus tollens, that the British are not coming by sea. I accept what you told me—if I did not, I would have no basis for concluding that the British won't be coming by sea. But I initially accepted, implicitly, the contrary open conditional, if the British are coming by sea (or however they come), there is only one lantern in the tower, and I may continue to do so. Despite the fact that I believed what you told me, and drew a conclusion from it, I continue to assent to a conditional that seems to contradict what you told me, and I continue to reject an open conditional that seems to be the same as the one you affirmed.

These puzzling points are well illustrated by an example invented by Allan Gibbard which he uses, first, to raise a problem for the principle of conditional noncontradiction, and then to argue that open conditionals do not express propositions at all. Here is Gibbard's example:

Sly Pete and Mr. Stone are playing poker on a Mississippi riverboat.

It is now up to Pete to call or fold. My henchman Zack sees Stone's hand, which is quite good, and signals its contents to Pete. My henchman Jack sees both hands, and sees that Pete's hand is rather low, so that Stone's is the winning hand. At this point the room is cleared. A few minutes later Zack slips me a note which says "if Pete called, he won," and Jack slips me a note which says "if Pete called, he lost. . . ." I conclude that Pete folded.[5]

If I know that the two notes come from my trusted henchmen but know nothing about the circumstances—about how they acquired the information that they pass on to me, then I can conclude *only* that Pete folded, and this conclusion is equivalent to the conjunction of the two *material* conditionals.

But despite the fact that I accept what both my henchmen tell me, I will myself affirm only one of the two opposite conditionals. Which I affirm will depend on my other beliefs and methodological policies. If, for example, I were to learn all the circumstances reported in the story, I would probably believe that if (contrary to what I believe) Pete called, then he lost (since we know that he had a losing hand). And it is clear that if I did believe this, I would *reject* the claim that if Pete called he won. But I still believe what Zack told me when he said "if Pete called, he won." How can this be?

Perhaps the paradox can be resolved by recognizing the context-dependence of open conditionals. Compare the case of such conditionals with a simple and unproblematic case of context-dependence: there is no paradox in the fact that I may consistently accept your claim when you say "I was born in Istanbul" while at the same time refusing to affirm, even denying, that I was born there. There is a straightforward sense in which the sentences "I was born in Istanbul" and "I was not born in Istanbul" are contradictories: when both are interpreted relative to the same context, they must have opposite truth-values. But different speakers create different contexts, and so two tokens of the respective sentences may both be true if spoken by different speakers. Since I accept what you say, I am prepared to assert the *proposition* you expressed, but I will have to use a different sentence to do so.

A parallel account of the relationship between sentences of the forms *if A then B* and *if A then not-B* might go like this: relative to a single context, the two sentences express contrary propositions. That is why one who affirms one must reject the other. But if you and I are in different epistemic situations, then the context in which I assert *if A then B* will be different from the context in which you assert *if A then not-B*, and so both may be true. I may accept what you say, but I will have to put it differently.

But to sustain the parallel, one would have to say what proposition is expressed by the open conditional, and what contextual factors it depends on. What makes the case of the pronoun "I" relatively unproblematic is that one can, in many contexts, give a neutral characterization of the proposition expressed in sentences using that pronoun, and one can give the rule relating sentences containing "I" and the contexts in which they might be used to the propositions which the sentences would express in such contexts.[6] One can also say how such propositions might be expressed by other speakers in other contexts. When NN says "I was born in Istanbul" I learn that NN was born in Istanbul. But when Zack says "if Pete called, he won," what (beyond the material conditional) do I learn? What sort of rule will assign contrary propositions to that sentence and its opposite, "if Pete called, he lost," relative to the context in which Zack was speaking? The following argument, due essentially to Allan Gibbard,[7] shows that any attempt to answer this question will face a serious difficulty.

Suppose I am in a context in which I don't know whether Pete called and won, called and lost, or folded. I ask someone the following question: "If Pete called, did he win?" That is, in effect, I ask my addressee—call him Mack—to affirm one of the two open conditionals, "if Pete called, he won," or "if Pete called, he didn't win." Now assume, first, that open conditionals play the methodological role we have been assuming they play, and second, that they express (possibly context-dependent) propositions. That is, assume that the conditional "if Pete called, he won" expresses (relative to the context) a proposition F which the speaker believes if and only if he is disposed to come to believe that Pete won upon learning that he called. Now consider an arbitrary possible world i in which Pete folded, and which is compatible with the context in which the question is asked. Is the proposition F true in world i? If Mack's answer is "if Pete called, he won," then F must be true in i, since his answer does not exclude that possibility. But if Mack gave the alternative answer, then F would be false in i. It follows that the conditional "if Pete called, he won" expresses one proposition when it is asserted, and a different one when it is denied.

In general, in any context in which *if A then B* and *if A then not-B* are (epistemically) possible answers, the questioner will have the contextual information necessary to interpret the answer only when he knows what it is. This seems to violate the following conversational maxim: speakers ought, in general, to assume that their addressees have whatever information is necessary to determine what they are saying. It seems that the assumption that open conditionals express propositions leads to the conclusion that in a very general kind of context, the assertion of indicative conditionals will always conflict with a very plausible principle of conversation.

Gibbard concludes from this kind of consideration that open conditionals do not express propositions at all, not even context-dependent propositions. One might avoid this conclusion by giving up, or modifying, the maxim. There are, surely, exceptions to it. Sometimes one may communicate without assuming that one's addressee can figure out exactly what one is saying because sometimes it does not matter *exactly* what one is saying. I might write an undated postcard saying "We arrived in Paris today. The weather is beautiful." To know exactly what I've said, you need to know what day the postcard was written, but even without knowing this you can infer that I made it to Paris and had good weather there, and this may be all that matters. A better analogy with the conditionals case would be a case in which the information necessary to interpret the statement is given by the making of the statement itself, as when you ask, in the dark, "Where are you?" and I reply, "I'm over here." In the conditional question case, as in this example, once you hear the answer, you know enough to know what is said.

One can, in this way, reconcile the hypothesis that open conditionals express propositions with the phenomena, but the propositions will be highly context-dependent. To play their methodological role, open conditionals must be too closely tied to the epistemic states of the agents who utter them for those conditionals to express propositions which could be separated from the contexts in which they are accepted. But *some* conditional sentences do seem to express such propositions. It is to these that I now turn.

Gibbard, in the paper I have been drawing on, argues that open conditionals and subjunctive conditionals have a common logic but that the similarity between them "hides a profound semantic difference." He suggests that the common syntactic devices and common logic are "little more than a coincidence" and that the two kinds of conditionals "have little of importance in common."[8] These claims seem to me seriously mistaken. I will argue that we can understand the meaning and role of subjunctive and counterfactual conditionals—more generally, of conditionals that express propositions that can be separated from their contexts—only by clarifying their connection with the open conditionals which express our epistemic policies.

To begin with, there is a *prima facie* implausibility in Gibbard's claim that the parallels between the two kinds of conditionals are mere coincidence, for the parallels are extensive. It is not just that in English, and most if not all other languages, the same words are used in both cases and that many of the same patterns of inference are valid. There

are other parallels and connections: open and counterfactual *ifs* combine
with other words—for example with *only, even,* and *might*—in the same
ways. There is no general agreement about exactly how one should
analyze *only, if, even if,* and *if . . . might* constructions, but the problems
such combinations present seem to be independent of whether the
conditional is subjunctive or indicative, open or counterfactual. Conditionals of both kinds can be paraphrased in similar ways. Instead of
"if Oswald hadn't shot Kennedy" (or "if Oswald didn't shoot Kennedy"),
I can say "suppose Oswald hadn't shot Kennedy" (or "suppose Oswald
didn't shoot Kennedy"). Some conditionals are appropriately paraphrased with *unless,* and these include conditionals of both kinds: "John
would not have come unless Mary had invited him" and "John didn't
come unless Mary invited him."

More generally, the contrast between open and proposition-expressing
conditionals can be seen as a special case of a wider contrast between
subjective and objective modal concepts. *Possibility* can be compatibility
with knowledge or compatibility with objective necessities. Probability
can be subjective degree of belief or objective chance. Certainty begins
as an attitude or epistemic state, but can also be some kind of objective
necessity. ("From that point, it was certain that the Shah would be
deposed, although no one recognized it at the time.") The contrast
between "if he killed the Pope," and "if he had killed the Pope"
parallels the contrast between "the Pope may have been killed" and
"the Pope might have been killed."

It would be unsatisfying to dismiss all these parallels as coincidences.
But, more important, to do so would be to ignore an important resource
for explaining the notoriously problematic objective modal concepts.
The empiricist and pragmatist traditions have always found the subjective modal concepts less problematic than their objective counterparts.
The possibilities that arise from ignorance and uncertainty are less
puzzling than the real possibilities that remain even when we know
they are unactualized. The connections between ideas that arise from
habits of inference are less puzzling than the connections that seem to
hold between events in the world. Similarly, the meaning and role of
conditionals that represent our dispositions to modify beliefs in response
to evidence are easier to understand than the meaning and role of
conditionals that seem to be trying to make objective claims about
what might have been, but was not. The recurring strategy of empiricists
and pragmatists for treating the cluster of objective modal concepts
has been to try to explain them either as illusory reflections or as
legitimate extensions of their subjective analogues. Whether such a
strategy can work in the case of open and proposition-expressing conditionals remains to be seen: the semantic contrast between the two

kinds of conditionals brought out by Adams and Gibbard shows that the relation between them is not a simple and straightforward one, but the systematic parallels between the two suggest at least the possibility of a deeper conceptual connection that developing the strategy might bring out. So I will adopt the working hypothesis that the parallels are more than merely coincidental.

To try to get at the relation between conditional belief, expressed in open conditional sentences, and belief in conditional propositions, I will look at an example which, at a certain level of abstraction, is exactly like Gibbard's story of Sly Pete and Mr. Stone, but which is in an important way strikingly different from it. The example is borrowed from Paul Grice who used it for a related but different purpose in his William James Lectures.[9]

You and I are discussing an approaching British national election (the time is the 1960s). Neither of us has a firm opinion about who will win, but I claim that the winner will be either Wilson or Thorpe. You, on the other hand, are convinced that it will be either Wilson or Heath. In a sense we disagree, and we might argue about the issue; we disagree about what it is reasonable to accept. But we don't, on the surface at least, necessarily disagree about the way the world is. Despite our disagreement, we might both be right.

The structure of the situation is like that of the Sly Pete story in the following respects: first, there are three relevantly different alternative possibilities in each context. In the Sly Pete story, they are (a) Pete folds, (b) Pete calls and wins, and (c) Pete calls and loses. In the British election example, they are (a) Wilson wins, (b) Heath wins, and (c) Thorpe wins. Second, each of the examples concerns two agents who have different beliefs with respect to the three alternative possibilities: Jack and Zack in the Sly Pete story and you and me in the election example. In both of the examples, one agent believes that the actual situation is either (a) or (b), while the other believes that it is either (a) or (c). As a result of their different disjunctive beliefs, the two agents have different conditional beliefs, and so accept contrasting open conditionals. One believes that if the actual situation is not (a) it is (b), while the other believes that if it is not (a) it is (c). But there is a crucial difference between the two examples. In the Sly Pete story, there is no conflict or disagreement; there is just a difference in the information that is initially available to the two agents. When their information is pooled, each will accept what the other says, and neither need change his mind in order to do so. But in the election example, the divergence persists after the agents pool their information. You and I disagree about how to respond to information available to both of us. Unlike the difference between Jack's and Zack's beliefs, the difference between your beliefs and mine looks more like a disagreement about the facts.

In both stories, the actual situation turns out to be (a). Pete folds, and Wilson wins. In the Sly Pete story, that is just what both Jack and Zack came to expect after they pooled their information. The facts confirmed what both believed. But in the election example, as Grice pointed out, we are reluctant to say that the facts—at least the fact that Wilson won—confirm either of us. Each of us may continue to insist that the other was wrong. If Wilson hadn't won, I insist, Thorpe would have. If the facts support *this* claim, then they show that I was right and you were wrong.

In any situation with the structure shared by these two stories, if the divergence between the beliefs of the two agents derives entirely from a difference in the information available to each, then it will disappear with an exchange of information. But where the divergence persists—when it becomes a disagreement—we inevitably treat it as a disagreement about what the world is like. In the normal case, the divergence will reflect other factual disagreements which will emerge as we argue about the issue. We cite opinion polls, statistics from previous elections, generalizations about major and minor parties or about the influence of unions, facts about recent by-elections or about the personalities of the candidates. If in the end we still disagree, this may be because one of us denies some of the factual claims the other affirms in support of his conditional belief, or because we disagree about the evidential significance of some of those claims. But both kinds of disagreement are regarded as disagreements about the way things are. If we do not disagree about the surface phenomena—about who said what or how many people voted for whom—then we disagree about the causal or explanatory relations that underly them. Through its evidential connections with other facts—facts which we agree are more or less independent of whether Wilson wins—the conditional question, "If not Wilson, then who?" takes on a life of its own. It becomes a question that can be detached from the particular context of our argument. We come to regard it as a question that will have an answer even if Wilson should win.

To detach the conditional question—to regard it as a question about the facts and not just about how to change one's beliefs in response to potential new information—is to recognize that the answers to the question may be judged by a purely external standard. Suppose that at the time we are arguing about the election, any reasonable and knowledgeable political observer would expect Heath either to win or to finish a close second. But then an unexpected last-minute scandal sinks Heath. Conservatives shift to Thorpe, who almost, but not quite, carries the election. In this situation, your conditional belief was the reasonable one to have; you were justified and I was not. But I, quite by accident, was proved right by the facts. (There is room for argument here about any particular case, but it is clear that one could fill in the details of the story so that the correct conclusion is that Thorpe would have won if Wilson had not.) Treating the disagreement as a factual one involves recognizing the possibility of a gap between being justified and being right.

Detaching the conditional question from its epistemic context requires that we recognize the possibility of another gap as well: a gap between acceptance of the conditional proposition and maintaining the methodological disposition in which, I am suggesting, the conditional proposition originates. Suppose, after the election but before I learn definitively who won, I see on television the end of what is obviously a concession speech by Thorpe. But I do not hear who he is conceding to. Since I believe that Wilson won if Thorpe did not, I conclude that Wilson must have won. Since I now know for sure that Thorpe lost, I also acquire the conditional belief that if Wilson didn't win, Heath did. But I haven't changed my mind about anything: I still believe that I was right and you were wrong. Wilson won, but I never denied that he would. I continue to believe that if Wilson had not won, Thorpe would have.

So what, then, is the connection between a conditional proposition and the methodological disposition expressed by the corresponding open conditional? In vague and impressionistic terms, the idea is this: our epistemic situation at any moment may be represented by the set of alternative possibilities compatible with what we accept, together with policies for modifying this set in response to new information. Some of these policies are relatively stable and systematically connected with our factual beliefs, while others are (and are recognized to be) unstable and dependent on the idiosyncrasies of our particular epistemic perspective. Purely epistemic relations which ignore this difference (such as the relation of epistemic relevance—the relation that holds between two propositions, one of which is evidence for or against the other) are too unconstrained to generalize about. Given the right context, any piece of information may be relevant to any other, and any open conditional with compatible parts may be justifiably accepted. For example, suppose I am given a list of unrelated propositions and told, reliably, that they all have the same truth-value. Against this background information, each of the propositions becomes relevant to each of the others. One will have good reason to accept any open conditional whose antecedent and consequent are both on the list. In such a case, that I accept the conditionals obviously says nothing about my beliefs about the relation between the facts that the propositions are about. Such cases show why we cannot plausibly project, in general, unrefined epistemic relations between propositions onto the world. But in more normal contexts in which such specialized information is not available, it is more plausible to identify evidential relevance with beliefs about connections and dependencies between the facts. If we could distinguish and filter out those aspects of our epistemic situation which derive more from our parochial perspective and less from the way we take the world to be, we might be able to explain the acceptance of conditional propositions in terms of the open conditionals that would be acceptable in idealized contexts which abstract away from those aspects. Inquirers have, in any case, a clear practical motivation for making such a distinction, since it would enable them to get at the aspects of epistemic policy which can be tested, refined, generalized, and widely applied.

I am not suggesting that one might give a reductive analysis of counterfactual conditional propositions in terms of epistemic or methodological concepts. The kind of projection I am suggesting requires that one hypothesize a fact of a certain kind: a fact that is identified by the methodological policies that it might justify, but which is not reducible to those policies. The idea is something like this: in accepting the proposition that Heath would win if Wilson did not, one is hypothesizing that there is a fact—a feature of the world—that is independent of whether Wilson wins, and which under normal conditions would give one reason to be disposed to accept that Heath will win, or has won, on learning that Wilson will not, or did not. This idea does not provide or point the way to a reductive analysis since the crucial notions of independence and normal conditions are themselves members of the family of notions that are problematic in the same way as conditional propositions. But while the projection strategy will not lead to the elimination of natural necessity, it may contribute to an explanation of why we have reason to describe the world in terms of dependencies and connections, of how we come to have concepts of such things, and of how beliefs about them play the roles they play in the process of inquiry.

My task in the remaining chapters will be to defend and discuss an account of conditional propositions which might help to clarify and sharpen the connection between conditional propositions and methodological policy. In chapter 7 I will discuss the general abstract semantic structure of conditional propositions, arguing that the hypothesis that conditional propositions are a projection of epistemic dispositions onto the world motivates and provides a foundation for the kind of semantic theory of conditional propositions that has been proposed in recent years by myself and Richmond Thomason, and by David Lewis. I will compare a number of closely related versions of this kind of semantic theory, and use facts about how conditional sentences are used to defend one of these theories against the others.

The abstract semantic analysis does not by itself solve the substantive problem of explaining what conditional propositions say, since it gives truth-conditions for such propositions only relative to an unexplained primitive parameter. (In the theory I will defend, it is a selection function selecting, for each potential antecedent, the possible situation in which the consequent is said to be true.) But while the abstract analysis does not solve the substantive problem of counterfactuals, it does give the problem a precise form. It transforms it into the problem of explaining the basis for the selection of possible situations that is relevant to the interpretation of counterfactual and other conditional propositions. In chapter 8, I will discuss various ways of approaching this problem, and consider to what extent a plausible solution to it would give us reason to be realists about counterfactuals.

Chapter 7
Conditional Propositions

In the last chapter I argued that we should try to understand conditional propositions in terms of a projection of epistemic policy onto the world. Conditional propositions should be understood as propositions about features of the world which justify certain policies for changing one's belief in response to potential new information. But I also argued that there could be no simple and straightforward relation between conditional belief and belief in conditionals. I suggested that the explanation of conditional propositions in terms of epistemic policy will require some distinctions between different aspects of epistemic policy, and between different epistemic contexts. To sharpen this problem and to provide a framework for solving it, we need an abstract account of conditional propositions. My task in this chapter will be to describe and defend a formal semantic theory of conditionals which I think provides both a plausible explanation for facts about how conditional sentences are used and a framework for an explanation of the role of conditional propositions in inquiry.

I will begin by using the projection hypothesis, together with the abstract model of an acceptance state sketched at the end of chapter 6, to motivate informally the abstract semantic analysis that I will defend. Then I will sketch the semantic theory, a theory developed in the late 1960s by Richmond Thomason and myself, and make some methodological remarks about the role of the abstract formal semantic theory in the solution of philosophical problems about counterfactual propositions. Finally, I will compare the theory with some of its competitors.

According to our abstract model of an acceptance state, an agent's open conditional beliefs are represented by a change function—a function taking a proposition (the potential new information) and a set of possible worlds (the initial acceptance state) into a set of possible worlds (the potential new acceptance state). A change function is a global feature of an acceptance state—a feature of the state as a whole which cannot necessarily be reduced to the properties of the individual possible worlds that are the components of the state. If conditional propositions are projections of such a function onto the world, then they must be interpreted in terms of a feature, shared by the individual possible worlds, which reflects and determines this global feature of the acceptance state. The projection of the change function onto the world is the attribution to the individual possible worlds in an acceptance state of a feature that will do this job.

To see what such a feature of individual possible worlds might be like, consider what happens as an agent learns more and more about the world. The set of possible situations compatible with what is accepted grows smaller and smaller. So, presumably, does the set that results from the application of the change function to some potential new information. At the limit of this process, where the agent knows everything relevant, the acceptance state will contain a single possible situation—one representing the way the agent knows the world to be. And one might expect the potential acceptance states that the agent is disposed to move to on learning some contrary information to contain a single possible situation as well.[1] Such a change function for omniscient states of knowledge would be equivalent to a world selection function of the kind proposed in our semantic analysis of conditional propositions. The information contained in such a function is information about the individual possible worlds, and it determines an ordinary change function for any set of such possible worlds.[2] Thus such a world selection function has the right formal properties to be a projection of a change function onto the world.

The abstract theory that I will defend takes such a selection function as given and provides truth conditions for conditionals in terms of it. According to this theory,[3] a conditional, *if A then B*, is true in a possible world i if and only if B is true in possible world $f_i(A)$. The abstract analysis says little about the basis for selection—without imposing some structure onto the possible worlds there is little it could say—but it does place three conditions on the function: for all propositions A and B, and possible worlds i,

(1) A is true in $f_i(A)$.

(2)   If A is true in i, then $f_i(A) = i$.

(3)   If B is true in $f_i(A)$ and A is true in $f_i(B)$, then $f_i(A) = f_i(B)$.

Condition (1) says that only possible situations in which the antecedent is true are eligible to be selected. To suppose that A is to consider a possibility in which A is true. This condition is uncontroversial, but it does raise a small problem: what do we do if the antecedent is impossible, in which case no possible world at all is eligible to be selected? For such antecedents, the selection function is undefined. One might leave conditionals undefined as well in this case, but our analysis stipulates that conditionals are vacuously true when the antecedent is necessarily false. The motivation for this decision is that it conforms to the intuition that when A semantically entails B, the conditional, *if A then B*, is true. The motivation is relatively weak, but so are the consequences of the stipulation. Anyone who prefers to leave conditionals undefined when the antecedent is impossible, or to give truth-conditions in such cases according to some other rule, may do so without affecting the rest of the theory.[4]

Conditions (2) and (3) are both motivated by the general intuitive idea that the selection function selects a possible world that, among the eligible worlds, is minimally different, in some sense, from the actual world. Without some specification of the relevant respects of similarity and difference, this idea will not do very much to constrain the selection, but it does imply these two conditions. To see that (2) is required, note that whatever respects of similarity and difference are relevant, it is clear that any possible world differs less from itself than it does from any other possible world. So if the actual world is eligible, it must be selected. This is what the second condition says. Condition (3) is less obvious intuitively and more controversial. The idea is this: the selection is to be based on two considerations: first, on which possible worlds are eligible to be selected; second, on which, among those that are eligible, is minimally different from the actual world. The only role of the antecedent of a conditional is to determine the class of eligible worlds. The relevant respects of difference between possible worlds can be assessed (it is assumed) independently of which worlds are eligible. This implies that if one possible world is preferred by the selection function to another, relative to one antecedent, it must be preferred to it relative to any antecedent for which both are eligible. This is what condition (3) says.[5]

As a response to the philosophical problem of counterfactuals, this semantic analysis and others like it contrasts sharply with the traditional approach to the problem exemplified in the classic papers of Nelson Goodman and Roderick Chisholm.[6] That approach began with a distinction between problematic and unproblematic concepts; the project was to give a reductive definition of the problematic counterfactual conditional construction using only unproblematic resources. From the point of view of this approach, formal semantic analyses look circular and question-begging. Rather than analyzing away a problematic notion, they cavalierly postulate primitive constructs such as possible worlds and selection functions which are at least as mysterious as what was supposed to be explained. A proponent of the traditional approach might complain that such an analysis does not solve the problem, but only packages and relabels it.

There would be merit in this complaint if the abstract analysis of conditionals were presented as a finished solution to the philosophical problem posed by Goodman and Chisholm, but a formal semantic analysis, by itself, is intended as neither a solution to nor a dismissal of the problem of counterfactual conditionals. What such an analysis purports to do is to clarify the abstract structure of a problematic concept in order to help separate formal problems about its logic from substantive problems. And it is intended to provide a framework for the formulation of the substantive problems, and for precise statements of alternative solutions to them. If formal semantic analyses seem to beg the interesting questions, this is, I think, only because such analyses seek to change the order in which questions are asked and to formulate them in new ways.

I hope to illustrate these points by examining some of the consequences of the semantic analysis and comparing it with some alternative analyses. I will do this by discussing three specific questions about the adequacy of the analysis. First, I will look at two classic inference patterns (the hypothetical syllogism and contraposition), long considered characteristic of conditionals, but judged invalid by the semantic analysis we are considering. I will compare the analysis with a more traditional one that judges them both to be valid. Second, I will look at the idea that some kind of comparative similarity or minimal difference is the basis for selection of the possible world relative to which truth-conditions for conditional propositions are given. I will consider some counterexamples to this assumption, and examine the criticism that the assumption, properly understood, is vague or vacuous. Third, I will look at the assumption that the selection function should select a single possible world. I will compare the semantic analysis with similar analyses, defended by David Lewis, John Pollock and others, which reject this assumption.

Throughout these discussions, we will find a recurring theme: conditional propositions are highly context-dependent, and they are often vague or semantically indeterminate. An adequate defense of any semantic theory will need an account of the way in which context interacts with content, and an account of semantic indeterminacy. So the comparison of alternative semantic analyses of conditionals will lead to some more general questions about the relation between semantics and pragmatics, about vagueness and indeterminacy, and ultimately, about realism.

Two familiar forms of argument—hypothetical syllogism and contraposition—are not valid according to the conditional semantics sketched above, or according to any of the standard variations on this semantics. This was a somewhat surprising result since these argument forms, valid for both the material conditional and the strict conditional, had previously been supposed to be paradigm cases of valid inferences involving conditionals. There are two ways to argue that these results fit the facts, despite the initial appearance. First, there are intuitive counterexamples: examples of sequences of conditionals fitting the argument form, but with premises that seem true and a conclusion that seems false. Second, there are some general arguments that the argument forms cannot be valid for any account of conditionals meeting certain very plausible conditions.

Consider the following argument:

If the Democrats has lost control of the House, the Republicans would be in control;

if the Socialist Labor Party had gained a majority in the House, the Democrats would have lost control;

therefore, if the Socialist Labor Party had gained a majority in the House, the Republicans would be in control.

This argument is obviously invalid. The sinister suggestion contained in the conclusion is nowhere implicit in the premises. Yet the argument has the form of the hypothetical syllogism: *if A then B; if B then C; therefore, if A then C*.

There is another argument form, closely related to the hypothetical syllogism and implied by it, which is more obviously invalid. This is the inference of strengthening the antecedent: *if A then B; therefore, if A&C then B*. If the hypothetical syllogism is valid, this argument form must be as well, since any proposition of the form *if A&C then A* will be a logical truth on any plausible theory of conditionals. But it is easy to construct counterexamples to strengthening the antecedent. A familiar example: if the match were struck, it would light; therefore, if the match were soaked in water overnight and then struck, it would light.

If such examples are not compelling enough, one can give a general argument that any theory of conditionals that makes two very weak assumptions must invalidate the hypothetical syllogism. The first assumption is that some conditionals are contingent: sometimes a conditional is true even though the antecedent does not entail the consequent. Any theory that purports to account for counterfactual conditionals must accept this assumption, since all of the interesting cases of counterfactuals are conditional statements that seem to make contingent claims. The second assumption is that any conditional whose antecedent is possibly true and whose consequent is logically incompatible with the antecedent is false. On any plausible account of conditionals, if one supposes something that might be true, one cannot legitimately draw a conclusion which would have to be false if the supposition were true. Any theory that makes these two rather cautious assumptions about conditionals must reject the validity of the hypothetical syllogism. For suppose *if A then B* is a contingently true conditional—one whose antecedent does not entail its consequent. Then the conjunction of the antecedent with the denial of the consequent (*A&not-B*) is possibly true, and so by the second assumption, *if A&not-B then B* is false. So the inference of strengthening the antecedent must be invalid, and as we have seen, this means that the hypothetical syllogism is invalid as well.

The following story is the background for a counterexample to the argument form of contraposition or transposition (*if A then B*; therefore *if not-B then not-A*.): My dog is a mutt. His paternity is in some doubt, but even if his father were a purebred dog, my dog would still be a mutt since his mother was one. Now consider the contrapositive of the conditional claim made in this remark: if my dog were a purebred, his father would be a mutt. (I assume that *mutt* and *purebred* are contradictory properties, as applied to dogs.) This conditional is not only false, but impossible, and so cannot be a consequence of the true conditional claim made in the story.

One might reject the counterexample on the grounds that the conditional contraposed is an "even if" conditional—a semifactual which should receive an analysis different from the one given to ordinary counterfactual conditionals. But it seems reasonable to assume, at least to begin with, that "even if" conditionals should be explained in terms of the interaction of "even" with the ordinary "if." If we look to nonconditional uses of "even" it seems plausible to conclude that this word has a purely pragmatic function. It does not change the semantic content—the truth-conditions of what is asserted—but serves only to indicate something about the speaker's presuppositions.[7] "Even Abe Lincoln lied to the American people" seems to assert exactly what is asserted by "Abe Lincoln lied to the American people." It is true if he lied to them and false if he did not. If this is right, then one may take "even if" conditional propositions to be ordinary conditional propositions, even if the contexts in which "even if" conditional sentences are appropriately used are different from those in which the corresponding conditional sentences without the "even" are used.

In any case, it is not as if the failure of contraposition is an unexpected anomaly. Our semantic theory predicts it, and besides, we have another general argument that the result must hold in any theory which meets one further condition: that the inference of weakening the consequent (if B entails C, then *if A then B* entails *if A then C*) is valid. This inference seems hard to deny. Suppose B would be true if A were. Then surely whatever B entails would be true as well. It would make no sense to say that B would be true but without its logical consequences.

Now suppose that contraposition is valid. Then we can argue validly from *if A then B* to *if not-B then not-A*. Then, using weakening the consequent, we can conclude *if not-B then not(A&C)*. Contraposing again, we get *if A&C then B*. So strengthening the antecedent is valid if contraposition is, but we have seen that this inference cannot be valid on any plausible theory of conditionals.

The upshot of this argument is that the two inferences we have been discussing are interconnected. One must choose between a theory in which both are invalid and one in which both are valid. Any theory that validates both, and also meets other minimal constraints on a theory of conditionals, will have the structure of a strict conditional, and so will be reducible to some kind of necessity operator. In a possible worlds semantics for such a conditional, the conditional will be true only if the consequent is true in *all* possible worlds (or all in some fixed set) in which the antecedent is true.

One can defend a strict conditional account of conditionals against the counterexamples and arguments we have given by emphasizing the context-dependence of conditionals. One may argue that the conditional is *semantically* a fixed strict conditional but that the domain of possible worlds relative to which it is defined varies with context. Apparent failures of hypothetical syllogism and contraposition are to be explained as fallacies of equivocation caused by shifts in context. For example, one may say of a counterexample to hypothetical syllogism that the first premise seems true because it suggests one context, while the second seems true because it suggests a different context. Perhaps no single plausible context will be one relative to which both premises are true. Therefore, it is argued, the counterexamples do not defeat the claim that the inference is, within any single context, valid.[8]

How would one who took this line respond to our general argument against the validity of the hypothetical syllogism? This argument too, it might be argued, depends on an equivocation—a shift in the notions of contingency and possibility. The first assumption of the argument— that some conditionals are contingently true—will be true according to a broad notion of contingency, but false relative to the context-dependent notion of contingency relative to which conditionals are defined. On the other hand, the second assumption—that conditionals with possibly true antecedents, and consequents incompatible with their antecedents, are false—will be true only for the context-dependent sense of possibility. This line of argument must accept the rather unpalatable conclusion that relative to the context used to interpret "if the match had been struck it would have lit," the conditional "if the match had been struck but hadn't lit, it would have lit" will be true (the antecedent being impossible, relative to that context). But it could explain why this last conditional seems false by saying that we never interpret such conditionals relative to such contexts. This last claim might be supported by invoking a pragmatic constraint requiring that conditionals be interpreted, whenever possible, relative to a set of possible worlds which includes some worlds in which the antecedent is true.

A suitable elaboration of this reply would build into the *pragmatics* of conditionals an apparatus similar to what is built into the *semantics* in the kind of theory I am defending. In our theory, context determines a semantic determinant which is itself a function taking the antecedent as argument. In the strict conditional theory, the antecedent is a part of the context which contributes to the determination of a semantic determinant which, once determined, does its work independently of the antecedent. Despite the differences in logic, the difference between a strict conditional theory and a theory of the general kind I am defending might be more superficial than it seems. The principal difference might be in where the line between semantics and pragmatics is drawn, which will determine at what level of abstraction one's notion of validity is defined. But this question is not arbitrary. If one draws the line in the wrong place, one may not only give a less efficient and perspicuous description of the phenomena, one may miss some significant generalizations. In general, if contexts shift too easily and often, then semantic validity will have little to do with the persuasiveness of arguments. Generalizations about the structure of arguments may be missed. On the other hand, if a simple semantics for a specific kind of construction, combined with general pragmatic principles governing the structure of discourse, can account for the complexities of the context shifts, one may have a better overall theory even if a purely semantic concept of validity loses its close connection with the phenomena of argument.

The second issue I will discuss concerns the role of a notion of similarity or minimal difference in determining the selection. Is it appropriate to think of the possible world selected by the selection function as the possible world that is, in some sense, the nearest or most similar one in which the antecedent is true? Can we make sense of this intuitive constraint? Is it doing any work in the analysis?

There are two kinds of criticisms that have been made of analyses which use a comparative similarity relation to explain the truth-conditions of counterfactual conditionals.[9] First, the notion of comparative similarity is too vague and empty to determine truth-conditions for conditionals. Second, there are counterexamples to the hypothesis that a counterfactual is true if and only if its consequent is true in the most similar world in which the antecedent is true.

To the first kind of criticism, David Lewis has replied by granting that comparative similarity is vague and highly context-dependent; but, he argued, this is a strength rather than a weakness of the analysis, since counterfactuals too are vague and context-dependent. He argued further that while the notion of overall comparative similarity is vague, it is not empty. We can make sense of comparative similarity judgments about large and complex entities (such as cities; Lewis's example was "Seattle is more like San Francisco than it is like Los Angeles") even without specifying explicitly the respects of similarity.

The second kind of criticism confirmed Lewis's point that the notion of comparative overall similarity does have some intuitive content. Various commentators on Lewis's book offered counterexamples of the following kind: counterfactuals which seem, intuitively, to be obviously true even though the consequent was false in all the possible worlds that seemed, intuitively, to be overall the most similar worlds in which the antecedent was true. Consider this example given by Kit Fine: "If Nixon had pushed the button, there would have been a nuclear war."[10] This seems true, given the right context, even though some possible worlds in which Nixon pushes the button and there is no war seem much more similar to the actual world. Consider a world in which after Nixon pushes the button something intervenes—perhaps in this world a switch is defective and the message fails to get through, and then Nixon changes his mind and things go on pretty much as they actually did. It does not seem that the fact that such a world is more similar to the actual world, overall, than one in which there is a nuclear war is a good reason for saying that these things would have, or even might have, happened.

The example, and others like it, do show decisively that the intuitive notion of overall similarity between possible worlds does have some content and that this notion is not the one that is relevant to the interpretation of counterfactual conditionals. But the abstract analysis is not committed to this intuitive explanation of the basis for selection. One can reply that selection is based on *some* notion of similarity, closeness, or minimal difference, leaving open the question of what the right respects of similarity are and how they are weighted.

The following example, offered by Pavel Tichy,[11] suggests that it may be wrong to say that the selection is based on any kind of similarity at all: suppose there is a man who always wears his hat when it rains, but when it does not rain, it is a matter of chance whether he wears his hat or not. Today, it rained and he wore his hat. What, in this situation, should we say about the counterfactual "if it hadn't rained, the man would have worn his hat"? According to the similarity analysis, Tichy argued, no matter how the different respects of similarity are weighted, the counterfactual will come out true. In choosing between possible worlds in which it rains and by chance the man wears his hat and possible worlds in which it rains and by chance the man does not, there is no question of trade-offs between different respects of similarity. One can choose a world in which the man wears his hat, as he does in the actual world, without giving up any respects of similarity at all.[12] But this is obviously the wrong result, intuitively. If it is really a matter of chance whether the man wears his hat when it doesn't rain, then we just cannot say whether he would have or not this time if it hadn't rained.

This kind of counterexample does cast further doubt on the intuitive role of the concept of similarity or difference in explaining the basis for selection, but it still does not threaten the abstract analysis. As Goodman has taught us, the *abstract* concept of similarity is too empty for its application to be refuted by counterexample. An account of the respects of similarity that are relevant to selection might say that some respects of similarity count for nothing at all, and so should be ignored even when there are no countervailing relevant respects of similarity.

If the counterexamples we have been discussing do not refute the abstract analyses which make use of the notion of comparative similarity, they do bring out how little work is being done by that notion in fixing truth-conditions for counterfactuals. Is the notion of similarity putting any constraint at all on selection? Perhaps the abstract analysis should just say that a conditional is true if the consequent is true in the selected world, leaving completely open what the basis for selection is. I will respond to this suggestion by making some remarks, first about the motivation for the thesis that selection is based on some kind of similarity or minimal difference, and second about the consequences of the thesis for the abstract semantic theory.

The principal motivation for the doctrine that the selected world is one that is, in some sense, minimally different from the actual world is that it seems necessary to explain how evidence about the actual world is relevant in the way that it is to the truth of counterfactual conditionals. For example, why is the fact that Sly Pete had a losing hand in the *actual* world a reason for saying that in a different possible world—the one that would have been actual if he had called—he lost? The answer, obviously, is that we assume that Pete's hand, and the hands of all the other players, are the same in that counterfactual world as they are here. In general, there is a presumption that what is true in the actual world is also true in the selected world. The presumption may be defeated; the substantive problem of counterfactuals can be seen as the problem of saying what (beyond logical incompatibility with the antecedent) defeats it. But the fact that the presumption exists in the first place suggests that the world selected is one that is, in some way, minimally different from the actual world.

The projection strategy suggests that we look to epistemic principles for a rationale for the doctrine that the selected world must be minimally different from the actual world. An epistemic analogue of this doctrine would be a principle of methodological conservatism. When changing beliefs in response to new evidence, you should continue to believe whatever the new evidence does not give you reason to give up. This principle is quite vague, and precise versions of it need to be carefully qualified. An incautious formulation of a principle of methodological conservatism would be subject to problems analogous to the problems raised by Tichy's counterexample. Suppose we came to believe that the man wore his hat today solely because we came to believe that it was raining. Then we learn that it was not raining. The new evidence does not conflict with the belief that the man wore his hat—it is not evidence *against* that belief—and so an incautious principle of methodological conservatism might direct us to continue to believe it. But it would clearly be irrational to do so since the basis of this belief has been undercut. Such examples show that conservative principles must be carefully qualified, but not that the general idea behind the principle—the idea that one should maintain one's beliefs unless one has reason to give them up—is mistaken. Similarly, Tichy's counterexample shows that the relevant conception of minimal difference needs to be spelled out with care, but not that the general idea that selection is based on minimal difference is wrong.

Despite the emptiness of the abstract concept of similarity, the doctrine that the selected world is minimally different does appear to have consequences for the abstract theory. It provides the rationale for two of the three formal constraints on the selection function. The first of these, the requirement that the actual world be selected if it is eligible (if the antecedent is true in it), is uncontroversial.[13] Even if we drop the intuitive similarity condition, we would need to keep this first constraint since without it modus ponens would not be a valid principle for conditionals. But the other formal constraint is more controversial. This is the requirement that if one possible world is selected over another relative to one antecedent, then it must be favored relative to any antecedent for which both are eligible. The assumption behind this condition is that the relevant kind of similarity is independent of the antecedent. Antecedents determine eligibility, but that is their only role in determining selection. The rest of the job is done by some antecedent-independent conception of similarity or minimal difference.

One way to test this assumption is to test the rules of inference that it implies. I will consider two closely related rules both of which are valid in conditional logic if and only if the semantic constraint is imposed. First, from $A > B$, $B > A$, $A > C$, to infer $B > C$. Propositions which are *counterfactually equivalent* in the sense that each would be true if the other were, are equivalent as antecedents. Second, from $A > B$ and $(A\&B) > C$, to infer $A > C$. This rule is an immediate consequence of the first. If $A > B$, then A and $A\&B$ are counterfactually equivalent, and so $(A\&B) > C$ will be equivalent to $A > C$.

The following example, a variation of Gibbard's Sly Pete scenario, provides a prima facie case for the validity of the second pattern of inference. This time there are three gamblers, Mr. Stone, Pete, and Ms. Jones. Stone raised, Pete folded, and Jones called, winning the hand. Jack, noting that Jones had Pete beat, says "Good thing Pete folded— he would have lost if he had called." "Not so," Zack replies. "He would have won, since if Pete had called, Jones would have folded. (She knew she had Stone beat, but she was worried about Pete). And if Pete had called and Jones folded, Pete would have won (since his hand was better than Stone's)." Zack's logic looks impeccable. Jack must either concede the point or challenge one of the premises. This suggests that the principle of inference in question is valid.

Of course examples cannot, by themselves, establish the validity of an inference pattern. But the way of reasoning about counterfactuals illustrated by the story is familiar and pervasive. If we reject the validity of the inference pattern, we need an alternative explanation for the force of the arguments.

On the other hand, if we accept the validity of the rule, there are counterexamples that will have to be explained away. Here is one such example, different from but modeled on one offered by Pavel Tichy.[14] The crown jewels are on an open display platform surrounded by electric eye sensors. A cat is sleeping on the platform, near the jewels but outside the circle of electric eyes. If anyone, human or cat, were to reach into the display area, an alarm would sound. If the alarm were to sound, it would wake up the cat. If the cat were to wake up, he would cross into the display area, setting off the alarm. That is, the following three counterfactuals are all true: if the alarm had sounded, the cat would have woken up; if the cat had woken up, the alarm would have sounded; if the cat had woken up, he would have set off the alarm. According to the first of the two inference patterns described above, it follows from these premises that if the alarm had sounded, it would have been the cat who set it off. But this shouldn't follow. It seems compatible with the story that if the alarm had sounded, it would have been a burglar, rather than the cat, who was responsible.

The right reply to this kind of counterexample, I think, is similar to the reply made by the defender of the strict conditional account to counterexamples to the hypothetical syllogism and contraposition. Given a fixed context, the argument form is valid, but the premises in the example are not all true relative to any one context. This kind of reply did not seem very persuasive when we considered it before; I will try to explain why I find it more plausible in this case.

Call a selection function which is based on some antecedent-independent ordering of possible worlds a *regular* selection function. The counterexamples present a triad of counterfactuals which seem true, given the story, but which cannot all be true relative to any regular selection function. The issue is whether one should describe the situation in terms of a single irregular selection function, or in terms of contextual shifts from one regular selection function to another. The question is one of how we distribute the burden of explanation between pragmatics and semantics. To some extent the issue may be one of simplicity and efficiency of formulation rather than substance, but there are some substantive issues underlying the question.

Suppose a speaker says something of the form *if A then B* and a hearer disagrees. There are two contrasting kinds of explanations for the conflict: (1) it may be that the hearer has misunderstood the speaker—he has not understood what sort of situation the speaker meant the hearer to consider; or (2) it may be that the speaker and hearer disagree about some relevant fact. In the first case, speaker and hearer disagree about what is being said. In the second, they agree about what is being said, but disagree about whether what was said is true. The two kinds of disagreement are possible, according to our semantic theory, because two components go into the determination of the selected possible world. First, there is the speaker's intention. When he says *if A, . . .* he has a certain sort of possible situation in mind. But the speaker's intentions alone cannot determine the selected possible world; the facts about the actual world must do part of the job. Otherwise counterfactual conditionals could not be factual statements—speakers could never be straightforwardly mistaken about them. That is why the theory assumes that what the context determines is not a selected possible world (relative to an antecedent), but instead a function from possible worlds (together with antecedents) to possible worlds. This is necessary so that two people who disagree about the truth of a counterfactual (and so about what possible world is the selected one) need not be disagreeing about the selection function. They may be disagreeing (as they must be if the disagreement is a factual one) about which possible world is actual. A single selection function may take i_1 to j_1 (relative to antecedent A) and i_2 to j_2. Speaker and hearer may disagree about whether the selected world is j_1 or j_2 because they disagree about whether the actual world is i_1 or i_2. The distinction between a factual disagreement and a misunderstanding of what is being said is obviously a significant one, and the way a theory draws the line between semantics and pragmatics will make a difference for how the theory makes this distinction.

In our most recent Sly Pete story, Jack and Zack disagreed about the counterfactual "if Pete had called, he would have lost." The disagreement, clearly, was a factual one, not a misunderstanding of what was intended. But consider the parallel story providing a context for the counterexample about the cat and the crown jewels.

You say, "If the alarm had sounded, it would have woken up the cat." Not so, I reply. "The cat would have been already awake. For if the alarm had sounded, it would have been the cat who set it off (no one else was around to set it off), and if the alarm had sounded because the cat set it off, it wouldn't have been what woke up the cat." My logic here is the same as Zack's, but the appropriate response seems neither a retraction nor a challenge to the premises, but instead an exasperated "That's not what I *meant*; I meant if the alarm had gone off while the cat was still asleep." There is clearly no factual disagreement here, but (as we would expect if the inference was valid) there is still a conflict to be resolved. Although perverse, my reply in the example is not a non sequitur. The conflict is resolved in this case by clarifying the speaker's intentions—by bringing out that the apparent disagreement results from a difference between what the speaker meant and what the hearer perversely took him to mean. This suggests that it is a context shift, a shift not just in the world selected but in the criteria for selection, which explains how the speaker and hearer can both be right. The same shift explains how the three counterfactuals in the counterexample can all seem true while a consequence of those premises seems false. The premises are true relative to different contexts, and so in no single context does the conclusion follow.

The third issue I will discuss concerns the assumption that the truth-value of a conditional depends on the truth value of the consequent in a single selected possible world. Some analyses of conditionals which are similar in spirit to the one I am defending have rejected this assumption, giving truth conditions in terms of a function that selects a *set* of possible worlds relative to the antecedent, or which gives truth-conditions directly in terms of a comparative similarity relation which allows that many possible worlds may be equally similar to the actual world. In discussing this issue, I will focus on the contrast between our semantic analysis and one defended by David Lewis in his book *Counterfactuals*. Lewis's theory states truth conditions for conditionals in terms of a three-place comparative similarity relation instead of a selection function. Let $C_i(j,k)$ mean that j is more similar to i than k is to i. For any fixed i, the relation is assumed to be transitive and connected, and so to determine a weak total ordering of all possible worlds with respect to each possible world. A counterfactual, *if A then B*, is then said by Lewis's theory to be true in i if and only if either there are no A-worlds, or there is an A-world j such that B is true in it and in all A-worlds which are at least as similar to i as j.[15]

These truth-conditions look quite different from the ones I have been defending, but part of the difference is superficial. Our world selection function is motivated by an idea of comparative similarity, and it is interdefinable with a comparative similarity relation meeting Lewis's conditions. But the theories are not equivalent since the defined comparative similarity relation has properties beyond those imposed by Lewis's theory; specifically, the comparative similarity relation defined in terms of a world selection function determines not just a weak ordering, but a well ordering of all possible worlds with respect to each possible world. So my theory, formulated in terms of a comparative similarity relation, is a special case of Lewis's.

Lewis identifies two assumptions about the comparative similarity relation which my theory makes and his does not: he calls them the *limit assumption* and the *uniqueness assumption*. The first is the assumption that for every possible world i and nonempty proposition A, there is *at least* one A-world minimally different from i. The second is the assumption that for every world i and proposition A there is *at most* one A-world minimally different from i. Lewis's theory, with the addition of these two assumptions, is essentially equivalent to mine.

Each of the two assumptions about the comparative similarity relation corresponds to an entailment principle in the semantics for conditionals. To accept the limit assumption is to accept the following consequence condition for conditionals: for any set of propositions Γ and propositions A and C, if Γ semantically entails C, then $\{A > B: B \in \Gamma\}$ semantically entails $A > C$.[16] To accept in addition the uniqueness assumption is to accept the validity of the principle of conditional excluded middle: $(A > C) \lor (A > \sim C)$.

Lewis argues that it is not reasonable to make the two assumptions which distinguish his theory from mine. I will argue that one of the assumptions is reasonable to make and that the other need not be made in application. I will also discuss a number of examples which I think tend to show that the analysis I have proposed gives a better account of the phenomena.

Let me look first at the uniqueness assumption. This is the assumption which rules out ties in similarity. It says that no distinct possible worlds are ever equally similar to any given possible world. This is, without a doubt, a grossly implausible assumption to make about the kind of similarity relation we use to interpret conditionals, and it is an assumption which the abstract semantic theory that I want to defend does make. But like many idealizing assumptions made in abstract semantic theories, it may be relaxed in the application of the theory. In general, to apply a semantic theory to the interpretation of language as it is used, one need not assume that every semantic determinant is completely and precisely defined. In application, domains of individuals relative to which quantifiers are interpreted, sets of possible worlds relative to which modal auxiliaries are interpreted, and propositional functions used to interpret predicates, all may admit borderline cases even though the abstract semantic theory assumes well-defined sets with sharp boundaries. To reconcile the determinacy of abstract semantic theory with the indeterminacy of realistic application, we need a general theory of vagueness. But given such a theory, we can reconcile the uniqueness assumption, as an assumption of the abstract semantics for conditionals, with the fact that it is unrealistic to assume that our conceptual resources are capable of well ordering the possible worlds.

The theory of vagueness that I will recommend is the theory of supervaluations first developed by Bas van Fraassen.[17] The main idea of the theory is this: any partially defined semantic interpretation will correspond to a set of completely defined interpretations—the set of all ways of arbitrarily completing it. For example, a partial ordering will correspond to a set of total orderings and a domain with fuzzy boundaries will correspond to a set of domains with sharp boundaries. The theory of supervaluations defines the truth-values assigned by a partial interpretation in terms of the corresponding set of complete, two-valued *classical valuations*. In this way, it explains the values under partial interpretations in terms of the kind of valuation assumed by idealized abstract semantic theories. A sentence is *true* in a supervaluation if and only if it is true on *all* corresponding classical valuations, *false* if and only if it is false on *all* corresponding classical valuations, and neither true nor false if it is true on some of the classical valuations and false on others.

Using the method of supervaluations, we may acknowledge, without modifying the abstract semantics for conditionals, that the selection functions that are actually used in making and interpreting counterfactuals correspond to orderings of possible worlds that admit ties and incomparabilities. In doing this, we are not resorting to an *ad hoc* device to save a theory since the method of supervaluations, or some account of semantic indeterminacy, is necessary anyway to account for pervasive semantic underdetermination in natural language. Whatever theory of conditionals one favors, one must admit that vagueness is particularly prevalent in the use of conditional sentences.[18]

What effect does the introduction of supervaluations have on the *logic* of conditionals? Very little: it is one of the virtues of this method of treating semantic indeterminacy that it leaves classical two-valued logic virtually untouched.[19] Classical logical truths are true in *all* classical valuations, and so will be true in all classical valuations determined by any partial interpretation. Therefore, they will be true in all supervaluations. Also, since classical valuations are themselves special cases of supervaluations, any sentence true in all supervaluations will be true on all classical valuations. So, whatever the details of the particular classical semantic theory, the concept of logical truth defined by it will not be changed by the introduction of this account of indeterminacy. For example, the principle of conditional excluded middle, $(A > C) \lor (A > \frown C)$, remains valid when truth and validity are defined in terms of supervaluations even though there may be cases where neither $(A > C)$ nor $(A > \frown C)$ is true. It may be that neither disjunct is made true by every arbitrary extension of a given partial interpretation, but it will always be true that each arbitrary extension makes true one disjunct or the other.[20]

What I have argued so far is just that one can neutralize one important objection to our semantic analysis—that it makes an implausible assumption about our conceptual resources: the assumption that we need a well ordering of all possible worlds with respect to each possible world in order to interpret conditional statements. I have argued that in the context of a general recognition of semantic indeterminacy, the dispute over the uniqueness assumption should be regarded not as a dispute about how much and what kind of structure there is in the actual contextual parameter we use to interpret conditionals, but rather a dispute about what degree and kind of structure that parameter is aiming at: about what would count as a determinate complete interpretation. On the surface, what the issue comes down to is a disagreement about whether certain counterfactuals are false or neither true nor false, and about whether certain inferences involving conditionals are valid.

Before looking at some examples of inferences and judgments which I think support the analysis I have proposed, I should point out, as Lewis does, that the limit assumption cannot be neutralized by the introduction of supervaluations in the same way as the uniqueness assumption. In my defense of the principle of conditional excluded middle, I shall take for granted that the limit assumption is a reasonable assumption to make. Later I will explain and defend this decision.

Let us look at some examples. I will begin with a familiar pair of counterfactual conditionals first discussed in 1950 by W. V. Quine.[21]

> If Bizet and Verdi had been compatriots, Bizet would have been Italian.

> If Bizet and Verdi had been compatriots, Verdi would have been French.

These examples have been taken, in the context of possible worlds analyses of conditionals, to illustrate the possibility of virtual ties in closeness of counterfactual possible worlds to the actual world. Worlds in which Bizet and Verdi are both French or both Italian, it seems plausible to assume, are more like the actual world than worlds in which both are Argentinian or Japanese. But there is no apparent reason to favor a world in which both are French over one in which both are Italian, or vice versa. This seems right. It would be arbitrary to require a choice of one of the above counterfactuals over the other, but as we have seen, this is not at issue. What is at issue is what conclusion about the truth-value of the counterfactuals should be drawn from the fact that such a choice would be arbitrary. On Lewis's and Pollock's analyses, both counterfactuals are false. On the analysis I am defending, both are indeterminate—neither true nor false. It seems to me that the latter conclusion is clearly the more natural one. I think most speakers would be as hesitant to deny as to affirm either of the conditionals, and it seems as clear that one cannot deny them both as it is that one cannot affirm them both. Lewis seems to agree that unreflective linguistic intuition favors this conclusion. He writes:

> Given Conditional Excluded Middle, we cannot truly say such things as this:
> *It is not the case that if Bizet and Verdi were compatriots, Bizet would be Italian; and it is not the case that if Bizet and Verdi were compatriots, Bizet would not be Italian; nevertheless, if Bizet and Verdi were compatriots, Bizet either would or would not be Italian. . . .*
> I want to say this, and think it is probably true; my own theory was designed to make it true. But offhand, I must admit, it does sound like a contradiction. Stalnaker's theory does, and mine does not, respect the opinions of any ordinary language speaker who cares to insist that it is a contradiction.[22]

Lewis goes on to say that the cost of respecting this "offhand opinion" is too great, but as I have argued, the introduction of supervaluations avoids the need to pay the main cost that he has in mind.

Quine originally presented this example, not to defend one analysis of counterfactuals against another but to create doubt about the possibility of any acceptable analysis. "It may be wondered, indeed," he writes, introducing the two Bizet-Verdi counterfactuals, "whether any really coherent theory of the contrafactual conditional of ordinary usage is possible at all, particularly when we imagine trying to adjudicate between such examples as these."[23] There is a problem, Quine suggests, because we are required to *adjudicate* between the two. But why are we required to adjudicate? The argument is implicit, but I suspect that what Quine had in mind might be reconstructed as follows: "It is clear that if Bizet and Verdi had been compatriots, then either Bizet would have been Italian or Verdi French. But then one (and only one) of the two counterfactuals in question must be true. How are we to adjudicate between them?" The crucial inference in this reconstructed argument relies on the distribution principle, $(A > (B \lor C))$, therefore, $(A > B) \lor (A > C)$, a rule of inference that is equivalent, in the context of conditional logic, to the principle of conditional excluded middle. Quine takes for granted, by tacitly using this principle of inference, that a counterfactual antecedent purports to represent a unique, determinate counterfactual situation. It is because counterfactual antecedents *purport* to represent unique possible situations that examples which show that they may fail to do so are a problem. One should respond to the problem, I think, not by revising the truth-conditions for conditionals so that it does not arise, but rather by recognizing what we must recognize anyway: that in application there is great potential for indeterminacy in the truth-conditions for counterfactuals.

The failure of the distribution principle we have been discussing is a symptom of the fact that, on Lewis's analysis, the antecedents of conditionals act like necessity operators on their consequents. To assert *if A then B* is to assert that *B* is true in every one of a set of possible worlds defined relative to *A*. Therefore, if this kind of analysis is correct, we should expect to find, when conditionals are combined with quantifiers, all the same scope distinctions that we find in quantified modal logic. In particular, corresponding to the distinction between $(A > (B \lor C)$ and $((A > B) \lor (A > C))$ is the quantifier scope distinction between $(A > (\exists x)Fx)$ and $(\exists x) (A > Fx)$. On Lewis's account, even when the domain of the quantifier remains fixed across possible worlds, there is a semantically significant difference between these two formulas of conditional logic, and we should expect to find scope ambiguities in English sentences that might be formalized in either way.

Before seeing if such ambiguities are found in conditional statements, let us look at a case where the ambiguity is uncontroversial. The following illustrates a quantifier scope ambiguity in a necessity statement:

> X: President Carter has to appoint a woman to the Supreme Court.
>
> Y: Who do you think he has to appoint?
>
> X: He doesn't have to appoint any particular woman; he just has to appoint some woman or other.

Y, perversely, gives the quantified expression, "a woman," wide scope in interpreting X's statement. X, in his response to Y's question, shows that he meant the quantifier to have narrow scope. The difference is, of course, not a matter of whether the speaker *knows* who the woman is. X might have meant the wide scope reading—the reading Y took it to have—and still not have known who the woman is. In that case, his response to Y's question would have been something like this:

> X: I don't know; I just know it's a woman that he has to appoint.

In this alternative response, the appropriateness of the question is not challenged. X just confesses inability to answer it. This alternative reply is appropriate only if the speaker intended the wide scope reading.

Now compare a parallel dialogue beginning with a statement that is clearly unambiguous:

> X: President Carter will appoint a woman to the Supreme Court.
>
> Y: Who do you think he will appoint?
>
> X: He won't appoint any particular woman; he just will appoint some woman or other.

X's response here is strange.[24] There must be a particular person that he will appoint, although the speaker need not know who it is. If he does not know, the analogue of the alternative response is the one he will give:

> X: I don't know; I just know it's a woman that he will appoint.

Now look at a corresponding example with a counterfactual conditional and consider which of the above examples it most resembles.

> X: President Carter would have appointed a woman to the Supreme Court last year if there had been a vacancy.
>
> Y: Who do you think he would have appointed?
>
> X: He wouldn't have appointed any particular woman; he just would have appointed some woman or other.

Or the alternative response:

> X: I don't know; I just know it's a woman that he would have appointed.

If Lewis's analysis is correct, you should perceive a clear scope ambiguity in X's original statement. Y's question, and X's alternative response, should seem appropriate only when the strong, wide scope reading was the intended one. I do not see an ambiguity; X's first response seems as bad, or almost as bad, as the analogous response in the future tense case. And I do not think there is any interpretation for which Y's question shows a misreading of the statement.

The test, however, is far from conclusive, since if the wording of X's reply is slightly different it sounds much better. Suppose he had said the following:

> X: There isn't any particular woman he would have appointed; he just would have appointed some woman or other.

This seems acceptable; the analogous reply in the future tense example also seems less bad. How is this to be explained? The problem is that while the account I am defending does not admit a quantifier-modal scope ambiguity, it does recognize the possibility of underdetermination. Because of this, X's original statement, in the counterfactual example, might be true even if there is no particular woman of whom it is true to say that she would have been appointed. The situation is analogous to familiar examples of underdetermination in fiction. The question, "Exactly how many sisters and cousins did Sir Joseph Porter have?" may have no correct answer. One might reply to it, "there is no particular number of sisters and cousins that he has; it's just that there are dozens of them." But the person who asked the question in response to the statement that his sisters and cousins numbered in the dozens did not exhibit a misunderstanding of the semantic structure of the statement.[25]

If there is a genuine scope ambiguity, then there ought to be a sense of X's question for which X's alternative reply is clearly inappropriate. If X means "has to" to have wide scope in "Carter has to appoint a woman," then he must reject Y's question and cannot appropriately reply, "I don't know; I just know it's a woman he has to appoint." But in the counterfactual case, I don't think there is any sense of the statement that rules out the alternative answer to the question. Compare this with the fiction case. To the question, "Exactly how many sisters and cousins does Sir Joseph Porter have?" one might reply, "We don't know—the story doesn't say. We just know that there were dozens of them."

It is not surprising, from the point of view of the analysis I am defending, that the possible situations determined by the antecedents of counterfactual conditionals are like the imaginary worlds created by writers of fiction. In both cases, one purports to represent and describe a unique determinate possible world, even though one never really succeeds in doing so.

As we have seen, Lewis agrees that the analysis I am defending respects, as his does not, certain "offhand" opinions of ordinary language speakers. He argues that the cost of respecting these opinions is too high. But Lewis also recognizes—in fact emphasizes—that counterfactual conditionals are frequently vague, and he adopts the same account of vagueness that allows the analysis I am defending to avoid implausible assumptions about our conceptual resources. Why, then, does Lewis still reject this analysis? "Two major problems remain," he writes. "First, the revised version [C2, revised by the introduction of supervaluations] still depends for its success on the Limit Assumption. . . . Second, the revised version still gives us no 'might' counterfactual."[26] I will conclude the defense of my analysis by responding to these two further problems. I will first argue that the limit assumption, unlike the uniqueness assumption, is a plausible assumption to make about the orderings of possible worlds that are determined by our conceptual resources and that the rejection of this assumption has some bizarre consequences. Second, I will say how I think *might* conditional should be understood and argue that Lewis's analysis fails to give a satisfactory account of the relation between *might* and *would* conditionals.

When the uniqueness assumption fails to hold for a comparative similarity relation among possible worlds, then the selection function in terms of which conditionals are interpreted in C2 is left underdetermined by that relation. Many selection functions may be compatible with the comparative similarity relation, and it would be arbitrary to choose one over the others. But if the limit assumption were to fail, there would be too few candidates to be the selection function rather than too many. Any selection function would be forced to choose worlds which were less similar to the actual world than other eligible worlds. This is why the supervaluation method does not provide a way to avoid making the limit assumption.

The limit assumption implies that for any proposition A which is possibly true, there is a nonempty set of *closest* worlds in which A is true. Is this a plausible assumption to make about the orderings of possible worlds which are relevant to the interpretation of conditionals? If one were to begin with a concept of overall similarity among possible worlds that is understood independently of its application to the interpretation of conditionals, this clearly would be an arbitrary and unjustified assumption. Nothing that I can think of in the concept of similarity, or in the respects of similarity that are relevant, would motivate imposing this restrictive formal structure on the ordering determined by a similarity relation. But, on the other hand, if one begins with a selection function and thinks of the similarity orderings as induced by the selection function, the assumption will not be arbitrary or unmotivated: the fact that it holds will be explained by the way in which the orderings are determined. To the extent that an intuitive notion of similarity among possible worlds plays a role, it is a device used for the purpose of selecting possible worlds. Given this rule, it is not unreasonable to require that the way respects of similarity are weighed should be such as to make selection possible.

Even if we take the selection function as the basic primitive semantic determinant in the analysis of conditionals, we still must rely on some more or less independently understood notion of similarity or closeness of worlds to describe the intuitive basis on which the selection is made. The intuitive idea is something like this: the function selects a possible world in which the antecedent is true but which otherwise is as much like the actual world, in relevant respects, as possible. So, one might argue, we still need to give some justification for the limit assumption. How can we be sure that it will be possible to select a world, or a set of worlds, on this basis? Consider one of Lewis's examples: suppose that this line, _____, were more than one inch long. (The line is actually a little less than one inch long.) Every possible world in which the line is more than one inch long is one in which it is longer than it needs to be in order to make the antecedent true. It appears that the intuitive rule to select a world that makes the minimal change in the actual world necessary to make the antecedent true is one that cannot be followed.[27]

The qualification in the intuitive rule that is crucial for answering this objection is the phrase, 'in relevant respects.' The selection function may ignore respects of similarity which are not relevant to the context in which the conditional statement is made. Even if, in terms of some general notion of overall similarity, i is clearly more similar to the actual world than j, if the ways in which it is more similar are irrelevant, then j may be as good a candidate for selection as i.[28] In the example, it may be that what matters is that the line is more than one inch long, and still short enough to fit on the page. In this case, all lengths over one inch, but less than four or five inches, will be equally good.

But what about a context in which every millimeter matters? If relative to the issue under discussion, every difference in length is important, then it is just inappropriate to use the antecedent, *if the line were more than an inch long*. This would, in such context, be like using the definite description, *the shortest line longer than one inch*. The selection function will be undefined for such antecedents in such contexts.

To summarize: from a naive point of view, nothing seems more obvious than that a conditional antecedent asks one to imagine a possible situation in which the antecedent is true. To say *if pigs could fly* is to envision a situation, or a kind of situation, in which pigs can fly. This is the motivation for making a selection function the basic semantic determinant. But it also seems true that the basis for the selection is some notion of similarity or minimal difference between worlds. The situations in which pigs can fly that you are asked to envision are ones which are as much as possible like the actual situation. The problem is that it is theoretically possible for these two intuitions to clash. There could be similarity relations and antecedents relative to which selection would be impossible. Lewis's response to this problem is to generalize the analysis of conditionals so that selection is no longer essential. The alternative response, which seems to me more natural, is to exclude as inappropriate those antecedents and contexts in which the relevant similarity relation fails to make selection possible. Given that the appropriate similarity notion is one that may ignore irrelevant respects of similarity altogether, this exclusion should not be unreasonably restrictive.

I think a closer look at our example will support the conclusion that Lewis's response to the problem is intuitively less satisfactory than the one I am suggesting. On Lewis's analysis, applied to his example of the line, every conditional of the following form is true: *if the line had been more than one inch long, it would not have been x inches long*, where *x* is any real number. This implies (given Lewis's analysis of *might* conditionals) that there is *no* length such that the line might have had that length if it had been more than one inch long. Yet, the line might have been more than an inch long, and if it had been, it would have had some length or other. The point is not just that there is no particular length that the line *would* have had. More than this, there is not even any length that it *might* have had. That conclusion seems, intuitively, to contradict the assumption that the line might have been more than one inch long, yet on Lewis's account, both the conclusion and the assumption may be true.[29]

The second problem that Lewis finds with the analysis I am defending is that it gives us no account of the *might* conditional. Lewis analyzes this kind of conditional in terms of his *would* ·conditional as follows: the *might* conditional, *if A, it might be that B*, is true if and only if the would conditional, *if A, it would be that not-B*, is false. In Lewis's notation, $(A \lozenge\!\!\rightarrow B) =_{df} \frown (A \,\square\!\!\rightarrow\, \frown B)$. Ordinary counterfactuals express a kind of variable necessity on the consequent, according to Lewis. *Might* counterfactuals express the corresponding kind of possibility.

It is clear that this definition conflicts with the analysis of conditionals I am proposing, since the principle of excluded middle, together with

Lewis's definition of *might* conditionals, implies that a *might* conditional is equivalent to the corresponding *would* conditional. This is obviously an unacceptable conclusion, so if Lewis's definition is supported by the facts, this counts against an analysis that validates the principle of conditional excluded middle. But I will argue that Lewis's definition has unacceptable consequences and that a more satisfactory analysis, compatible with the principle of excluded middle, can be given.

Note that Lewis's definition treats the apparently complex construction, *if . . . might*, as an idiom which cannot be explained in terms of the meanings of *if* and *might*. This is not a serious defect, but it would be methodologically preferable—less *ad hoc*—to explain the complex construction in terms of its parts. So I will begin by looking at uses of *might* outside of conditional contexts and then consider what the result would be of combining the account of *might* suggested by those uses with our analysis of *if*.

Might, of course, expresses possibility. *John might come to the party* and *John might have come to the party* each say that it is possible, in some sense, that John come, or have come, to the party. I think the most common kind of possibility which this word is used to express is epistemic possibility. Normally, a speaker using one of the above sentences will be saying that John's coming, or having come, to the party is compatible with the speaker's knowledge. But *might* sometimes expresses some kind of nonepistemic possibility. *John might have come to the party* could be used to say that it was within John's power to come, or that it was not inevitable that he not come. The fact that the sentence *John might come to the party, although he won't* is somewhat strange indicates that the epistemic is the dominant one for this example. There is less strangeness in *John could come to the party, although he won't*. The epistemic interpretation seems less dominant in the past tense example: *John might have come to the party, although he didn't* is not so strange.

What I want to suggest is that *might*, when it occurs in conditional contexts, has the same range of senses as it has outside of conditional contexts. Normally, but not always, it expresses epistemic possibility. The scope of the *might*, when it occurs in conditional contexts, is normally the whole conditional and not just the consequent. This claim may seem *ad hoc*, since the surface form of English sentences such as *if John had been invited, he might have come to the party* certainly suggests that the antecedent is outside the scope of the *might*. But there are parallel constructions where the wide scope analysis is uncontroversial. For example, *if he is a bachelor, he must be unmarried*. Also, the wide scope interpretation is supported by the fact that *might* conditionals can be paraphrased with the *might* preceding the antecedent: *It might be that if John had been invited, he would have come to the party.*

The main evidence that *might* conditionals are epistemic is that it is unacceptable to conjoin a *might* conditional with the denial of the corresponding *would* conditional. This fact is also strong evidence against Lewis's account, according to which such conjunctions should be perfectly normal. On Lewis's account, *might* conditionals stand to *would* conditionals as ordinary *might* stands to *must*. There is no oddity in denying the categorical claim *John must come to the party* while affirming that he might come. But it would sound strange to deny that he would have come if he had been invited, while affirming that he might have come.

Consider a variation on the Supreme Court appointment dialogues discussed above:

> X: Does President Carter have to appoint a woman to the Supreme Court?
>
> Y: No, certainly not, although he might appoint a woman.

This is perfectly okay. Now compare:

> X: Would President Carter have appointed a woman to the Supreme Court last year if a vacancy had occurred?
>
> Y: No, certainly not, although he might have appointed a woman.

On Lewis's analysis, one should expect Y's second response to be as acceptable as his first.

One should not conclude from the conflict between the denial of the *would* conditional and the affirmation of the *might* conditional that these two statements contradict each other. To draw that conclusion would be to confuse pragmatic with semantic anomaly. On the epistemic interpretation, what Y does is to represent himself as knowing something by asserting it, and then to deny that he knows it. The conflict is thus like Moore's paradox, rather than like a contradictory assertion.

My account predicts, while Lewis's does not, that the example given above should seem Moore-paradoxical. I think it is clear that the evidence supports this prediction. Rich Thomason has pointed out that there are also examples of the reverse: cases for which Lewis's account predicts a Moore's paradox, while mine does not. Here too, I think it is clear that the evidence supports my account. Consider any statement of the form *if A, it might be that not-B, although I believe that if A then it would be that B.* Lewis's definition implies that such a statement is equivalent to a statement of the form *not-C, although I believe that C,* and so implies that such a statement should seem Moore-paradoxical.

But there is nothing wrong with saying *John might not have come to the party if he had been invited, but I believe he would have come.* As my account predicts, this statement is as acceptable as the parallel statement with nonconditional *might: John might not come to the party, although I believe that he will.*[30]

Lewis considers and rejects a number of alternatives to his analysis of *might* counterfactuals, including an analysis which treats them as *would* counterfactuals prefixed by an epistemic possibility operator. Here is his counterexample: Suppose there is in fact no penny in my pocket, although I do not know it since I did not look. "Then *'If I had looked, I might have found a penny'* is plainly false." But it is true that it might be, for all I know, that I would have found a penny if I had looked.[31]

I do not think that Lewis's example is *plainly* false since the epistemic reading, according to which it is true, seems to be one perfectly reasonable interpretation of it. I can also see the nonepistemic sense that Lewis had in mind, but I think that this sense can also be captured by treating the *might* as a possibility operator on the conditional. Consider not what is, in fact, compatible with my knowledge, but what would be compatible with it if I knew all the relevant facts. This will yield a kind of quasi-epistemic possibility—possibility relative to an idealized state of knowledge. If there is some indeterminacy in the language, there will still remain some different possibilities, even after all the facts are in, and so this kind of possibility will not collapse into truth. Propositions that are neither true nor false because of the indeterminacy will still be possibly true in this sense. Because *if Bizet and Verdi had been compatriots, Verdi would have been French* is neither true nor false, *if Bizet and Verdi had been compatriots, Verdi might have been French* will be true in this sense of *might.*

Now this interpretation of *might* conditionals is very close to Lewis's. It agrees with Lewis's account that *if A, it might be that B* is true if and only if *if A, it would be that not-B* is not true. But my explanation has the following three advantages over Lewis's. First, it treats the *might* as a kind of possibility operator on the conditional—an operator that can also operate on other kinds of propositions—rather than treating *if ... might* as a semantically unanalyzed unit. With Lewis's analysis of the *would* conditional, this cannot be done. Second, it treats this particular kind of *might* as a special case of a more general analysis—one that includes the ordinary epistemic interpretation as another special case. Third, it explains, as Lewis's analysis cannot, why it is anomalous to deny the *would* conditional while affirming the corresponding *might.*

It may seem strange that I have called the use of *might* that expresses semantic indeterminacy a quasi-epistemic use, but I think that there is a general tendency to use epistemic terminology to describe indeterminacy as a limiting case of ignorance—the ignorance that remains after all the facts are in. On the supervaluation account, indeterminacy is represented in the same way as ignorance—by a plurality of possibilities. Where we draw the line between indeterminacy and ignorance is often an empirical question—a question about the extent to which the world answers to our conception of it. This question concerns realism about counterfactuals, a question I will consider in the next chapter.

Chapter 8

Realism about Counterfactuals

In our discussion of the abstract semantic structure of conditional propositions, we have frequently run up against the fact that counterfactuals are, first, context-dependent and, second, vague. Both of these facts have been taken as reasons to be skeptical about a realistic understanding of counterfactuals—about the thesis that counterfactual conditionals can state genuine facts about the world. In this chapter I want to confront some of the antirealist arguments. I will try to clarify the issue between realism and antirealism and to argue for an interpretation that I think can be correctly described as a realist interpretation of counterfactual and causal dependencies but also recognizes the indeterminacy and irreducible context-sensitivity of sentences expressing propositions about such dependencies.

I will begin with some arguments of John Mackie and Bas van Fraassen concerning conditionals and context-dependence. I will argue that the context-dependence of conditionals does not, by itself, provide a reason to say (as Mackie does) that counterfactuals lack determinate truth-conditions, or (as van Fraassen does) that a correct scientific description of the world would not contain or imply counterfactuals. Second, I will consider whether counterfactuals might be in some sense reducible to, or supervenient on, some less problematic set of facts. In this context I will examine David Lewis's project of trying to specify, in a noncircular way, the respects of similarity relative to which counterfactuals are interpreted. Third, I will consider Michael Dummett's claim that if the realist rejects, as I will, a reductionist account of counterfactuals, then he must be a *naive* realist: he must say that counterfactuals are "barely true"—true, but not in virtue of something else. The notion of bare truth is difficult to pin down, but I will argue that on a plausible construal of that notion there is a middle ground for the realist between reduction and bare truth. Finally, I will look at the relation between realism and the principle of bivalence. I will agree with Michael Dummett that our rejection of bivalence for counterfactuals is a concession to antirealism, but I will argue that this rejection is compatible with the thesis that counterfactuals express irreducible propositions about the world, propositions which sometimes are determinately true. This, I think, is a realist conclusion.

John Mackie, criticizing David Lewis's account of counterfactuals, argues that such possible worlds analyses fail to provide objective truth conditions for counterfactuals because they fail to eliminate vagueness and context-dependence.

> Lewis himself admits that counterfactuals as he interprets them are like such statements as 'Seattle resembles San Francisco more closely than it resembles Los Angeles,' since the truth of a counterfactual depends upon the relative closeness of possible worlds, i.e. their relative similarity to the actual world. . . . As Lewis says, the relative similarity between towns depends on whether we attach more importance to the physical surroundings, or the architecture, and so on. Likewise the relative similarity between these worlds depends on what we attach importance to. But then neither the statement about Seattle nor the counterfactual thus interpreted is capable of being true or false. The claim to have supplied truth conditions fails. What have been supplied are still only acceptability conditions; someone who *regards* the first of the two possible worlds as more like the actual world will *accept* or *use* the counterfactual, someone who *regards* the second as more like the actual world will *reject* it.[1]

There are, I think, two mistakes in Mackie's criticism. First, it is a mistake to interpret Lewis to be attempting to remove the indeterminacy in counterfactuals. Lewis's account is not, as Mackie says, "a proposed linguistic reform . . . which enables them to be determinately true or false."[2] Lewis recognizes, and emphasizes, the pervasive indeterminacy of conditional sentences as they are ordinarily used, and intends his analysis to capture rather than to eliminate it. To the objection that comparative similarity is "hopelessly imprecise," he replies: "Imprecise it may be, but that is all to the good. Counterfactuals are imprecise too. Two imprecise concepts may be rigidly fastened to one another, swaying together rather than separately, and we can hope to be precise about their connection."[3] So while Mackie is right that in Lewis's theory "the indeterminacy is not removed but only relocated,"[4] he is wrong to think that this is incompatible with the success of Lewis's project.

Second, and more importantly, it is a mistake to think that the context-sensitivity and indeterminacy which Lewis and Mackie point to is incompatible with the hypothesis that counterfactuals express propositions which are objectively true or false. The truth of the *sentence* "Seattle resembles San Francisco more closely than it resembles Los Angeles" depends on what respects of similarity are presupposed to be important by the speaker because what is said by the sentence—what proposition is being expressed—depends on those presuppositions. But once the relevant respects of similarity are fixed, once it is determined what is being said, there remains the factual question: which city is Seattle more like, in the relevant respects? The answer to *this* question obviously depends on the properties the three cities have, and this has nothing to do with what any speaker accepts. A speaker can be straightforwardly wrong about such facts, and so the distinction between truth and acceptability remains. The same is true for counterfactuals. As we have seen, criteria for selection alone do not determine selection: they determine a function from a possible world (the putative actual world) to a possible world. A speaker's intentions and presuppositions may be a factor in determining the criteria for selection, but the speaker may still be factually mistaken about the results of applying those criteria since he may be wrong about the possible world to which they are applied.

Mackie concludes his criticism by saying that the possible worlds analysis, with its dependence on the subjective, context-sensitive notion of comparative similarity, is "too shaky a foundation for the truth of counterfactual statements *detached from their users.*"[5] The last phrase, I have been suggesting, contains an ambiguity. Mackie is right that we cannot detach subjunctive conditional *sentences* from their users and then interpret them. But this does not imply that there are not conditional *propositions* expressed, in context, by those sentences, propositions that can be detached from their users and seen to make objective factual claims.

Bas van Fraassen, in arguing for an antirealist philosophy of science which recognizes "no objective modality in nature,"[6] also cites the context-dependence of conditionals as a reason for banishing them from the resources proper for sober description of the way the world is. The truth-conditions of counterfactuals are, he suggests, so context-dependent "that we must conclude that there is nothing in science itself—nothing in the objective description of nature that science purports to give us—that corresponds to these counterfactual conditionals."[7] "The hope that the study of counterfactuals might elucidate science is quite mistaken: scientific propositions are not context-dependent in any essential way, so if counterfactual conditionals are, then science neither contains nor implies counterfactuals." The argument for this bold conclusion is brief and blunt: "The truth-value of a conditional depends in part on the context. Science does not imply that the context is one way or another. Therefore science does not imply the truth of any counterfactual—except in the limiting case of a conditional with the same truth-value in all contexts."[8]

On the face of it, this argument seems to be guilty of the same equivocation that we saw in Mackie's criticism of Lewis. If science says nothing about the way the context is, then it may not say or imply that any context-sensitive *sentence* is true, but it may still imply that the *proposition* expressed by context-sensitive counterfactual utterances are true. The distinction is clearer in simpler cases of context-dependence: despite the context-sensitivity of personal pronouns and referential definite descriptions, Daniels might correctly say to O'Leary, "Medical science has shown that your condition is caused by a dietary deficiency." Still, O'Leary will search in vain if he turns to the medical journals for the statement "your condition is caused by a dietary deficiency."

One might still think that van Fraassen's argument can be used, without equivocation, to show that conditional *sentences*, and concepts and distinctions analyzed in terms of conditionals (perhaps causation and the distinction between lawlike and accidental generalizations), have no place in a sober scientific description of the world. This might be enough to show that "the hope that the study of counterfactuals might elucidate science is quite mistaken." But the claim that scientific statements are never context-dependent seems to me questionable. Van Fraassen's argument employs the premise that "science does not imply that the context is one way or another." If this means that it is not part of the *content* of scientific propositions that any context is one way or another, this may be right, but one need not *say* what the context is in order to use context-dependent sentences in a determinate way. When O'Leary says "I am hungry" he does not say who is speaking or when, but he still succeeds in expressing a proposition which depends on who is speaking and when. For scientific statements to be both determinate and context-dependent, all that is required is that scientific practice provide a context for the interpretation of the language it uses to describe the world.

Does the institution of science provide such a context, and do scientific claims depend on it for their interpretation? It may be that the kind of extreme context-dependence exemplified by personal pronouns, demonstratives and tenses is out of place in scientific description. Physics does not distinguish *now* from other times, and anthropology should not be expected to designate some person as *me*. But there are all degrees of context-dependence. While it may be inappropriate for scientific theory to express propositions in a way that is dependent on parochial perspectives, priorities and presuppositions, it may be that the way science describes the world is dependent on a broad, stable, and widely shared context. This kind of context-dependence seems difficult to avoid. It would seem, for example, that even the more sober descriptive parts of science will include quantified statements, and these depend for their interpretation on a contextually determined domain of discourse. It might be objected that while some quantified statements (for example, "everyone is here so we can start the meeting") are context-dependent, some are interpreted relative to a big, context-independent domain of all the things that there really are, a domain of which all more specific context-dependent domains are restrictions. But the hypothesis that there is such a domain seems to me a metaphysical extravagance. The distinction between obviously context-dependent quantifications such as the statement about the meeting and scientific claims (for example, "there are three colors of quarks") that can be interpreted without knowing the local circumstances in which they were made is, I think, a matter of degree. The same contrast between statements dependent on a more local context and those dependent only on a broad, stable, and perhaps more carefully and precisely fixed context might be illustrated with counterfactuals. The example van Fraassen uses to illustrate the context-dependence of conditionals (Lewis Carroll's barbershop paradox) involves *indicative* conditionals which, as we have seen, are in general very sensitive to the particular epistemic situation of the speaker and his audience. But the existence of such examples should not be taken to show that all conditionals are infected with this dependence on local circumstances.

I have been assuming in this discussion that context-dependence is a matter of the relation between expressions and their content. Van Fraassen, in his discussion of contexts and propositions, seems to make the same assumption.[9] But in his argument about counterfactuals and science, he says that "scientific *propositions* are not context dependent *in any essential way*," while counterfactuals are. The suggestion is that the dependence on speaker interests and attitudes that infects counterfactuals, unlike the more superficial and easily eliminated context-dependence exhibited by tenses, pronouns, and demonstratives, is somehow essential to the thought expressed and not just to the means used to express it. This is why they do not belong in an objective scientific description of the world.

The idea of essential context-dependence is difficult to pin down. One might think that context-dependence is deeper and more essential if it is more difficult to eliminate—that is, if it is more difficult to replace the context-dependent statement with one expressing the same proposition without relying on context. But it is too easy to eliminate context-dependence for this to be right. For any proposition expressed in context *c* by context-sensitive sentence *s*, one may simply stipulate that some other sentence s' shall express, in all contexts, that same proposition. In general, it is a simple matter to shift the job of determining content from pragmatics to semantics by using a particular context to fix the meaning of an expression. (Compare the way that, according to causal theories of reference, one may use demonstratives or indexicals to fix the reference of a proper name or the meaning of certain common nouns.) One might think that the proposition remains, in some deeper sense, essentially context-dependent, since the context was essential to fixing the meaning of the context-independent sentence. But this notion of essential context-dependence remains to be explained. And it seems likely that a plausible explanation of it will show quantified and other purely descriptive constructions, along with counterfactuals, to be essentially context-dependent.

Although the idea of essential context-dependence is elusive, I think there is a notion here that we can get at least an impressionistic grip on. Let me try to say what I have in mind. The interests, projects, presuppositions, culture, and community of a speaker or writer provide resources for the efficient expression of content, but they also provide something more fundamental: they provide resources which contribute to the construction of content itself. Content, I have been suggesting, can be represented as a subset of some set of possible states of the world. Relative to a given set of possibilities, one can contrast sentences that determine such subsets simply in virtue of meaning (context-independent sentences) with those that rely on context as well as meaning (context-dependent sentences). But if the space of possible states of the world itself, the way it is possible to distinguish one possible state from another, is influenced by the situations and activities of the speakers (or more generally, the agents) doing the distinguishing, then we have a kind of context-dependence that infects content itself and not just the means used to express it. It is this deeper dependence on context that I think van Fraassen is pointing to. The whole framework, with its possible worlds and selection functions, which provides the resources necessary to the interpretation of counterfactuals, is not something simply found in nature, but arises from certain human concerns and activities: specifically, the concern to have reliable expectations to guide us in moving about in the world, and the activities which are directed to acquiring these expectations. I think this is right; the projection strategy suggests it. But it is no retreat from a reasonable realism to admit that the way we describe the world—the features and aspects of reality that we choose to focus our attention on—is not entirely dictated by the reality we purport to describe. However we arrive at the concepts we use to describe the world, so long as there is something in the world in virtue of which our descriptions are true or false, the realist will be vindicated.

One might grant that counterfactuals and causal and explanatory statements do make factual claims about the world but argue that the propositions they express are, despite appearances, quite ordinary unproblematic descriptive propositions. Such a thesis might be defended by giving some kind of reduction of counterfactuals to propositions which uncontroversially satisfy some condition which counterfactual propositions appear not to satisfy: for example, propositions that are directly verifiable by sense experience, or propositions which make no claims about connections and dependencies between facts. The reductionist strategy has been applied to many classes of problematic statements: statements about material bodies, about mental phenomena, about unobservable theoretical entities. It is not obvious that such projects are antirealist since they involve a defense of rather than an attack on the legitimacy of the problematic class of statements, but such reductionist projects—phenomenalism, behaviorism, positivist accounts of scientific theory—have something in common with less constructive antirealist theses: they deny a dimension that others purport to find in reality, even if the reductionist softens this conclusion with an argument that the dimensions of reality that remain are richer than has usually been supposed. The reductionist, like the antirealist who argues that the problematic statements in question fail to describe the world at all, requires a clear distinction between the problematic statements to be reduced or rejected, and an unproblematic factual basis. And both require the assumption that the unproblematic factual basis is autonomous—that we can make sense of the world, and of the unproblematic statements describing the world, without relying, explicitly or implicitly, on the propositions whose status is in question. Attacks on reductionist projects of various kinds have often taken the form of attacks on the relevant autonomy assumption. Phenomenalism fails, it has been argued, because we need a conception of an objective material world in order to have the resources to describe our sense experience. Positivist reductions of theoretical entities to observation reports are doomed, according to one familiar argument, because observation reports themselves are theory laden. This kind of attack, if successful, cuts deeper than a refutation by counterexample of a particular reduction, or even than an argument that a reduction is impossible, since it counts against the antirealist part of a reductionist program, and not only against the constructive part. I will raise some questions below about the plausibility of the autonomy assumption that is required for a reductionist account of counterfactuals.

Earlier in the century, reductionist projects were usually formulated as theses about language. Statements involving certain problematic vocabulary were said to be replaceable by semantically equivalent statements not involving that vocabulary. More recently, reductionist theses, or at least theses with a similar motivation, have been formulated as theses about the subject matter of a problematic class of statements rather than about the statements themselves. These more liberal projects require only that propositions in the problematic class be supervenient on the unproblematic propositions. The claim is that possible worlds which are indiscernible with respect to the unproblematic propositions must be indiscernible with respect to the problematic ones as well. No claim is made about the expressive power of a part of the language; the liberal reductionist may grant that the problematic vocabulary makes it possible to say things that couldn't be said without it. And no claim is made about the possibility of matching up particular problematic statements with particular unproblematic ones. The liberal reductionist makes only a holistic claim: if one could describe the world completely in unproblematic terms (in terms, for example, of actual and possible sense experience, of behavior, or of observable properties of observable things), one would leave no room for variation in the correct description of the world in certain other terms (in terms, for example, of material bodies, of mental states, or of theoretical properties of unobservable entities). A liberal reductionist leaves himself more flexibility, but like the traditional reductionist, his thesis depends for its intelligibility on a clear line between the problematic and the unproblematic and for its plausibility on the assumption that the unproblematic propositions form an autonomous class.

The classic statement of the problem of counterfactuals posed it as a demand for a reduction in the narrow sense. Counterfactuals were thought problematic because they seemed to express a mysterious kind of connection between antecedent and consequent—a connection that was neither truth-functional nor logical. They seemed not to be directly verifiable, to be about merely possible situations, to be contingent statements yet not ordinary statements of fact. To clarify such statements, according to the traditional formulation of the problem, one must show that they say something different from what they seem to say: one must reduce the subjunctive to the indicative,[10] the merely possible to the actual,[11] necessary connection to a combination of logical implication and empirical regularity.

I argued in the last chapter that the abstract formal semantic analyses of conditional propositions are not intended as complete solutions to the problem of counterfactuals as defined by Goodman and Chisholm, that they should be seen as attempts to reformulate rather than to solve, dismiss, or avoid the substantive problem. The abstract theory gives truth-conditions for counterfactuals in terms of a semantic determinant—a selection function or relation of comparative similarity—at least as problematic as counterfactuals themselves, and it leaves open the question of how that semantic primitive is to be explained. The abstract theory neither requires nor forecloses a reductionist answer to this question. Whether such an answer would be appropriate depends on the broader philosophical context in which the abstract theory is applied.

I want to suggest that David Lewis's overall theory of counterfactuals and related notions is a reductionist one, in this broad sense.[12] This may appear paradoxical, since Lewis's extreme realism about possible worlds seems to be at the opposite end of a spectrum from Goodman's extreme skepticism about mere possibilities. But I believe that Lewis's project is motivated by the same Humean assumptions that gave rise to Goodman's problem. For Lewis, as for Hume, what is problematic is the idea of necessary connection—connections and dependencies between facts and events. Such connections and dependencies are to be explained away in terms of a less problematic kind of relation, resemblance. The project has a number of different parts. One is a reduction of cause and causal dependence to counterfactuals. Another is the abstract analysis of counterfactuals in terms of a primitive relation of comparative similarity between possible worlds. But the most crucial step for the Humean project is the explanation of the respects of similarity that are relevant, and of the priorities among them. To succeed, the project must give a noncircular account of the way a possible world must resemble the actual world in order for it to be a world that might have been actual if some particular proposition had been true.

Before looking at Lewis's explanation of comparative similarity, I want to consider a general argument, made independently of the details, that any such project is misconceived. Pavel Tichy has argued that projects such as Lewis's must fail since they presuppose, mistakenly, that "the notion of subjunctive—or counterfactual—conditionals is logically prior to that of causation." He points out that, for example, if the striking of the match did not have the causal power to bring about the lighting of the match, then the subjunctive conditional "if the match were struck it would light" would not be true. He concludes from this that "it is causal facts which sustain subjunctive conditionals rather than *vice versa*, and any attempt to explicate the former in terms of the latter is inevitably circular."[13]

I have three comments on this argument. First, I don't think one can show that a reductionist program must fail simply by appealing to intuitions about logical priority. For example, one could not refute phenomenalism simply by pointing to the fact that (in an ordinary perceptual situation) if the physical object were not there, the perceiver would not be having the sense experiences he is having, and then concluding from this that any analysis of the former in terms of the latter is inevitably circular. The phenomenalist agrees that sense experience normally depends on the presence of physical objects; his analysis tries to explain the nature of this dependence. The analysis may be wrong or circular but one must consider the details to show that it is. Second, logical priority is not in any case a transparent notion. There may be different kinds of priority which go in different directions. *A* may be prior to *B* in some intuitive sense, even if *A* is usefully analyzed in terms of *B*. Consider ordinary dispositional properties. If sugar were not soluble in water it wouldn't dissolve. It dissolves only because it is soluble. The state of being soluble sustains the activity of dissolving rather than *vice versa*. But an explanation of solubility as a tendency or disposition to dissolve is not thereby wrong or circular. Third, even if, in the end, one decides that Lewis's Humean project cannot succeed because it is not possible to give a noncircular analysis of comparative similarity, one might still accept that part of the project that analyzes causation in terms of counterfactuals. Such an analysis might be right, and illuminating, even if it does not form a part of a reduction. If the logical status of counterfactuals is clear, then one might use them to help clarify the structure of causal relations even if there is no defensible conceptual hierarchy according to which counterfactuals are more basic than causal relations, dependencies and powers. There might be some sense in which such an analysis is circular, but it need not follow that it is trivial or uninformative.

Now let's take a brief look at Lewis's account of similarity. How does one tell what respects of similarity are relevant to the evaluation of counterfactuals? By looking at what counterfactuals are true. "The thing to do," Lewis writes, "is not to start to deciding, once and for all, what we think about similarity of worlds, so that we can afterwards use these decisions to test [the analysis]. Rather, we must use what we know about the truth and falsity of counterfactuals to see if we can find some sort of similarity relation—not necessarily the first one that springs to mind—that combines with [the analysis] to yield the proper truth conditions."[14] This remark does not imply any circularity in the analysis. The suggestion is not that we should *explain* the relevant respects of similarity in terms of the truth and falsity of counterfactuals. Rather, the suggestion is a methodological one. We should use our knowledge of what counterfactuals are true and false to help find and evaluate specific proposals about the way various respects of similarity should be ordered and weighed for the purpose of evaluating counterfactuals. This procedure is no more objectionable than the procedure of finding and modifying an analysis of "x knows that p" by considering intuitive judgments about what we know.

Following this discovery procedure, Lewis came up with a specific list of priorities among respects of similarity that are relevant to the evaluation of counterfactuals. The list is not, and is not intended to be, a precise decision procedure—there remains a lot of vagueness and room for disagreement over interpretation—but it does respond to the demand for a more substantive explanation of the truth-conditions for counterfactuals. I will describe the general idea of Lewis's notion of similarity and then discuss whether the development of this idea can bear the weight that the Humean project puts on it.

In selecting possible worlds, the most important priority is to avoid massive, widespread deviation from the laws of nature that hold in the actual world.[15] The second priority is that one should try to maximize the spatiotemporal region over which there is an *exact* match of particular fact between the chosen world and the actual world. Approximate match of the course of history counts for very little—perhaps for nothing—but exact agreement over a part of history counts for a lot. Small, isolated deviations from the laws of nature that actually hold are less important than this kind of agreement of particular fact.

This choice of priorities was guided by examples (such as Kit Fine's Nixon example discussed in the last chapter) which showed that Lewis's analysis of conditionals yielded the wrong results when it was interpreted in terms of an impressionistic idea of overall similarity between possible worlds. Whether the analysis, interpreted in terms of this new notion of similarity, yields the right results for these examples and avoids problems with further counterexamples that might be devised is a question I will set aside.[16] My concern about the project is a different one: whether Lewis's explanation of similarity avoids circularity. I will express some skepticism about the possibility of clarifying the respects of similarity he describes without relying on descriptions of the possible worlds which presuppose causal relations, dependencies and powers.

One might worry about circularity because the problematic notion of laws of nature plays a prominent role in Lewis's conception of similarity, but this is not my main concern. Lewis recognizes that his project requires a Humean account of laws of nature in terms of regularities of particular fact, and he has made some suggestions about how such an account might go.[17] My worry is about the notion of particular fact itself. The reductionist program presupposes that the causal dependencies between events and the causal powers of things in a possible world derive from *relational* properties of the possible world, properties defined in terms of the way the possible world resembles other possible worlds. The notion of resemblance relative to which the relational properties are defined obviously cannot, without circularity, involve resemblance with respect to the relational properties themselves. To avoid circularity, the project requires the isolation of a level of pure categorical particular fact relative to which possible worlds are compared—the same kind of level of particular fact that is required by more traditional Humean reductionist projects.

Of course the relational properties of a possible world as a whole, the properties in terms of which causal powers and connections are defined, will be supervenient on the *intrinsic* properties of that world—on the level of particular fact. It is not, according to either Hume's or Lewis's program, that we are looking for a level of fact that is *causally neutral*, since the reductionist claims that the particular facts determine the causal facts. But for both Hume and Lewis, the determination of causal and explanatory facts by particular facts is *global*. Event *c* causes event *e*, not in virtue of facts about *c* and *e*, but in virtue of the overall pattern of events in the possible worlds in which *c* and *e* occur. Even though the particular facts about the world as a whole cannot be causally neutral, the particular facts about individual events will be.[18]

A. J. Ayer, in his discussion of the problem of conditionals, gives an admirably clear account of the Humean picture of this level of particular fact. Ayer is not himself defending a reductionist account of counterfactuals—his thesis seems to be more uncompromisingly antirealist[19]—but as I have argued, the antirealist and the reductionist both require the same kind of autonomy assumption, and Ayer makes this assumption quite explicit. He writes:

> I propose, then, to look upon the world as constituting a bedrock of fact, and the only statements which I shall regard as being strictly factual will be those that are limited in their content to supplying true or false descriptions of the world, together with such statements as are obtainable from them by quantification or by the use of extensional operators. All other empirical statements, or at least all those that function at a higher level, will be construed as relating to the arrangement, or the explanation, of what are taken to be the primary facts.[20]

Ayer recognizes, in fact emphasizes, that the commonsense notion of particular fact is not sufficiently pure to provide the unproblematic bedrock of fact that he needs. Ordinary factual descriptions are, he points out, "overcharged with references to causal properties." They do have some factual content, but "they overflow into a secondary system, which is concerned with the arrangements of facts or what are taken to be so." The distinction that Ayer and, I think, Lewis need is one that "ordinary language blurs." To get to the pure factual level, we need to subtract out from our descriptions of things "any logical implications about their powers." While the factual world contains ordinary physical objects, they "are meant to be identified only by their phenomenal properties."[21]

But Ayer does not explain how the factoring of ordinary descriptive concepts into factual and causal components is to be accomplished, and it is not obvious that it can be done. There is a unique way to *add* a component to a concept—by conjunction—and at one point Ayer suggests that this procedure can easily be put in reverse: "If a property f has been included in the connotation of an expression E which applies to the members of a class K, all we have to do is invent an expression E' which applies to just those things that have the defining properties of K other than f."[22] But this procedure works only if the connotation of the expression E comes already analyzed into components. If we know only that satisfying predicate E entails having property f, then there is no unique way to define the concept expressed by that part of E which does not entail f.[23] In special cases, it may be intuitively natural to think of the property expressed by E as having independent components, one of which is the property f. But even then, the other components may be highly theoretical.

The problem is bad enough when there is some specific consequence of a concept that one wants to bracket or subtract out. But it is even less clear that one can make sense of the idea of subtracting out from a property all "logical consequences about their powers." Consider any ordinary property such as the property of being blue, or having a mass of 73 grams. Now try subtracting out of it, not just a particular causal power associated with the property (the power to reflect and absorb light of certain frequencies, the power to be accelerated at a certain rate by a certain force), but *all* causal powers. I think that such thought experiments about examples suggest what is persuasively argued on more general grounds, that "what makes a property the property it is, what determines its identity, is its potential for contributing to the causal powers of the things that have it."[24] On this conception of properties, if we abstract away from the causal consequences of a property, there will be nothing left. The levels at which we describe the world are causal all the way down.

I should emphasize that I am not arguing in general against all reductionist projects, but only against one kind of reduction—one that purports to reduce causal and explanatory properties and relations to a level of particular fact. My argument is not directed, for example, at a physicalist program which argues that all facts about the world are supervenient on microphysical facts about the distribution of elementary particles in some abstract property space. But this kind of reduction could serve Lewis's purposes only if it were plausible to identify statements of particular fact with the ascription of such properties as mass and charge to elementary particles, and this is plausible only if those properties can be separated, conceptually, from the laws in which they occur and from the causal powers which they confer on the objects that instantiate them. Such a level of description may be primary in some sense and complete. But I don't think it could be plausibly argued that it is a level of particular fact suitable for the Humean project.

"It is only at some level of theory," Ayer writes, "that we can form any picture of an objective world." But he argues that there is a lower level of theory—his primary system of fact—more theoretical than the phenomenal world but less theoretical than the world of common sense that "overflows into a secondary system."[25] I am suggesting that the hypothesis that there is such a level of fact—itself a rather high-level theoretical hypothesis—is a dubious one. In fact, the whole hierarchical picture, which is essential to this reductionist project, seems to me questionable. There may be different ways to rank levels of description and explanation, and there may be conceptual dependencies between them that go in both directions. Such mutual dependencies will be fatal to a project of reduction—even a liberal reductionist project such as Lewis's—but not to a more modest project of charting the relation between the members of the cluster of concepts that Humeans find problematic.

If we give up the reductionist program, what alternatives for the explanation of counterfactual conditionals are we left with? Michael Dummett has argued that there is no plausible alternative other than antirealism. For if we reject the reductionist thesis, he argues, we must either reject realism or else say that counterfactuals are *barely* or *simply* true. But Dummett takes it to be obvious that "a counterfactual conditional could not be simply true: if it is true, it must be true in virtue of the truth of some categorical statement."[26] I will argue that Dummett has posed a false dilemma for the realist, a dilemma with presuppositions which should be rejected along with the reductionist project.

The dilemma that Dummett presents the realist is a general one. A realist about any class of statements must choose, he argues, between naive realism—the view that statements in the class are barely or simply true—and reductionist realism—an explanation of the truth of the statement in terms of statements in some more basic class. The idea is that if the members of any class of statements are to be true or false, there must be something in the world in virtue of which they are true or false, something that renders them true when they are true and false when they are false. Sometimes it suffices to use the statement itself, or some trivial paraphrase of it, to state the fact that would render the statement true. One might, for example, when asked to say what facts render true statements about the past, say simply that there are facts about the past and leave it at that. It is true that Queen Victoria was born in 1837 in virtue of the fact that she was born then. Such statements, one might plausibly say, are barely true. But in other cases we require a more revealing answer. Dummett suggests, for example, that it would be excessively naive to be a naive realist about ascriptions of character. If it is true that some person is brave or vain or complacent, it must be true in virtue of something more basic: either facts about the behavior of the person or perhaps facts about the state of the person's brain. If we are to be realists about ascriptions of character, we must reduce such statements to statements of the more basic kind. If the reduction fails, then we must conclude that such statements do not make determinately true or false factual claims at all.

The problem with Dummett's argument, I think, is that the notion of bare truth is characterized in several different ways, all vague and subject to different interpretations, and not obviously equivalent to each other. At one point, bare truth is defined in terms of reducibility. "A statement is barely true if it is true, but there is no class of statements not containing it or a trivial variant of it to which any class containing it can be reduced."[27] But then it is said that "this amounts to holding that we cannot expect a non-trivial answer to the question 'In virtue of what is a statement . . . true when it is true?' "[28] These characterizations do not seem to me equivalent and I think Dummett's argument requires an equivocation between them. If one defines bare truth strictly as irreducibility, then it is obviously right to argue that every truth must be either reducible or barely true. And if one defines it more loosely in terms of the kinds of facts that render the statement true, then it may be obvious that counterfactuals are never barely true. But I doubt that there is a single interpretation of this notion which would support both premises of Dummett's argument.

Let me use two familiar examples, neither of which directly concerns the problem of counterfactuals, to bring out some of the differences between different ways of understanding bare truth and reducibility. Consider the statement that England declared war on Germany in 1939. It seems clear, using a loose intuitive notion of bare truth, that this statement cannot be barely true. The statement is true in virtue of certain facts which are, in some sense, more basic: facts about individuals saying things, casting votes, signing documents, in a certain setting. The more basic facts about individual actions *render true* the statement that England declared war on Germany in 1939. But is the statement reducible to statements about individual actions? It would obviously be unreasonable to expect a reduction of the traditional sort: a procedure for replacing the statement with a semantically equivalent one from a more basic class of statements. First, there may be no finite specification, in terms of more basic statements, of all the possible ways of declaring war. Second, the fact that certain individual acts constitute a declaration of war will be an empirical fact and not something that can be unpacked from the meaning of the expression "to declare war." Third, the more basic facts that render the statement true may not be expressible in some more basic vocabulary.

One can avoid some of these problems by retreating to the more liberal supervenience thesis, but even this thesis might be questioned on the grounds that an adequate description of the actions of individuals requires reference to institutions and institutional action. One might argue that there is no noncircular conceptual hierarchy with an autonomous level of individual action below the level of institutional action. But this is compatible with saying that of course there are, and must be, nontrivial answers to the questions, "How did England declare war?" or "In virture of what individuals performing what actions did England declare war?"

For a second example, consider statements of the form "x perceives that p." A defender of a causal theory of perception might say that such statements are not barely true: they are true in virtue of the fact that the fact that p causes (in a certain way) a certain present tense sense datum statement to be true of x. One prominent defender of the causal theory of perception suggested that the relevant use of the technical term "sense datum" be explained in the following way: "Its use would be explicitly defined by reference to such supposedly standard locutions as 'so-and-so looks Φ (e.g., blue) to me,' 'It looks (feels) to me as if there were a Φ so-and-so,' 'I seem to see something Φ' and so on."[29] Now if this project were one of reduction, even of the most liberal kind, then this sort of definition of sense data would be unacceptable because of its blatant circularity; the suggestion is to define sense data in terms of perception. But even if one needs the concept of perception to characterize sensation, it still may be that facts about sensation, together with facts about their causes, are what render statements about perception true. One may deny that perceptual statements are barely true in the rough intuitive sense which is explained in terms of the way one answers questions about what makes a statement true, while at the same time rejecting a reduction and the conceptual hierarchy which reduction presupposes. To reject reduction is not necessarily to treat a concept as an unstructured given. A causal analysis of perception, even if it fails to yield any kind of reduction, may still clarify the relations between perception and sense experience in a way that contributes to solutions to problems in epistemology and the philosophy of mind.

If "barely true" means that a statement is not only irreducible but also simple, unproblematic, and true in virtue only of itself, then it is clear that counterfactuals are not barely true. They are, after all, complex statements. According to our semantic analysis, a counterfactual, *if P then Q*, is true in virtue of the fact that Q is true in a different possible world, one that stands in a certain relation to the actual world, a relation that is a function of P. But this is not quite the answer we want when we ask what fact it is in virtue of which a counterfactual is true. Counterfactuals make factual claims—claims about the actual world and not just about some fictitious situation. If we are to defend a realist interpretation of counterfactuals, we must defend that claim that there is a fact about the actual world which renders a true counterfactual true.

There is no conflict between the semantic analysis, which says that a counterfactual is true in virtue of the truth of the consequent in some different possible situation, and the realist thesis that a counterfactual is true in virtue of some fact about the actual world. Consider two people who disagree about the truth of a counterfactual. I think that Thorpe would have won if Wilson hadn't, while you think that Heath would have. According to the analysis, this means that I think Thorpe did win in the selected possible world while you think that Heath won there. But the selected world is selected in virtue of its relation to the actual world, and so our disagreement may have its source in a disagreement about that world. If the disagreement is in fact a factual one, it will be a disagreement not about how to select a possible world but about what world the selection is made from. It is like when two people disagree about which way to go to get home, not because they disagree about where they live but because they disagree about where they are.

Is there an informative way to say what the fact about the actual world is in virtue of which a true counterfactual is true? In particular cases, there surely is. Sly Pete would have lost if he had called in virtue of his losing hand; Heath would have won if Wilson hadn't in virtue of the dispositions of the voters; the match would have lit if struck in virtue of its chemical composition and the presence of oxygen in the environment. These are substantive answers, but for several reasons they do not point the way toward any kind of reduction. First, there may be no useful way to generalize these answers, no way to give an answer to the question "in virtue of what is a counterfactual true when it is true?" which is both general and substantive. Second, the claim that a certain fact renders a counterfactual true is itself a factual claim and not something to be unpacked from the meaning or content of the counterfactual. Third, the facts that render counterfactuals true are often stated in terms that are as problematic as counterfactuals themselves and for which analysis in terms of counterfactuals may seem natural. As is clear from examples, this does not make the explanation trivial or incorrect, but it does undercut any project of reduction.

If we claim that for every true counterfactual there is a nontrivial answer to the question "in virtue of what is it true?" then we are claiming that counterfactuals are never barely true in a broad and rather vague sense of this term. But it is not obvious that this claim distinguishes counterfactuals from other statements. Aren't there always nontrivial answers to questions about the facts that render statements true? Can't we ask, in virtue of what is snow white, what fact is it that renders it true that water is wet, that Jack is walking down the street, that the cat is on the mat? Of course such questions might be asking for a causal explanation—what *causes* it to be true that . . . —and this, presumably, is not the relevant sense of the question. But even if one makes clear that one is asking about the fact itself—about what constitutes it and not just about what brought it about—there will be few if any cases where the question cannot be asked and answered. Our conceptual resources are rich; there are always other nontrivially related ways to characterize what is, in some loose sense, the same phenomenon. So it may be that the vague sense in which counterfactuals are never barely true is a sense in which nothing is.

Even if there are few or no pure cases of bare truths in the loose sense, there are surely differences in degree. Some facts stand more or less on their own, while others seem to depend for their legitimacy on an answer to the question, in virtue of what is it a fact? Consider the following two contrasting stories:

(1) Tweedledee and Tweedledum tossed a fair coin, but before they could see how it landed someone picked it up and ran away with it. Tweedledee is convinced that it landed heads, Tweedledum that it landed tails. Neither has any reason for his belief, but each still feels quite certain. Neither belief is justified, but one of them—we will never know which—is surely correct.

(2) This time someone ran off with the coin before it was tossed. Having no other coin, Tweedledee and Tweedledum argue about how it would have landed if it had been flipped. Tweedledee is convinced that it would have landed heads, Tweedledum that it would have landed tails. Again, neither has a reason—they agree that the coin was a normal one and that the toss would have been fair. This time, there is little inclination to say that one of them must be right. Unless there is a story to be told about a fact that

renders one or the other of the counterfactuals true, we will say that neither is.[30]

If we recognize (as I argued in the last chapter we must) that such questions may and often do have no answers, are we abandoning realism about counterfactuals? Michael Dummett has suggested that we are: "Realism concerning a given class of statements" he suggests, may be characterized "as the assumption that each statement of that class is determinately true or false."[31] I think it is right that the recognition of a certain kind of semantic indeterminacy is a concession (although not a capitulation) to antirealism, but I think Dummett's identification of realism with bivalence needs to be qualified in two ways.

First, one needs to distinguish different kinds of semantic indeterminacy. It is no concession to antirealism to admit that sentences may be vague or ambiguous. Vagueness and ambiguity arise from indeterminacy in the relation between words and the reality they purport to describe, and need have no significant consequences for the character of the reality itself. But the indeterminacy in counterfactuals seems deeper than this. To clarify the relation between bivalence and realism, we need to clarify the distinction between deeper and more superficial sources of truth-value gaps.

Second, even if some counterfactuals are neither true nor false, that does not foreclose the possibility that others are both irreducible and determinate. Dummett's characterization of realism seems to leave no room for being a realist about some members of a given class of statements and not about others. Dummett seems to assume that if some counterfactuals fail to be barely true or false, then all must; or at least, I think Dummett would say, we can reasonably permit some but not all counterfactuals to be irreducible only if we have a general criterion for drawing the line between the two kinds of counterfactuals, and a justification for drawing it where we do.

As to different sources of indeterminacy: given the possible worlds framework for representing propositional attitudes, we can make a clear distinction between two kinds of semantic indeterminacy, one deeper and one more superficial. The distinction is clearer in the model than it is in application, but it is a distinction that has intuitive content and that I think helps to illuminate Dummett's idea that the denial of bivalence, when it has its source in the deeper kind of indeterminacy, is a retreat from realism.

Suppose, as we have been supposing, that a person's attitudes and the contents of his statements are represented in terms of a space of alternative possibilities. The content of a statement, for example, is characterized by a function from the points in this space to truth-values, a function which, in effect, divides the space into two parts. A statement can be vague or indeterminate by expressing only a partial function, a function which, relative to some possible situations, takes no value. Such a vague statement, in effect, uses a fuzzy line to divide the space of possibilities. If the actual world lies on the fuzzy boundary, the statement will be neither true nor false. So, for example, Jack, and other people, have various heights in different possible situations. The statement that Jack is tall is clearly true in some of them and clearly false in others. But many situations that we can easily imagine do not fall clearly on either side of the line. We might say, because of such cases, either that "Jack is tall" expresses a vague proposition (a partial function) or that there is some indeterminacy in the relation between the sentence (as used in a given context) and the proposition it expresses. Either way, the indeterminacy is relatively superficial.

But now consider this contrasting kind of representation of indeterminacy. Suppose the content of our statement is determinate relative to the relevant set of possibilities: it draws a sharp line between the points so that, for each possible world in the space, the proposition is true or false. But when we ask, is the statement true in the *actual* world, we find that the question has no answer for the following reason: there are no facts which determine which of several points (some on each side of the sharp line) is the actual world. Our conceptual space of possibilities, I am supposing, has cut things up too finely, making distinctions to which nothing in reality answers.

This would, of course, make no sense on an extreme realist conception of the space of possible worlds. If the actual world—the reality which our conceptions are intended to represent—just *is* one of the points in logical space, then there could be no indeterminacy of this kind. But the moderate realist distinguishes the actual world as the designated "way things might be" from the actual world as "I and all my surroundings"—the reality itself which representations purport to represent. There is no reason to expect the distinctions reality allows for to coincide with those our conceptions of reality make.

As I said, I think the distinction I am making is sharper in the model than it is in its application. Possible worlds, as I understand them, are abstractions from the dispositions of rational agents; they are part of a device for representing and relating those dispositions to each other, to the actions (linguistic and otherwise) of the agents, and to the world. There may be some arbitrariness in the way we individuate possible situations in characterizing a person's attitudes, and as a result some arbitrariness in whether a given truth-value gap is reconstructed as a deeper or as a more superficial indeterminacy. But the distinction is not simply an artifact of the model; its intuitive basis is evident, I think, in examples.

Consider Tweedledee and Tweedledum again. *We* may think it absurd to assume that the counterfactual "if the coin had been tossed it would have landed heads" is either barely true or barely false, but Tweedledee and Tweedledum obviously do make this assumption. They not only make apparently conflicting statements, they have genuinely conflicting beliefs. Their conflicting beliefs may make contrasting actions rational, and may lead to different attitudes of other kinds. Maybe Tweedledee believes that because the coin would have landed heads, he will have an unlucky day, in which case he ought, given his beliefs, to be cautious. Perhaps Tweedledum, although he believes that the coin would have landed tails, wishes that Tweedledee had been right. We may need a distinction between possible situations in which the coin would have landed heads and possible situations in which it would have landed tails in order to give an adequate description of the attitudes of Tweedledee and Tweedledum, even if we don't need or want such a distinction in order to locate the actual world in a space of possibilities.

Or consider a more realistic example: Dummett's case of Jones, the man, now dead, who never in his life encountered danger.[32] We consider whether Jones was a brave man, assuming that Jones was brave if and only if he would have acted bravely had he encountered danger. In asking the question, we don't (as Tweedledee and Tweedledum do) assume that the counterfactual is barely true or false in the loose sense; we assume that if Jones was brave, there must be facts about Jones's physical and psychological makeup in virtue of which he was brave. But even if we do not have much idea what the relevant physical and psychological facts are, we still may have a whole cluster of attitudes towards Jones's character, attitudes that require distinguishing the possible situations in which he was brave from those in which he was not. We may have reasons for believing that Jones was brave, or not, and we may have other attitudes towards Jones as a result of believing that he was brave, or not. For example, we may admire Jones because he was, as we think, a brave man; we may regret that Jones never had the opportunity to display the bravery that we are sure he had. If we follow Dummett in rejecting *naive* realism about states of character—the assumption that there *must* be a fact of the matter about whether Jones was brave—then we will recognize that the facts may not decide the question of whether Jones was brave. If they do not, then there will be possible situations which our beliefs and other attitudes distinguish between, but which the facts do not.

The possibility of this kind of indeterminacy reflects, I think, a tension between a pragmatic theory of propositional attitudes and a realist theory of truth. On the one hand, a space of possibilities is a framework for representing the mental states of agents. Possibilities are distinguished if they need to be distinguished in order to give a certain kind of account of why agents behave the way they do. On the other hand, the space of possibilities is a logical space in which we locate the world itself. Possible worlds are possible totalities of facts—everything that is or might be the case. These two roles that possible worlds play are interdependent. On the one hand, the causal dimension of propositional attitudes, which I argued in chapter 1 is essential to understanding attitudes as representational, requires that the conceptual space we use to characterize attitudes be one in which we locate the actual world. On the other hand, our locating the actual world in logical space is itself constituted by a state of belief—our own. But the mutual dependence of these two roles of a conceptual space of possibilities does not ensure that they will individuate the possibilities in the same way. To recognize that our conception of the alternative possibilities may raise questions which the facts cannot answer is, as Dummett suggests, a retreat from an excess of realism.

The second qualification that I think we need to make to Dummett's identification of antirealism with the denial of bivalence is to recognize that commitment to bivalence can be a matter of degree. Even if some counterfactuals are neither true nor false, others may be both irreducible and true, and so, in one of Dummett's senses, barely true.

The all or nothing position that I have attributed to Dummett would be reasonable if it were reasonable to identify irreducibility with bare truth in the loose sense. Suppose irreducible truths were all simple truths, true in virtue only of themselves and in need of no further explanation. Suppose further that *some* counterfactuals were barely true in this way. Then, one might reasonably argue, there would be no nonarbitrary basis for denying that status to any counterfactual. If a counterfactual is the kind of statement about which it is sometimes reasonable to say that we do not need an answer to the question "What makes it true?" then what basis could we have for requiring an answer to the question in other cases? But if we recognize that even irreducible facts need to be connected with other facts, need answers to the question "In virtue of what is it a fact?" then we have a basis for distinguishing, case by case, determinate from indeterminate counterfactuals.

Consider again the question of Jones's bravery. Suppose that a correct general psychological theory would explain patterns of brave behavior in terms of a broader cluster of character traits that always go together, a cluster that manifests itself in many different ways. Jones never encountered danger, but, let us suppose, he had many opportunities to demonstrate his stable possession of the broader type of character of which bravery is only one part. This outcome would, I think, justify one in saying that it was a fact that Jones was brave. But it does not point toward any general criterion for distinguishing types of counterfactuals, of identifying "if Jones had encountered danger, he would have acted bravely" as a counterfactual of the type that can be barely true or false. Nor does it suggest anything remotely like a reduction of the counterfactual, or of the character trait, to something more basic. It is just that one character trait is discovered to be a special case of another. In general, what is required to justify the hypothesis that there is a fact of the matter whether Jones was brave is that it be reasonable to hypothesize that there is a property of people which is more or less independent of whether they in fact encounter danger, and which tends to cause them to act bravely when they do. Such a hypothesis will very often be highly plausible in cases where counterfactuals play an essential part in defining or fixing the referent of a predicate.

According to the modest realist thesis that I have been defending, at least some counterfactuals are both irreducible and determinately true or false. From the point of view of the possible worlds conception of content and the possible worlds analysis of conditionals, the claim that some counterfactuals are not reducible, even in a liberal sense, is the claim that the introduction of counterfactuals allows for finer discriminations between possible worlds than could be made without counterfactuals. The selection functions relative to which counterfactuals are interpreted do not simply select on the basis of facts and criteria of similarity that are intelligible independently of counterfactuals. Rather, the claim is, the fact of selection gives rise to new ways of cutting up the space of possibilities, and so to a richer conception of the way the world is. The second part of the modest realist thesis— that irreducible counterfactuals are sometimes determinately true or false—is the claim that the world can live up to our richer conception of the way it is or might be. This claim will be justified if the new distinctions between possibilities that the inquirer makes connect with each other and with other facts and are reinforced by further interactions between the inquirer and the world.

Notes

Chapter 1

1. The suggestion that propositions be identified with functions from possible worlds into truth-values was, I believe, originally made by Saul Kripke. Rudolf Carnap suggested identifying propositions with sets of state descriptions. See Carnap (1947), 181. C. I. Lewis identified the *comprehension* of a sentence with the set of possible worlds in which the sentence is true (C. I. Lewis, 1947: 57).
2. Cf. Geach (1957), section 18.
3. Dummett (1973), 362.
4. Wilfrid Sellars in Sellars and Chisholm (1958), 521.
5. Davidson (1975), 9.
6. Gilbert Harman (1973), 57.
7. See Sellars and Chisholm (1958) for an interesting debate that focuses on just this issue.
8. Field (1978).
9. Ibid., 10.
10. The analogy between numbers and propositions has been noted and discussed by a number of philosophers including Paul Churchland (1979: 105) and Daniel Dennett (1982: 7). Field (1981) discusses the analogy, which was suggested to him by David Lewis.
11. Fodor (1978), 47.
12. Ibid., 61.
13. Ibid., 46.
14. Field (1981), 112–114.
15. Ibid., 114.
16. Stampe (1977).
17. Field (1978), 31.
18. I recognize that the definition sketches that I have given do not really define *physical* relations between objects and propositions. The notions defined are like functional notions in that they might be realized in physically different ways: two systems might indicate that *P* or tend-to-bring-about that *P* because of different physical mechanisms. But in the case of simple systems to which these relations apply, it is easy to see what the mechanism is and to see how to characterize it in terms of a physical relation between an object and a proposition.
19. For an excellent exposition and discussion of this kind of account of belief and desire, see Dennett (1971).
20. Donald Davidson (1975:11) suggests that "attributions of belief and desire ... are supervenient on behavior more broadly described." His reasons seem to be basically verificationist: "If we were to ask for evidence that [a belief-desire] explanation is

correct, the evidence would in the end consist of more data concerning the sort of event being explained—namely further behavior which is explained by the postulated beliefs and desires."

21. Richard Boyd has pointed out that there may be some constraints required to ensure that the objects of Mary's belief are propositions. Perhaps, for example, it makes no sense to say that a mathematical point insulted Mary. So if we take Mary's belief to be about a mathematical point, we will have to reinterpret the *insulting* relation as well. But it is still clear that the pragmatic analysis leaves too much freedom to allow it to explain how mental states can represent.

22. There may be other elements of mental representation left out as well. One might, for example, argue that something like our concept of *need* puts some constraints on the desires of rational creatures.

23. Davidson (1977), in Platts (1980), 136.

24. Salmon (1981), 66.

25. Harman (1973), 45.

26. Ibid., 58.

27. Ibid., 55.

Chapter 2

1. Field (1978), 12.

2. Ibid., 12.

3. Ibid., 12.

4. Let me mention just one problem. In sketching a possible account of the belief* relation, Field invokes a distinction between the *core* belief*s—sentences explicitly stored as belief*s—and belief*s generally. "One believe*s a sentence," he suggests, "if and only if that sentence is an obvious consequence of sentences that are explicitly stored" (ibid., 17). But developing this suggestion would require spelling out the apparently semantical notion of an *obvious consequence* independently of the meanings of the sentences.

5. Field (1972).

6. Field (1978), 23.

7. Field (1972), 363.

8. The main technical interest of Tarski's theory of truth is in the devices for explaining quantification and variable binding generally. But the abstract philosophical issues concerning the status of truth theory as a reduction of truth to nonsemantic terms, and thus as part of a solution to the problem of intentionality, are independent of these devices and can be seen more easily by considering simpler languages.

9. Scott Soames (1984) gives a similar argument against this part of Field's project.

10. I am thinking, of course, principally of work on meaning and conversation by Paul Grice (1957, 1969). See also Schiffer (1972), Bennett (1976), and D. Lewis (1969).

11. This is of course greatly oversimplified in many ways. In a more careful statement of this idea, one qualification would be this: in any language with context-dependent sentences, the meaning of a sentence will not by itself determine a proposition. It will be something like a function from contexts into propositions. For such a language, one would explain what it is for a sentence S to mean f in terms of a convention in a population of speakers that S should be used in context c to mean proposition x, where $x = f(c)$.

12. This idea is developed in D. Lewis (1969).

13. Both Noam Chomsky and Donald Davidson have long emphasized that this is a central fact about language use which syntactic and semantic theories must explain.

14. Field (1972), 367.
15. In widely cited disclaimers, Kripke emphasized that he was not presenting a reductive theory of reference. He noted that if his account were understood in this way, it would be circular since he characterizes the causal condition partly in terms of speakers' intentions to preserve reference. See, for example, Kripke (1972), 302: "Notice that the preceding outline hardly *eliminates* the notion of reference; on the contrary, it takes the notion of intending to use the same reference as given."

On the other hand, see Devitt (1981) for a detailed development of a causal theory of reference which attempts to remove the intentional elements in the analysis of the relevant causal relation. Devitt sees his project as a part of the kind of reductive project which Field proposed. He analyzes *designation* in terms of certain kinds of causal chains, which he calls *d-chains*, between a referring token and the object referred to. A d-chain must be "grounded" in the object through an act or event which involves perception of the object, and through which the perceiver acquires the ability to refer to the object. Other links in the chain involve the transfer of the ability through causal interactions between someone with the ability and others.

The characterization of d-chains presupposes the notion of a *thought*, by which Devitt means a sentential attitude such as Field's belief*. Thus this part of the project requires a satisfactory solution to Field's subproblem (a). It also takes for granted the notion of the perception of an object. To be successful, the project requires an explanation of what it is to perceive an object which does not presuppose the idea of acquisition of information about the object.
16. Dummett (1973), 4-5.
17. For example, "My way of trying to give an account of language and meaning makes essential use of such concepts as those of belief and intention, and I do not believe it is possible to reduce these notions to anything more scientific or behaviouristic" (Davidson, 1976: 38).
18. The following papers by Davidson are relevant: Davidson (1973), (1974), and (1975).
19. Davidson (1975), 15.
20. Ibid., 9.
21. Ibid., 22.
22. Grandy (1982), 331.
23. Burge (1982), 286.
24. Davidson (1975), 22.

Chapter 3

1. Mackie (1973), 84.
2. Powers (1976), 95.
3. D. Lewis (1973b), 84.
4. Ibid., 86.
5. Ibid., 85.
6. Ibid., 85-86.
7. Ibid., 85.
8. D. Lewis (1979a), 533.
9. Augustine (399), 276 (Book 11, chapter 20).
10. D. Lewis (1973b), 88.
11. Mackie (1973), 90, 92.
12. R. Adams (1974), 224.
13. Ibid., 225.
14. Ibid., 225.

15. In the earlier published version of this chapter I claimed otherwise. Philip Bricker, in his dissertation (Bricker, 1983), pointed out my mistake in assuming that (W4) followed from (W1)–(W3). Bricker's dissertation contains a clear, detailed and interesting investigation, both technical and philosophical, of the relation between proposition-based theories such as Adams's world-story theory and world-based theories such as the analysis I am defending.
16. R. Adams (1974), 228.

Chapter 4

1. Fodor (1978), 503.
2. Stephen Stich (1982) develops this idea.
3. Harman (1973), 55.
4. Fodor (1978), 505–506.
5. Stich (1982), 159.
6. Stich (1979), 18.
7. Dennett (1969), 183.
8. Stich (1982), 185–189.
9. Burge (1979).
10. Burge's example raises some other interesting problems. For example, it illustrates the problem of belief in necessarily false propositions, since what Mabel seems to believe—that she has arthritis in her thigh—is impossible. I discuss this later in this chapter.
11. Stich (1982), 158.
12. Cf. Hintikka (1962) for an early formal development of this kind of account of belief states.
13. Cf. Dummett (1973), 286, and Powers (1978).
14. Cf. Dray (1957), chapter v.
15. If this suggestion is to help, it must be that the semantical propositions about the relation between statements and what they say are themselves contingent propositions. For example, it would not work if it were a necessary truth that "2 + 2 = 4" says that two plus two equals four. If one defines a language and identifies sentences in terms of their semantical properties, then such semantical propositions will not be contingent. If, on the other hand, one defined a language in terms of the community of speakers that speak it, and identifies linguistic expressions in terms of their physical properties, then the semantical propositions will be contingent. It might seem then that I am committed to the second approach, but I don't think there is a substantive issue here. However utterances or sentences are identified across possible worlds, it is enough for my purposes that there be possible worlds in which some epistemic counterpart of the expression "2 + 2 = 4" says something different than that two plus two equals four. One can set aside the question of whether such counterpart sentence tokens (which sound and look the same as our "2 + 2 = 4") are really instances of the same sentence type.
16. I discuss some devices that I think would be useful in the development of such a theory in Stalnaker (1978) and (1981a).
17. Essentially this argument was pressed by Larry Powers (1976), and by Saul Kripke in conversation. A related argument is given by Hartry Field (1978), 15.

Chapter 5

1. I discuss a notion of presupposition which is a social acceptance concept of this kind

in Stalnaker (1974). For discussions of closely related notions of mutual knowledge and common knowledge, see D. Lewis (1969) and Schiffer (1972).

2. David Lewis discusses a theory for representing fragmented states of belief, as he calls them, in D. Lewis (1982).

3. There will inevitably be a certain arbitrariness in drawing the line between the propositions an agent believes "straightaway" and those he is disposed to come to believe after perfunctory calculation. Where one draws this line will depend in part on what one is interested in explaining.

4. The example comes from Dretske (1970), 1015–1016. See also Dretske (1981), 123–134. For an interesting discussion of Dretske's example and argument, see Stine (1976).

5. Kyburg (1970), 56.

6. Ibid., 74.

7. Ibid., 76. This remark was made about two particular systems, one developed by Jaakko Hintikka and Risto Hilpinen and the other by Keith Lehrer, but Kyburg says that "any global system in which the conjunction principle is satisfied will suffer from these shortcomings" (ibid., 76).

8. Ibid., 77.

9. Goodman (1947), which is also chapter 1 of Goodman (1955).

Chapter 6

1. Armstrong (1973), 3–6.

2. Ibid., 5

3. This qualification points to an important problem about the relation between beliefs and dispositions to act. Let me use the map analogy to say what the problem is. Suppose there are two maps at two different entrances to the zoo. They are exactly the same, except that they have their "you are here" arrows tacked on at different points. You, after consulting the map at the south entrance, go north to get to the small mammal house, while I, after consulting the map at the north entrance, go south to get there. We have the same beliefs about the layout of the zoo, and the same desire: to get to the small mammal house. But we do, and obviously should do, different things. Our maps of reality are the same in relevant respects, but we locate ourselves at different points on the map, and as a result have different rational dispositions. This suggests that dispositions to act are given not by our maps of reality alone, but by this together with the agent's identity—by where he locates himself.

But isn't my locating of myself on my map of reality itself a belief? Don't I believe, not only that the zoo is laid out thus and so, but also that I am at the south entrance? Can *that* belief be explained as a belief that some proposition is true? This kind of problem was first noted by Hector-Neri Castañeda, and has recently received a lot of attention from philosophers. I argue in Stalnaker (1981a) that we can understand self-locating beliefs as beliefs with propositions as objects. Others have responded to the problem in different ways: John Perry used a distinction between belief states and objects of belief to account for the phenomenon of self-locating belief. David Lewis has argued that we should take the objects of belief to be properties rather than propositions. To believe a property is to ascribe it to oneself. I suspect that some of the differences between these alternative approaches are less substantive than they seem to be. See Perry (1979) and D. Lewis (1979a).

4. E. Adams (1970).

5. Gibbard (1981), 231.

6. As recent work on indexicals and egocentric belief has shown, the pronoun "I" is far from unproblematic in all contexts. See Perry (1979), D. Lewis (1979a) and Stalnaker (1981a).

7. Gibbard (1981), 231–234.
8. Ibid., 211, 239.
9. Grice (1967).

Chapter 7

1. One might question this last assumption. If one does not make it, the change function for omniscient states of knowledge will correspond to a *set* selection function, which yields a slightly different abstract semantic theory. The difference between this kind of theory and the one I will defend is discussed later in this chapter.
2. A change function can be defined in terms of a world selection function in the following way. If K is a set of possible worlds representing an initial belief state, and f is a world selection function taking possible worlds and propositions into possible worlds, then c_K, a function taking propositions into potential new acceptance states, may be defined as follows: for any proposition A, $c_K(A) = \{f_i(A):i \in K\}$.
3. The theory was sketched informally and defended in Stalnaker (1968). A version of it was presented more formally in Stalnaker and Thomason (1970).
4. One might object to this stipulation because one believes that there are counterfactuals with impossible antecedents which express nonvacuously true propositions, for example conditionals which express dependencies between mathematical propositions. The problem here is similar to the problem of mathematical belief and I think must be solved in a related way: by finding a sense in which mathematical suppositions are contingent. If we can make sense of the supposition that, say, there are only finitely many primes, we will have to do it in terms of a possible situation in which it is true that there are only finitely many primes.
5. The arguments for condition (3) are far from decisive. I will discuss later in this chapter some intuitive counterexamples to it, and a theory like the one I am defending which leaves it out.
6. Goodman (1947), and Chisholm (1946).
7. See Horn (1969) for a general analysis of "even."
8. See Warmbrod (1981) for a development of this kind of argument.
9. The notion of comparative similarity is most prominent in David Lewis's analysis, and many of the criticisms come from reviews and other discussions of his book *Counterfactuals* (Lewis, 1973b).
10. Fine (1975b).
11. Tichy (1976).
12. Or at least without giving up any respects of similarity that are not completely contrived. One can always construct artificial respects of similarity which favor any object over any other. For example, whatever a, b and c are, b is more similar to a than c is with respect to membership in the set $\{a,b\}$.
13. Within a theory in which a *set* of possible worlds, rather than a single possible world, is selected, the corresponding constraint might be either a stronger or a weaker condition: (s) that the selected set be the unit set containing the actual world, or (w) that the selected set be some set containing the actual world. The weaker condition is sufficient to validate modus ponens but not the more controversial principle that a conditional is always true when both antecedent and consequent are true. If the specification of the relevant respects of similarity allowed certain respects to be completely irrelevant (as was suggested above), then the weaker condition might be more appropriate.
14. Tichy (1978), 453–454.
15. This is the truth-condition only on the assumption that there are some A-worlds,

which is to say, on the assumption that the antecedent is not necessarily false. Both Lewis's theory and mine stipulate that a counterfactual is vacuously true when its antecedent is impossible.

16. This principle is uncontroversial and independent of the limit assumption in the case where Γ is finite.

17. See van Fraassen (1966). This theory and theories based on the same general idea have been widely applied. See, for example, Field (1974), Fine (1975a), Kamp (1975), D. Lewis (1972), and Thomason (1970) and (1972).

18. Lewis emphasizes the vagueness and context-dependence of counterfactuals in his discussion of resemblance. See D. Lewis (1973b), 91–95.

19. This statement needs qualification when the language has a truth operator or other resources capable of expressing the fact that a statement lacks a truth-value. In such cases, there will be a divergence between the validity of an argument from A to B and the logical truth of a statement $A \supset B$. See van Fraassen (1966).

20. The relationship between the semantics for C2 with supervaluations and Lewis's semantics is explored by Bas van Fraassen (1974). A C2 model with supervaluations is defined as a family of determinate C2 models. Van Fraassen shows that Lewis models which satisfy the limit assumption are equivalent to what he calls *regular* families of C2 models—families meeting certain restrictions. I believe that if one drops the regularity restriction, then the same equivalence holds between families of C2 models and the models of the semantic theory of simple subjunctive conditionals favored by John Pollock. For an exposition of Pollock's theory, see Pollock (1976).

21. Quine (1959), 14.

22. D. Lewis (1973b), 80.

23. Quine (1959), 14.

24. Philosophers who deny truth to statements about future contingents may disagree. They may want to say that X's reply makes sense and might be true. Readers who are inclined to this view may substitute a past tense example.

25. This example from Gilbert and Sullivan's *H.M.S. Pinafore* is borrowed from D. Lewis (1978).

26. D. Lewis (1973b), 82–83.

27. D. Lewis (1973b).

28. D. Lewis (1979b) suggests that the similarity ordering relevant to interpreting counterfactuals may, in some cases, give zero weight to some respects of similarity.

29. See Herzberger (1979) and Pollock (1976: 18–20) for arguments against the limit assumption.

30. This argument was suggested by Richmond Thomason.

31. D. Lewis (1973b), 80.

Chapter 8

1. Mackie (1973), 89–90.
2. Ibid., 88.
3. D. Lewis (1973a), 420–421.
4. Mackie (1973), 89.
5. Ibid., 90 (emphasis added).
6. van Fraassen (1980), 202–203.
7. Ibid., 115–116.
8. Ibid., 118.
9. Ibid., 134–137
10. Chisholm (1946)

11. Goodman (1955).
12. The most explicit expression of Humean sympathies that I know of in Lewis's writings is in D. Lewis (1980), in Harper, Stalnaker, and Pearce (1981), 294: "A broadly Humean doctrine (something I would very much like to believe if at all possible) holds that all the facts there are about the world are particular facts, or combinations thereof."
13. Tichy (1978), 433.
14. D. Lewis (1979b), 466–467.
15. More precisely, we should say the base world rather than the actual world.
16. Jonathan Bennett (1984) discusses this problem.
17. D. Lewis (1973b), 73.
18. I am not sure how to make sense, in general, of my talk of facts being *about* particular events, but the following constraint seems reasonable: if a proposition has consequences for what happens at parts of the world that are spatially or temporally distant from an event or a sequence of events, then that proposition does not state a particular fact about the event or sequence. If this is right, then (according to Lewis) propositions describing causal connections between events will not state particular facts about those events, since they depend on laws, which depend on the overall pattern of events in the universe. So even though (according to the Humean program) the totality of particular facts about the world will not be causally neutral, the particular facts about individual events and sequences of events will be.
19. Ayer's position on counterfactual and causal propositions seems to be a rather extreme form of noncognitivism. Near the end of his essay, he makes the following remarks:" . . . in a certain sense, causes are what we choose them to be. We do not decide what facts habitually go together, but we do decide what combinations are to be imaginatively projected. The despised savages who beat gongs at solar eclipses to summon back the sun are not making any factual error. . . . They see what goes on as well as we do." (Ayer, 1972, 138–139)
20. Ibid., 115.
21. Ibid., 115.
22. Ibid., 8.
23. Robert Jaeger (1973) makes this point and discusses its significance for a number of philosophical problems.
24. Sydney Shoemaker argues for this account of properties in Shoemaker (1980), 114.
25. Ayer (1972), 114–115.
26. Dummett (1963), 148.
27. Dummett (1976), 94.
28. Ibid., 94.
29. Grice (1961), 123. Grice, in this paper, is not defending a particular version of the causal theory of perception, but is just responding to some general objections to all theories of a certain kind.
30. Ayer (1972), 121.
31. Dummett (1976), 93.
32. Dummett (1959), in Dummett (1978) 15–17.

References

Adams, Ernest (1970). "Subjunctive and Indicative Conditionals," *Inquiry*, 6, 39–94.

Adams, Robert M. (1974). "Theories of Actuality," *Nous*, 5, 211–231.

Armstrong, D. M. (1973). *Belief, Truth and Knowledge*. Cambridge: Cambridge University Press.

Augustine (399). *Confessions*, translated by F. J. Sheed (1943). New York: Sheed and Ward.

Ayer, A. J. (1972). *Probability and Evidence*. New York: Columbia University Press.

Bennett, Jonathan (1976). *Linguistic Behavior*. Cambridge: Cambridge University Press.

Bennett, Jonathan (1984). "Counterfactuals and Temporal Direction," *Philosophical Review*, 93. 57–97.

Block, Ned, ed. (1981). *Readings in Philosophy of Psychology*, vol. II. Cambridge, Mass.: Harvard University Press.

Bricker, Philip (1983). *Worlds and Propositions: The Structure and Ontology of Logical Space*. Unpublished Ph.D. dissertation, Princeton University, Princeton, N.J.

Burge, Tyler (1979). "Individualism and the Mental," *Midwest Studies in Philosophy, IV: Studies in Metaphysics*. Minneapolis: University of Minnesota Press.

Burge, Tyler (1982). "Two Thought Experiments Reviewed," *Notre Dame Journal of Formal Logic*, 23, 284–293.

Carnap, Rudolf (1947). *Meaning and Necessity*. Chicago: University of Chicago Press.

Chisholm, Roderick (1946). "The Contrary-to-Fact Conditional," *Mind*, 55, 289–307.

Churchland, Paul (1979). *Scientific Realism and the Plasticity of Mind*. Cambridge: Cambridge University Press.

Davidson, Donald (1973). "Radical Interpretation," *Dialectica*, 27, 313–328.

Davidson, Donald (1974). "Belief and the Basis of Meaning," *Synthese*, 27, 303–324.

Davidson, Donald (1975). "Thought and Talk," in Samuel Guttenplan, ed., *Mind and Language*, 7–24, Oxford: Clarendon Press.

Davidson, Donald (1976). "Reply to Foster," in Evans and McDowell (1976), 33–41.

Davidson, Donald (1977). "Reality Without Reference," *Dialectica*, 31, 247–258. Reprinted in Platts (1980), 131–140.

Davidson, Donald, and Harman, Gilbert, eds. (1972). *Semantics of Natural Language*. Dordrecht: Reidel.

Dennett, Daniel C. (1969). *Content and Consciousness*. London: Routledge and Kegan Paul.

Dennett, Daniel C. (1971). "Intentional Systems," *Journal of Philosophy*, 68, 87–106. Reprinted in Dennett (1978), 3–22.

Dennett, Daniel C. (1978). *Brainstorms*. Montgomery, Vermont: Bradford Books.

Dennett, Daniel C. (1982). "Beyond Belief," in Woodfield (1982), 1–95.

Devitt, Michael (1981). *Designation*. New York: Columbia University Press.

Dray, William (1957). *Laws and Explanation in History*. Oxford: Oxford University Press.

Dretske, Fred I. (1970). "Epistemic Operators," *Journal of Philosophy*, 67, 1007–1023.

Dretske, Fred I. (1981). *Knowledge and the Flow of Information*. Cambridge, Mass.: Bradford Books, MIT Press.

Dummett, Michael (1959). "Truth," *Proceedings of the Aristotelian Society*, n.s. 59, 141–162. Reprinted in Dummett (1978), 1–19.

Dummett, Michael (1963). "Realism," in Dummett (1978), 145–165.

Dummett, Michael (1973). *Frege: Philosophy of Language*. London: Duckworth.

Dummett, Michael (1976). "What is a Theory of Meaning, II," in Evans and McDowell (1976), 67–137.

Dummett, Michael (1978). *Truth and Other Enigmas*. Cambridge, Mass.: Harvard University Press.

Evans, Gareth, and McDowell, John, eds. (1976). *Truth and Meaning*. Oxford: Clarendon Press.

Field, Hartry (1972). "Tarski's Theory of Truth," *Journal of Philosophy*, 69, 347–375. Reprinted in Platts (1980), 83–110.

Field, Hartry (1974). "Quine and the Correspondence Theory," *Philosophical Review*, 83, 200–228.

Field, Hartry (1978). "Mental Representation," *Erkenntnis*, 13, 9–61. Reprinted in Block (1981), 78–112.

Field, Hartry (1981). Postscript to "Mental Representation," in Block (1981). 112–114

Fine, Kit (1975a). "Vagueness, Truth and Logic," *Synthese*, 30, 265–300.

Fine, Kit (1975b). "Critical Notice of Lewis, *Counterfactuals*," *Mind*, 84, 451–458.

Fodor, Jerry A. (1978). "Propositional Attitudes," *The Monist*, 61, 501–523. Reprinted in Block (1981), 45–63.

Geach, Peter (1957). *Mental Acts, Their Content and Objects*. London: Routledge and Kegan Paul.

Gibbard, Allan (1981). "Two Recent Theories of Conditionals," in Harper, Stalnaker and Pearce (1981), 211–247.

Goodman, Nelson (1947). "The Problem of Counterfactual Conditionals," *Journal of Philosophy*, 44, 113–128. Reprinted in Goodman (1955), 3–27.

Goodman, Nelson (1955). *Fact, Fiction and Forecast*. Cambridge, Mass.: Harvard University Press.

Grandy, Richard (1982). "Semantic Intention and Linguistic Structure," *Notre Dame Journal of Formal Logic*, 23, 327–332.

Grice, H. P. (1957). "Meaning," *Philosophical Review*, 66, 377–388.

Grice, H. P. (1961). "The Causal Theory of Perception," *Proceedings of the Aristotelian Society*, Supplementary Volume 35, 121–152.

Grice, H. P. (1967). *Logic and Conversation*. Unpublished but widely circulated typescript from the William James Lectures, Harvard University.

Grice, H. P. (1969). "Utterer's Meaning and Intention," *Philosophical Review*, 78, 147–177.

Harman, Gilbert (1973). *Thought*. Princeton, N.J.: Princeton University Press.

Harper, W. L., Stalnaker, R., and Pearce, G., eds. (1981). *Ifs: Conditionals, Belief, Decision, Chance and Time*. Dordrecht: Reidel.

Herzberger, Hans (1979). "Counterfactuals and Consistency," *Journal of Philosophy*, 76, 83–88.

Hintikka, Jaakko (1962). *Knowledge and Belief*. Ithaca, N.Y.: Cornell University Press.

Horn, Laurence (1969). "A Presuppositional Analysis of 'Only' and 'Even,' " *Papers from the Fifth Regional Meeting of the Chicago Linguistics Society*, 318–327.

Jaeger, Robert A. (1973). "Action and Subtraction," *Philosophical Review*, 82, 320–329.

Kamp, Hans (1975). "Two Theories of Adjectives," in Edward Keenen, ed., *Formal Semantics of Natural Language*, 123–155. Cambridge: Cambridge University Press.

Kripke, Saul (1972). "Naming and Necessity," in Davidson and Harman, (1972), 253–355.

Kyburg, Henry E. (1970). "Conjunctivitis," in Marshall Swain, ed., *Induction, Acceptance and Rational Belief*, 55–82. Dordrecht: Reidel.

Lewis, C. I. (1947). *Knowledge and Valuation*. La Salle, Ill.: Open Court Press.

Lewis, David (1969). *Convention*. Cambridge, Mass.: Harvard University Press.

Lewis, David (1972). "General Semantics," in Davidson and Harman, (1972), 169–218. Reprinted in D. Lewis (1983).

Lewis, David (1973a). "Counterfactuals and Comparative Possibility," *Journal of Philosophical Logic*, 2, 418–446. Reprinted in Harper, Stalnaker and Pearce (1981), 57–85.

Lewis, David (1973b). *Counterfactuals*. Oxford: Blackwell.

Lewis, David (1978). "Truth in Fiction," *American Philosophical Quarterly*, 15, 37–46. Reprinted in D. Lewis (1983).

Lewis, David (1979a). "Attitudes De Dicto and De Se," *Philosophical Review*, 88, 513–543. Reprinted in D. Lewis (1983).

Lewis, David (1979b). "Counterfactual Dependence and Time's Arrow," *Nous*, 13, 455–476.

Lewis, David (1980). "A Subjectivist Guide to Objective Chance," in R. C. Jeffrey, ed., *Studies in Inductive Logic and Probability*, II, 269–293. Berkeley: University of California Press. Reprinted in Harper, Stalnaker and Pearce (1981), 267–297.

Lewis, David (1982). "Logic for Equivocators," *Nous*, 16, 431–441.

Lewis, David (1983). *Collected Papers, I*. Oxford: Oxford University Press.

MacKay, Alfred F., and Merrill, Daniel D., eds. (1976). *Issues in the Philosophy of Language*. New Haven, Conn.: Yale University Press.

Mackie, John L. (1973). *Truth Probability and Paradox*. Oxford: Clarendon Press.

Perry, John (1979). "The Essential Indexical," *Nous*, 13, 3–21.

Platts, Mark, ed. (1980). *Reference, Truth and Reality: Essays in the Philosophy of Language*. London: Routledge and Kegan Paul.

Pollock, John (1976). *Subjunctive Reasoning*. Dordrecht: Reidel.

Powers, Larry (1976). "Comments on Stalnaker, 'Propositions,' " in MacKay and Merrill (1976), 93–103.

Powers, Larry (1978). "Knowledge by Deduction," *Philosophical Review*, 87, 337–371.

Putnam, Hilary (1981). *Reason, Truth and History*. Cambridge: Cambridge University Press.

Quine, W. V. (1959). *Methods of Logic* (revised edition). New York: Holt, Rinehart and Winston.

Salmon, Nathan U. (1981). *Reference and Essence*. Princeton, N.J.: Princeton University Press.

Schiffer, Stephen (1972). *Meaning*. Oxford: Oxford University Press.

Sellars, Wilfrid, and Chisholm, Roderick, (1958). "Correspondence on Intentionality," in H. Feigl, M. Scriven, and G. Maxwell, eds., *Minnesota Studies in the Philosophy of Science, II: Concepts, Theories and the Mind-Body Problem*, 521–539. Minneapolis: University of Minnesota Press.

Shoemaker, Sydney (1980). "Causality and Properties," in Peter van Inwagen, ed., *Time and Cause*, 109–135, Dordrecht: Reidel.

Soames, Scott (1984). "What is a Theory of Truth?" *Journal of Philosophy*, forthcoming.

Stalnaker, Robert (1968). "A Theory of Conditionals," in N. Rescher, ed., *Studies in Logical Theory*, 98–112, Oxford: Blackwell. Reprinted in Harper, Stalnaker, and Pearce (1981). 41–55.

Stalnaker, Robert (1974). "Pragmatic Presuppositions," in Milton Munitz and Peter Unger, eds., *Semantics and Philosophy*, 197–214. New York: New York University Press.

Stalnaker, Robert (1976a). "Propositions," in MacKay and Merrill (1976), 79–91.

Stalnaker, Robert (1976b). "Possible Worlds," *Nous*, 10, 65–75.

Stalnaker, Robert (1978). "Assertion," *Syntax and Semantics,* 9, 315–332.

Stalnaker, Robert (1981a). "Indexical Belief," *Synthese,* 49, 129–151.

Stalnaker, Robert (1981b). "A Defense of Conditional Excluded Middle," in Harper, Stalnaker and Pearce (1981), 87–104.

Stalnaker, Robert, and Thomason, Richmond (1970). "A Semantic Analysis of Conditional Logic," *Theoria,* 36, 23–42.

Stampe, Dennis W. (1977). "Toward a Causal Theory of Linguistic Representation," *Midwest Studies in Philosophy, II: Studies in the Philosophy of Language,* 42–63. Morris, Minn.: University of Minnesota at Morris.

Stich, Stephen (1979). "Do Animals Have Beliefs?" *Australasian Journal of Philosophy,* 57, 15–28.

Stich, Stephen (1982). "On the Ascription of Content," in Woodfield (1982), 153–206.

Stich, Stephen (1983). *From Folk Psychology to Cognitive Science: The Case Against Belief.* Cambridge, Mass.: Bradford Books, MIT Press.

Stine, Gail (1976). "Skepticism, Relevant Alternatives, and Deductive Closure," *Philosophical Studies,* 29, 249–261.

Thomason, R. H. (1970) "Indeterminist Time and Truth-value Gaps," *Theoria,* 36, 246–281.

Thomason, R. H. (1972). "A Semantic Theory of Sortal Incorrectness," *Journal of Philosophical Logic,* 209–258.

Tichy, Pavel (1976). "A Counterexample to the Stalnaker-Lewis Analysis of Counterfactuals," *Philosophical Studies,* 29, 271–273.

Tichy, Pavel (1978). "A New Theory of Subjunctive Conditionals." *Synthese,* 37, 433–457.

van Fraassen, Bas (1966). "Singular Terms, Truth-value Gaps, and Free Logic," *Journal of Philosophy,* 63, 481–495.

van Fraassen, Bas (1974). "Hidden Variables in Conditional Logic," *Theoria,* 40, 176–190.

van Fraassen, Bas (1980). *The Scientific Image.* Oxford: Clarendon Press.

Warmbrod, Ken (1981). "Counterfactuals and Equivalent Antecedents," *Journal of Philosophical Logic,* 10, 267–289.

Woodfield, Andrew, ed. (1982). *Thought and Object.* Oxford: Clarendon Press.

Index

Abstract object, 8, 46
Acceptance
  conditions (for conditionals), 107
  contrasted with belief, 79–81, 93
  of a proposition, 77, 79, 99
  of a sentence, 37
  state, 81
Actual world, 2, 43, 45–46, 48–50, 76, 149, 163, 166
Adams, Ernest, 106, 113
Adams, Robert, 51, 53
Antirealism, 147, 149, 153, 158, 160
Armstrong, David, 101
Assent (to a sentence), 37, 38, 69, 104
Assertion, 5, 92
Assertive utterance, 37
Assumption, 79, 80
Atomism (in semantics), 34
Augustine, Saint, 47–48
Autonomous semantics, 40
Autonomy, 162
Autonomy assumption, 153
Ayer, A. J., 158, 159, 160

Bare truth, 147, 160–164, 167–168
Bayesian decision theory, 91
Behaviorism, 16, 153
Belief, 7, 13, 15, 19, 20, 23, 27, 32, 60, 79, 80
  active, 89
  of animals, 62, 64, 72
  attribution, 59, 62, 73
  change, 96, 98, 99, 104
  conditional, 102–103, 106, 115, 119
  degree of, 98
  disjunctive, 113
  general, 101
  factual, 102

holistic nature of, 64
inconsistent, 25, 81
justified, 90
mathematical, 72
partial, 80, 98
perceptual, 66, 70
shared, 40
skepticism about, 64
social character of, 67
tacit, 68, 104 (see also Presupposition)
unconscious, 81
Belief-desire explanations, 23, 60, 79
Belief states, 60, 69, 82, 83, 96, 98
  integration of, 87, 98
  separate or fragmented, 86–87
Bivalence, 147, 165, 168
Burge, Tyler, 39, 67, 75

Carnap, Rudolf, 32
Carroll, Lewis, 151
Causal and explanatory statements, 153
Causal connection, 14, 102, 155
Causal powers, 155, 157, 159
Causal-pragmatic analysis, 23–24, 38
Causal-pragmatic picture, 32
Causal theory of perception, 162
Causal theory of reference, 18–20, 28, 34
Causation (analysis in terms of counterfactuals), 155–156
Change function, 99, 102, 119
Chisholm, Roderick, 154
Comparative similarity. See Similarity
Compositional semantic theory, 35
Conceptual hierarchy, 162
Conceptual priority, 54
Conditional excluded middle, principle of, 133, 135–137
Conditional noncontradiction, principle of, 108

Conditional propositions, 61, 103, 115, 116, 117, 120
Conditional questions, 110, 114–115
Conditionals. *See also* Counterfactuals
  abstract analysis of, 119, 122, 128, 134, 147, 154
  indicative, 106, 151
  material, 70, 106–108
  open, 106–108, 111–112, 115–116
  proposition-expressing, 112
  strict, 125
  subjunctive, 106, 111, 112, 155
  truth-conditions for, 106
Conditional sentences, 99, 103, 104
Conjunction condition (on belief and acceptance), 82, 90, 93, 94
  global, 94–95
Consequence condition (on belief and acceptance), 82, 88–90
Consistency, 52
Consistency condition (on belief and acceptance), 82–83
Content, 7, 18, 21, 23, 25, 59, 85, 152
Context-dependence
  of belief attributions, 65
  of comparative similarity, 127
  of conditionals, 109, 111, 125, 132, 147–148, 150
  essential, 151–152
  of justification, 90
  of quantifiers, 151
Context-dependent language, 40
Contradictory, 52
Contraposition, 122, 124–125
Convention, 32–33
Conversational maxims, 110
Counterfactuals, 14, 131, 138, 148–150, 156, 168. *See also* Conditionals
  Goodman on, 97
  philosophical problem of, 117, 121, 129, 154
  realism about (*see* Realism)
  reduction of (*see* Reduction)

Davidson, Donald, 20, 21, 36–38
Deduction, problem of, 25, 72, 75
Deductive closure (of belief and knowledge), 76
Deductive conditions (on belief and acceptance), 94
Deductive inquiry, 76, 86–87, 99

Deductive reasoning, 25
Deductive relations, 86, 87
de Finetti, Bruno, 103
Definition by enumeration, 30
Dennett, Daniel, 10, 64, 65, 71
Denotation, 28–29
Dependence, causal and counterfactual, 14, 97, 116. *See also* Independence
Desire, 15, 19, 20, 23, 60, 79, 80, 101
Dispositional concepts, 103
Dispositional properties, 16, 156
Dispositional states, 19, 38
Dispositions
  to assent, 69
  conditional, 82, 101
  linguistic, 37
  methodological, 103–104
  rational, 83
Domain of discourse, 58
Dretske, Fred, 90
Dummett, Michael, 35, 147, 160, 165, 167, 168

Empiricists, 112
Entailment, 10, 71, 97
Enthymematic reasoning, 81
Epistemic policy, 111, 119
Epistemic relevance, 115
Epistemic situation, 116, 151
Equivalence, problem of, 24–25, 72
Even if conditionals, 124
Extreme realism. *See* Realism about possible worlds

Fact, particular, 101, 157, 158
Feedback mechanisms, 12
Fidelity conditions, 12, 37, 66
Field, Hartry, 7, 10, 14–15, 27–29, 32–34, 41
Fine, Kit, 127, 157
Fodor, Jerry, 10, 59, 60, 71
Frege, Gottlob, 3, 35, 68
Function (mathematical), 2–3
Functionalism, 15, 22
Functional state, 15
Fusion, 8

Gibbard, Allan, 108, 110, 111, 113, 130
God, 43
Goodman, Nelson, 97, 103, 128, 154, 155

Grandy, Richard, 39
Grice, Paul, 113

Harman, Gilbert, 22, 60, 71
Hume, David, 98, 103, 155, 157, 158, 160
Hypothetical syllogism, 122–123, 125

Idealizing assumptions, 93
Implication, 53
Independence
  causal and epistemic, 97, 116
  logical, 10, 97
Indeterminacy (semantic), 122, 134–135, 137, 145–146, 148, 165, 167
  of belief attributions, 65
  deep vs. superficial, 166
Indexical analysis of actuality, 45, 47
Indication, 18–19, 24, 35, 66
Individuals, 3, 71
  analogy with possible worlds, 57–58
Inductive inquiry, 92, 94
Inference, 70–72
Information, 13, 25, 65, 73, 85, 87
  contextual, 110
  metalinguistic, 74
  new, 99, 101, 106, 119
  total, 106
Intention, 7, 19, 32, 149
  conditional, 32–33
Intentionality, problem of, 6–7, 15, 25, 27–28, 32–33, 35–36
Intentional mental states, 13–15, 27
Interpretation, theory of, 36–37, 41

Justification, 90

Knowledge, mathematical, 74
Kripke, Saul, 34
Kyburg, Henry, 90, 94–95

Language, dependence of mental representation on, 3, 40
Language of thought, 6, 22–23, 27, 41, 63
Laws of nature, 157
Leibniz, Gottfried, 43
Lewis, David, 44–47, 49, 116, 122, 127, 133, 135, 136, 139–140, 142, 144–145, 147–148, 150, 155–157, 160
Limit assumption, 133, 140–141

Linguistic dispositions, 37
Linguistic picture (of mental representation), 5–6, 27, 59, 71, 94
Linguistic structure, 41, 61, 75
Logical form, 61, 62. See also Structure, semantic
Logical relations, 60, 71. See also Relations, propositional
Logical space, 166, 168. See also Possibilities, space of
Logic of conditionals, 107, 135
Lottery paradox, 90

Mackie, J. L., 42, 51, 147–150
Mathematical ignorance, 76
Mathematical inquiry, 72–77, 85–87
Maximal consistent sets (of propositions), 53
Meaning, 28, 32, 40
  theory of, 36
Measurement theory, 9
Mental language. See Language of thought
Metaphysics, methodology of, 49–50
Methodological conservatism, 129
Methodological policy, 98, 116
Might conditionals, 112, 140, 142–145
Minimal difference (between possible worlds), 122. See also Similarity
Moore, G. E., 144
Moore's paradox, 144

Natural kind terms, 21
Necessary connection, 98, 112, 155
Necessary truth, 25, 72, 73, 75, 76, 85
Necessity
  metaphysical, 64
  natural, 103
Need, 11, 14
Normal or optimal conditions, 12, 13, 19, 37, 66
Now, 48, 150

Objective modal concepts, 112
Omniscient states of knowledge, 120
Ontological commitment, 3, 57–58

Paradox of the preface, 92
Phenomenalism, 153, 155–156
Philosophical analysis, 54
Physicalism, 30, 159

Pollock, John, 122, 136
Popper, Karl, 32
Positivism, 153
Possibilities, space of, 112, 165, 167
Possibility
    epistemic, 24, 143
    quasi-epistemic, 145
Possible objects, 49
Possible worlds, 2, 3, 27, 28, 43, 76, 85,
    120, 149, 166. See also Propositions;
    Realism; Reduction
    structure of, 97
Powers, Larry, 43
Pragmatic analysis of belief and desire,
    17–18, 22
Pragmatic picture (of mental
    representation), 4, 6, 15, 20, 22, 41,
    59, 65, 68, 79, 81, 101
Pragmatics, 124
    contrast with semantics, 106, 122, 126,
    131, 144
Pragmatists, 112
Presupposition, 68, 79, 80, 81, 99, 149,
    150, 152
Primitive denotation, 28–29
Pro attitude, 4, 13, 80
Probability, 80, 91–93, 98, 103, 112
Projection strategy, 103, 116, 119, 120,
    129, 152
Properties, 159
    causal, 16
    dispositional, 16, 156
    intentional, 11
    intrinsic vs. relational, 9, 158
    representational, 6, 13
Propositional functions, 61
Propositions
    analogy with numbers, 8–9, 11, 61
    basic, 56
    conditional, 61, 103, 115, 116, 117, 120
    constituents of, 63, 71
    fine-grained conception of, 10
    identity conditions for, 3, 24, 54–55, 64,
    76
    mathematical, 3, 25, 73–76, 86
    minimal theory of, 52–54
    possible worlds analysis of, 2, 22, 25,
    41, 54, 56, 61, 65, 71–72, 97
    relations between persons and, 27
    structure of, 54
Psychology, commonsense, 62, 71

Putnam, Hilary, 21

Quantities, physical, 9, 11
Quine, W. V., 136, 137

Ramsey, Frank, 101
Rationality conditions (on belief and
    acceptance), 81, 84, 94
Realism, 165, 168
    about causal connections, 98
    about counterfactuals, 117, 122,
    146–147, 152, 168
    naive, 147, 160, 167
    about possible worlds, 44, 57, 49–50,
    155, 166
Reasoning, 70, 92
    deductive, 72
Reduction, 153–155, 158–160, 164, 168
    of counterfactuals, 116, 121, 147
    of possible worlds, 45, 51–53
    of reference, 29, 34
Relation between thought and language,
    21
Relations
    between persons and propositions, 11,
    14
    between sentences and propositions, 32,
    74
    intentional, 6, 11, 13
    logical, 60, 71
    propositional, 15, 52–54
    semantic, 27, 29
Relativity of content, 20
Representation
    linguistic, 22, 23, 33, 34
    mental, 4, 11, 12, 39
Revision (of belief), 96
Russell, Bertrand, 3, 68

Salmon, Nathan, 21
Scope distinctions and ambiguities,
    137–139, 143
Selection function, 120–122, 131–132,
    134, 140–141, 149, 155, 169
Semantic analysis of tenses, 48
Semantic complexity, 63, 71. See also
    Structure, semantic; Logical form
Semantics, contrast with pragmatics, 106,
    122, 126, 131, 144
Semantic theory, 21
Semifactuals, 124

Sentential attitudes, 27–28
Similarity
  abstract concept of, 128–129
  of beliefs, 65
  of possible worlds, 121–122, 126–127,
    133–134, 140, 156–157
Skepticism, 90
  about belief, 64
Solipsism, 47
Speaker, 5, 19, 21, 32, 36, 37, 59, 149,
    152
Speech, 5, 6, 39
Speech acts, 37, 59
Speech community, 32, 59
Stampe, Dennis, 12, 13, 66
Stich, Stephen, 62, 63, 65, 68, 71
Strengthening the antecedent, 123
Structure
  of possible worlds, 97
  semantic, 61–62, 74, 86
Supervaluations, 134–135
Supervenience, 147, 154, 162

Tarski, Alfred, 28, 29, 30, 31, 32, 33, 35
Tarski truth characterization, 29, 30, 31,
    32, 33, 35
Tautology, 74
Tendency-to-bring-about, 12, 15, 19, 24
Thomason, Richmond, 116, 119, 144
Tichy, Pavel, 127, 129, 130, 155
Times, analogy with possible worlds, 47
Total information, 105
Translation, 5
Transposition. See Contraposition
Truth-conditions, 30, 32, 40–41
  for conditional propositions, 117, 120,
    126, 148
Truth definition. See Tarski truth
  characterization
Truth functions, 56, 74
Truth-value, 2, 30, 71
Truth-value gaps, 166

Uniqueness assumption, 133–135, 140

Vagueness, 127, 134, 166
  of counterfactuals, 122, 147–148
Validity, 126
van Fraassen, Bas, 134, 147, 149, 150,
    151
Verificationism, 16, 49

Wanting, 89. See also Desire
Ways things might have been, 44
Weakening the consequent, 124
Wittgenstein, Ludwig, 3
World-story theory, 52, 55–56

Lightning Source UK Ltd.
Milton Keynes UK
UKOW02f1009070616

275766UK00001B/84/P